SALVATION THROUGH INFLATION

Other Books by Gary North

Marx's Religion of Revolution (1968, 1989)
An Introduction to Christian Economics (1973)
Puritan Economic Experiments (1974, 1988)
Unconditional Surrender (1981, 1988)
Successful Investing in an Age of Envy (1981)
The Dominion Covenant: Genesis (1982, 1987)
Government by Emergency (1983)
Backward, Christian Soldiers? (1984)
75 Bible Questions Your Instructors Pray You Won't Ask (1984)
Coined Freedom (1984)
Moses and Pharaoh (1985)
The Sinai Strategy (1986)
Conspiracy: A Biblical View (1986)
Honest Money (1986)
Fighting Chance (1986), with Arthur Robinson
Unholy Spirits (1986)
Dominion and Common Grace (1987)
Inherit the Earth (1987)
Liberating Planet Earth (1987)
Healer of the Nations (1987)
The Pirate Economy (1987)
Is the World Running Down? (1988)
When Justice Is Aborted (1989)
Political Polytheism (1989)
The Hoax of Higher Criticism (1990)
The Judeo-Christian Tradition (1990)
Tools of Dominion: The Case Laws of Exodus (1990)
Victim's Rights (1990)
Westminster's Confession (1991)
Christian Reconstruction (1991), with Gary DeMar
The Coase Theorem (1992)
Politically Incorrect (1993)
Rapture Fever: Why Dispensationalism Is Paralyzed (1993)

SALVATION THROUGH INFLATION
The Economics of Social Credit

Gary North

Institute for Christian Economics

Library of Congress Cataloging-in-Publication Data

North Gary.

Salvation through inflation : the economics of social credit / Gary North

p. cm.

Includes bibliographical references and index.

ISBN 0-930464-64-8 (pbk): $12.95 (alk)

ISBN 0-930464-66-4 (hdbk) $25.00 (alk)

1. Social Credit. 2. Inflation (Economics) 3. Douglas, C. H. (Clifford Hugh), 1879-1952. 4. Economics – Religious aspects – Christianity I. Title

HG355.N67 93-18285

332.4'1–dc20 CIP

Institute for Christian Economics
P. O. Box 8000
Tyler, TX 76711

This book is dedicated to

Don Bell

whose journalistic integrity is matched only by his dogged persistance – a model for all of us professional scribblers.

TABLE OF CONTENTS

Foreword ix
Preface xxi

Introduction 1
1. Testing the Prophets 17
2. The Origins of Social Credit 31
3. Scarcity and Wealth 41
4. Social Credit's Blueprint 55
5. Who Represents the Consumers? 81
6. Who Should Control Distribution? 106
7. Falling Prices and Capitalist Profits 119
8. A False Prescription 141
9. Dividends Under Capitalism 165
10. Social Credit Means State Monopoly Credit 185
11. Sanctions: From Economics to Politics 209
Conclusion 226

Appendix A: Major Douglas' A + B Theorem 241
Appendix B: My Challenge to Social Credit Leaders 264
Appendix C: A Bibliography of Fiat Money
Reforms 277
Appendix D: A Bibliography of Free Market
Monetary Theory 285

Scripture Index 288
Index 290

About the Author 301

There are men who are commonly stigmatized as *monetary cranks*. The monetary crank suggests a method for making everybody prosperous by monetary measures. His plans are illusory. However, they are the consistent application of a monetary ideology entirely approved by contemporary public opinion and espoused by the policies of almost all governments. The objections raised against these ideological errors by the economists are not taken into account by the governments, political parties, and the press.

It is generally believed by those unfamiliar with economic theory that credit expansion and an increase in the quantity of money in circulation are efficacious means for lowering the rate of interest permanently below the height it would attain on a nonmanipulated capital and loan market. This theory is utterly illusory. But it guides the monetary and credit policy of almost every contemporary government. Now, on the basis of this vicious ideology, no valid objection can be raised against the plans advanced by Pierre Joseph Proudhon, Ernest Solvay, Clifford Hugh Douglas and a host of other would-be reformers. They are only more consistent than other people are. They want to reduce the rate of interest to zero and thus to abolish altogether the scarcity of "capital." He who wants to refute them must attack the theories underlying the monetary and credit policies of the great nations.

Ludwig von Mises*

---

*Mises, *Human Action: A Treatise on Economics* (New Haven, Connecticut: Yale University Press, 1949), p. 186.

FOREWORD

And Jesus answering them began to say, Take heed lest any man deceive you (Mark 13:5).

This book is an antidote for economic deception. It is designed to help you understand economics. Read it, pay attention to it, and follow its arguments. When you have finished it, you will have learned to "think economically." You will never again be easily deceived by politicians and other professional deceivers when talk about taxes, prices, and money. Especially money. I am trying to help you keep more of your money.

If you hold a Ph.D. in economics, you are not likely to have been deceived by the version of inflationism that I do my best to refute in this book. Major Douglas' version of inflationism is long forgotten within the economics profession. Even in its heyday in the 1930's, it was considered terribly unfashionable by economists. Far be it from me to suggest that you are unfashionable. While you probably hold some version of inflationism, unless you are an Austrian School economist, you will probably find this book a curiosity. You need to read my book on the Coase theorem more than you need to read this one.[1]

My targeted reader for this book is a sincere Christian, probably a layman, who has stumbled into some branch of the Social

1. Gary North, *The Coase Theorem: A Study in Epistemology* (Tyler, Texas: Institute for Christian Economics, 1992).

Credit movement and has been persuaded (though not by reading the complete works of Major Douglas) that Social Credit economics is Christian. He has been woefully deceived about this. I see my task as that of instructor in biblical economic truth. What the Bible teaches about economics in general and monetary policy specifically is utterly opposed to Social Credit economics. I intend to prove this to him. This may be you.

I receive no money from the sale of this book. I wrote it free of charge as a service. Why? As we ask in the United States: "What's the catch?" There is no catch. I was trained to be a teacher. Teachers teach. Once they begin a career teaching, it is difficult for them to stop. But unlike most teachers, I teach in front of a computer screen, not in front of a classroom.

I have devoted my adult life to studying the Bible. I have also devoted much of my career to studying economics. Having learned some things, I feel compelled to teach them to others. The things I have learned are simple, such as the old rule, "You rarely get something for nothing,"[2] and its corollary, "you sometimes get nothing for something." As a businessman, I have learned that the solutions to personal poverty are hard work, long hours, personal thrift, honesty, and a commitment to serve others by selling them what they want at a price they can afford. Prayer is also a gooda idea. These are also the solutions to world poverty. I have learned, above all, that there are no shortcuts to lasting wealth. This principle applies to societies as well as to individuals.

---

2. The exception is salvation, a free gift of God. "For by grace are ye saved through faith; and that not of yourselves: it is the gift of God: Not of works, lest any man should boast" (Ephesians 2:8-9). But salvation ceases to be free once it is freely received. "For we are his workmanship, created in Christ Jesus unto good works, which God hath before ordained that we should walk in them" (Ephesians 2:10). Grace is a form of debt. We receive more from God than we can ever pay for, but we are nevertheless required by God to pay what we can in order to verify the reality of our faith. "But wilt thou know, O vain man, that faith without works is dead?" (James 2:20). "Ye see then how that by works a man is justified, and not by faith only" (James 2:24).

The trouble is, while people say they believe these simple principles, they find it difficult to act on them when confronted with deception. They are easily sidetracked. They are easily deceived. They seek out wealth formulas that supposedly have been hidden to others. This book is about one such formula.

I agree with the words of Jesus: "Take heed lest any man deceive you." It is very easy for people to be deceived by false economic ideas. Most people know a little bit about economics, but they think they know far more than they really do. Therefore, they are easily deceived. A charlatan would have a difficult time making a living by deceiving the average person about nuclear physics because the average person knows that he knows almost nothing about nuclear physics. He is unlikely to become a crusader for a new, revolutionary view of nuclear physics. He is not going to read a monthly newsletter on the "new" nuclear physics. He is unlikely to send large portions of his income to support a new nuclear physics movement. But he may do all these things and more if the promoter comes in the name of a revolutionary new view of economics, especially money. The average man believes he understands money.

An Antidote to Economic Deception

This is a book about a deception: a social reform program known as Social Credit. It began with one man's self-deception: Clifford Hugh Douglas (1879-1952). It moved rapidly to a more comprehensive form of deception. It continues to deceive, though on a scale much smaller than in 1935. Today, the details of Social Credit economics no longer interest anyone outside of one of the tiny, struggling national organizations that still call themselves "Social Credit." Meanwhile, the whole world has adopted some version of salvation through inflation. *Faith in fiat money remains a universal faith.* What was regarded by most Western economists and politicians in 1918 or 1927 as a bizarre conclusion – the need for continual injections of fiat money in order to keep a national economy productive – is today the universal orthodoxy.

With the transformation of monetary heresy into orthodoxy, the "ministry" one of the chief prophets of the older heresy has been forgotten. Academic historians and economists prefer to pay retroactive homage to John Maynard Keynes rather than Major Douglas. Keynes, for all his bizarre personal behavior, was a scholar; Douglas was not. Keynes served as a high government official; Douglas did not. Keynes' *General Theory* was incoherent in a scholarly fashion; Douglas' little books were incoherent in an amateurish fashion. Style counts for a great deal in academia and in fashionable intellectual circles. Keynes had style; Douglas did not.

Yet Major Douglas' call for salvation through inflation recruited tens of thousands of people, 1918-1936, when Keynes' monetary ideas were anything but stable. Beginning late in World War I, it was C. H. Douglas, not J. M. Keynes, who heralded the West's new age of fiat money and price inflation.

The Curse of Self-Deception

Self-deception is the most difficult form of deception to overcome, both for the deceived and his opponents. The deceiver is convinced that he is telling the truth. This makes him confident. His aura of confidence impresses others. People are also impressed with his great sincerity and his utter devotion to his ideas or his cause. This is why the deception of Social Credit spread rapidly, first to literary figures: editors, poets, and social critics; then to clerics, evangelists, and youth leaders. From there it spread to the tens of thousands of these people's disciples. Alberta, the Canadian province, overwhelmingly voted in a Social Credit government in 1935. Eventually, the appeal of this deception faded when most people lost interest in pursuing what increasingly looked like a lost cause. But the cause still simmers in Canada, Australia, New Zealand, and South Africa.

The problem is, those who remain impressed with this deception are very often well-meaning Christians. Those who profess faith in the divinity of Jesus Christ, the divine-human incarnation in history of the Second Person of the Trinity, find themselves on the fringes of Western society. Protestant fundamentalists, who seem to make up the bulk of Social Credit's Christian supporters, have been consigned to the cultural outer darkness of poorly typeset newsletters, AM radio broadcasts, and tiny Bible colleges. They are not taken seriously by those who publicly shape the modern world.

In self-defense, these culturally isolated Christians have tried to build psychological and cultural walls around themselves and their families. They live in the equivalent of cultural ghettos, or perhaps more accurately, broken-down cultural castles. Occasionally they lower the drawbridge to bring in some harried pilgrim, but then they immediately raise it. The problem is, in order to march out to attack the enemy outside, they must lower the drawbridge for considerable periods of time. This offers the enemy an opportunity to invade, and most Christians are so paralyzed by an intellectual inferiority complex that they refuse even to consider an offensive campaign outside the castle. Meanwhile, television, government schools, and the news media break through the flimsy castle walls on a daily basis, but still Christians comfort themselves that they have not been totally corrupted by the world around them. Small comfort!

Today, Christians communicate mainly with each other. More accurately, many tiny pockets of believers within this larger conglomeration of cultural rejects today communicate only within their isolated regional subdivisions of the Church International. They do not take seriously those from outside the local camp of the faithful who dare to criticize their beliefs, whether the critics are Christians or humanists. Their very isolation from Establishment culture comforts them. It also makes them vulnerable to charlatans and deviants who proclaim some bizarre "new thing" in the name of Christ.

The Lure of the Bizarre

This is why Christians often revel in ideas that members of the Establishment's humanist culture regard as utterly bizarre. Their willingness to embrace the culturally and intellectually bizarre becomes their point of vulnerability. There are many bizarre fringe groups within the humanist camp. Leaders inside the Christian camp can and do import very strange ideas from these humanist fringes, ideas that have nothing to do with the Bible but which can be wrapped in the swaddling clothes of conservative religion. In this form, these imports can and have deceived many. One such import is Social Credit.

Because the importers are Christians, the typical disciple does not expect them to be familiar with the details of academic, scientific, and intellectual matters. Here is the problem: because the Christian importers are intellectually unable to recognize the nature of the deception when they see it, they pass along its errors to their followers in the name of their own anti-Establishment commitment. They do not perceive that *they have been deceived by humanists, occultists, and charlatans from outside the camp*. They say: "Weren't the originators also persecuted by the Establishment? Didn't they also suffer for their beliefs? Well, then, let Christians also warmly receive these new ideas!" Result: Christians rarely recognize that these ideas are very often ancient errors that had once been the common coin of the realm within the humanist camp, but which fell out of favor when they were found to be incorrect and, more to the point, totally unworkable.

A growing minority of Christians have grown weary of their status as political observers and victims. They have become restless. They want to make a difference in history. But they have no experience in "worldly" matters. They are aware of no biblical working models, no Bible-based blueprints for social transformation. But they are no longer content to serve as doormats, paying taxes to finance their spiritual enemies' endless State-funded projects. So, they begin to listen to those who promise solutions, especially quick-fix, one-shot, "turn-key" solutions – solutions they hope will patch things up temporarily until Jesus returns in glory to take them bodily to heaven.

Different Christian subdivisions embrace different reform projects. What is significant is that all of these proposed reforms have been imported from the humanist camp. Academic neo-evangelical Christians tend to become enthusiastic promoters of liberal humanist fads that fell out of favor a decade or two earlier. Fundamentalist Christians, in contrast, tend to be skeptical about social reform in general, so they are less likely to adopt these decade-old reform schemes. This does not make a fundamentalist immune to discarded humanist fads. It makes him vulnerable to much older discards – discards so ancient that even the humanists have forgotten about them. Unaware that these ideas were exposed as erroneous or even fraudulent two or more generations earlier, a fundamentalist may embrace these ideas as the wave of the future, to the extent that he believes that this dispensation has a future. A good example of this sort of long-forgotten discard is Social Credit.

Social Credit and "Real Bills"

The Social Credit movement began in 1917. The fundamental idea of Social Credit is that capitalism suffers from a major flaw: it does not create sufficient bank credit to allow consumers to buy the entire output of industry. The origin of this idea goes back to the long-forgotten "real bills" doctrines of the early nineteenth century. This was an arcane debate between two groups of English economists: the Banking School ("real bills" advocates) and the Currency School (anti-inflation). What is not understood is that *Social Credit is a logical extension of the case for real-bills banking, but without private banks*. Under Social Credit, the State would take over the bankers' economic function: creating credit and deciding which businesses should receive it.

The terminology of "real bills" commercial banking was popularized by Adam Smith in 1776, who referred to a "real bill of exchange drawn by a real creditor upon a real debtor, and which, as soon as it becomes due, is really paid by the debtor; . . ."[3] The process works as follows: a bank offers credit (issues a bank note or writes a check) to a businessman who is owed money in the future. The bank discounts the promised future payment today, and the businessman must pay the face value of this "real bill" to the bank when the debtor pays the businessman. The discount constitutes the rate of interest.

"Elastic" Counterfeit Currency

Banking School economists called for a so-called "elastic currency," one which can expand or contract according to "the needs of business." They regarded short-term bank credit as an appropriate response to the demand by business for capital. They did not perceive that *short-term money creation by a fractional reserve banking system has unwanted repercussions*, such as the creation of a boom-bust economic cycle. They also did not perceive that "the needs of business" cannot be separated from "the price of loans," meaning the interest rate.

Fractional reserve banking creates credit (money) out of nothing. The law allows the banking system to lend out more money than the banks have taken in from depositors: fractional reserves. Thus, in the short run, banks can lower the short-term interest rate by increasing the supply of loanable funds: *monetary inflation*. Businesses then take advantage of this short-term subsidy by borrowing more money than they would have borrowed otherwise. So, the so-called "needs of business" rise when interest rates are forced down by fiat money (called *fiduciary* money) created by the banking system. As these "needs" rise, banks create more money to satisfy these "needs."

The process of borrowing and money creation becomes self-reinforcing until the increase in the money supply begins to

---

3. Adam Smith, *Wealth of Nations*, edited by Edwin Cannan (New York: Modern Library, [1776] 1937), p. 288.

raise prices. Then interest rates will rise, "the needs of business" will slow down or even shrink, and a recession begins. Depositors may even begin withdrawing their deposits and demanding cash: a "banking panic." The money supply then shrinks.

The reduced interest rate condition is *a temporary phenomenon created by the expansion of bank credit*. Rates will rise later on, then fall because of the recession. A bank run will shrink the money supply. In the short run, however, the creation of bank credit does increase the supply of money. This "elastic credit" system has long been basic to the modern economy, and most economists, including Adam Smith, have accepted the legitimacy of this system. The "real bills" doctrine plus the legalization of fractional reserve banking constitute a license for banks to counterfeit money. The result is the boom-bust business cycle.[4]

Social Credit

Defenders of Social Credit today, not one of whom is a trained economist, have never heard of the real-bills doctrine. Neither had Social Credit's founder, Major Douglas. For that matter, only specialists in the history of banking theory have heard of it. So, those enthusiasts who announce Social Credit as both a breakthrough economic theory and a practical monetary reform program operate from a profound ignorance of the history of the erroneous idea which they so enthusiastically proclaim: fiat credit money, i.e., *legalized counterfeiting*.

Following the logic of the real-bills doctrine, they proclaim the need for continual new injections of fiat money by the State in order to avoid economic slumps. They also call for the replacement of the fractional reserve banking system by the State. They become apologists for long-term monetary inflation, but always in the name of stable prices and economic growth. They ask "merely" for the general public to get in on the issue of

4. Ludwig von Mises, *Human Action: A Treatise on Economics* (New Haven, Connecticut: Yale University Press, 1949), ch. 20.

credit, not just businesses. What they rarely acknowledge is that the rise of consumer credit has accomplished just this, but without a reform of the banking system or monetary policy. They choose to ignore this development, perhaps because their real economic goal is to eliminate interest from all loans: a utopian economic demand which goes back to Aristotle.[5]

The intellectual roots of Social Credit are in the real-bills school of monetary opinion. This was first pointed out by Louis Spadaro in his 1955 doctoral dissertation, but who read it even then? Only his dissertation advisors.[6]

As the reader will see, I regard the real-bills doctrine as erroneous and fractional reserve banking as immoral: legalized counterfeiting. Thus, I am also opposed to Social Credit economics and all of its inflationary first-cousins.[7]

To Immunize the Elect

Why should I devote a book to the idea of Social Credit? First, because the movement's primary victims today are Christians. They have been deceived. They deserve to know the truth. Second, because in the 1930's, in the midst of a worldwide economic collapse, the monetary reform ideas of Social Credit and other very similar inflationist schemes spread like wildfire in the English-speaking world. Economic errors always spread rapidly in periods of economic breakdown. I regard this book as a kind of inoculation for a coming period of economic breakdown.

---

5. The Old Testament forbade interest on charitable loans made to fellow believers and resident aliens, as a requirement of mercy, but it did not abolish interest on business loans, which were not morally mandatory. On this point, see Gary North, *Tools of Dominion: The Case Laws of Exodus* (Tyler, Texas: Institute for Christian Economics, 1990), ch. 23.

6. Louis Spadaro, "Salvation Through Credit Reform: An Examination of the Doctrines of Proudhon, Solvay, and C. H. Douglas," unpublished Ph.D. dissertation, Graduate School of Business Administration, New York University, 1955.

7. See Appendix C, below: "A Bibliography of Fiat Money Reforms."

Will anyone in authority ever take seriously the ideas of Social Credit? Admittedly, this seems highly unlikely today. But we can never be sure about the future of any idea, especially one which appeals to the spark of larceny (not divinity!) in everyone's heart: to pay off his debts with depreciated money. In 1975, Soviet dissident and scholar Igor Shafarevich made a very important observation in his book on the history of the idea of socialism. He pointed out that peculiar little socialist groups discussed in isolation their economic ideas for decades during the nineteenth century. Then, without warning, these ideas would sweep across a nation and become the basis of a successful political reform. He wrote:

> At the moment of their inception, socialist movements often strike one by their helplessness, their isolation from reality, their naïvely adventuristic character and their comic, "Golgolian" features (as Berdyaev put it). One gets the impression that these hopeless failures haven't a chance of success, and that in fact they do everything in their power to compromise the ideas they are proclaiming. However, they are merely biding their time. At some point, almost unexpectedly, these ideas find a broad popular reception, and become the forces that determine the course of history, while the leaders of these movements come to rule the destiny of nations.[8]

In an economic crisis, frightened and confused people will embrace any mistaken belief, any proposed cure. This is why economic crises are always a time ripe for economic innovation. The economic ideas of John Maynard Keynes, another apostle of fiat money and government fine-tuning of the economy, triumphed because he offered them in the middle of the worst depression in modern history. The popularity of Social Credit in the 1930's was also the product of the Great Depression.

---

8. Igor Shafarevich, *The Socialist Phenomenon*, translated by William Tjalsma (New York: Harper & Row, [1975] 1980), p. 129.

I expect the next economic crisis to be inflationary, not deflationary. Social Credit is a system designed for a deflationary era, not an inflationary one. For a time, people will get their fill of inflationary nostrums during the next major crisis. But on the far side of mass inflation there could be a deflation. In fact, there will surely be a post-inflation depression unless the government imposes price controls during the period of inflation, thereby destroying production so thoroughly that a deflationary monetary reform will produce prosperity, as it did in Germany in the summer of 1948: the famous "German miracle." During a painful deflationary period, Social Credit's ideas, along with other inflationary proposals, will once again be entertained by unsophisticated readers. While I do not expect Social Credit to become the basis of a new economic orthodoxy, its ideas could easily sidetrack tens of thousands of Christians and conservatives for years.

This would be a terrible waste. Dedicated Christians who are concerned with developing and implementing self-consciously biblical reforms, including economic reforms, need to avoid wasting their time, money, and hopes on a State-deifying humanist import such as Social Credit, even though it has been baptized by some of its followers in the name of Christianity. As we shall see, its moral and theological roots were self-consciously opposed to what Jesus Christ preached about God, man, law, and time.[9] Whenever Christians proclaim some humanist error in the name of Christ, His church suffers. So does the preaching of the gospel. Those who take up such a cause have good reason to fear that their life's work will become what the Apostle Paul warned against: wood, hay, and stubble (I Corinthians 3:12). I wrote this book to counter the wood, hay, and stubble of Social Credit and its many first-cousins, all of which proclaim economic salvation through monetary inflation.

---

9. On these four topics, see my book, *Unconditional Surrender: God's Program for Victory* (3rd ed.; Tyler, Texas: Institute for Christian Economics, 1988), Part I.

PREFACE

> The capitalistic system in the form in which we know it has served its purpose, and may be replaced with advantage; . . .
>
> C. H. Douglas (1921)[1]

Major C. H. Douglas, retired engineer and inventor of an economic philosophy and reform program he called Social Credit, did his readers a great service by announcing in his first book exactly what he intended to accomplish: the replacement of traditional capitalism. As I hope to show from a careful analysis of his books, with extensive word-for-word citations, he intended to replace capitalism with a peculiar variant of what has come to be known as the mixed economy: part capitalist, part government-planned. He was not an advocate of full-scale socialism, but certain features of his system could easily lead to an economy resembling the one imposed by Germany's National Socialism, 1933-38. The Nazi economy relied on centralized monetary manipulation, price controls, and government subsidies to favored industries.[2] So does Social Credit, as we shall see.

---

1. C. H. Douglas, *Economic Democracy* (2nd ed.; London: Cecil Palmer, 1921), p. 23.

2. Hans Sennholz, "The Second German Inflation and the Destruction of the Mark," *Journal of Christian Reconstruction*, VII (Summer 1980), pp. 53-63.

In other respects, Douglas' system resembles the mixed economy of Keynesianism's "New Economics." John Maynard Keynes was Douglas' contemporary, and in 1936 he praised with faint damns the economics of Social Credit, as we shall see. It is worth noting that in that same year, in the Preface to the German edition of his *General Theory*, Keynes admitted that his own system could more easily be applied in a totalitarian state.[3] I do not expect the reader to take my word for all this at this point. But since Major Douglas was forthright early in *Economic Democracy*, I thought it would be wise to be equally forthright early in this book.

The Goal of This Book

Every author has a primary goal in writing a book. There are numerous motivations for book authors. A brand-new author may just want to get his first book into print. After thirty books, the novelty of this wears off, I assure you from experience. An academic who is hoping to receive tenure at a university on the basis of his book has a different goal. A popular novelist has book royalties and a movie contract in mind.

What about me? What is my goal? A book on Major C. H. Douglas will not earn me book royalties; the market is too small. Besides, I do not accept royalties from books of mine published by the Institute for Christian Economics. This book will not win me an academic post; in any case, I am not seeking one. Then why write a book like this? Because I am concerned that many well-meaning conservative and Christian people have stumbled into the writings of men who claim to be intellectual disciples of Major Douglas, men who honestly believe themselves to be conservatives, Christians, or both. They may well be conservatives or Christians, but their economic views are neither conservative nor Christian. Major Douglas' system is un-

3. This appears in *The Collected Writings of John Maynard Keynes* (New York: St. Martin's, 1973), Vol. VII, p. xxvi.

sound, both logically and theologically. My goal is to persuade honest people of this fact – people who are willing to spend some time examining the actual words of Major Douglas, and who are willing to think through my arguments and Major Douglas' arguments before making a decision.

Nevertheless, we need more than negative goals in life. We need positive goals. This book is more than a critique of an obscure and long-forgotten English author of the 1920's and 1930's. It sets forth a positive case for free market economics, and specifically *Christian* free market economics. After you read it, you should have a better understanding of how the economic world works.

There will be some readers who think, "I don't care anything about theology or religion." Others may think, "I don't care anything about a lot of technical economics." The problem I face is that so many of those who identify themselves as followers of Major Douglas do so in the name of Christianity. I am a Christian. I am the author of a four-volume (as of early 1993) economic commentary on the Bible, with another 1,300-page volume due out later this year. Over the last quarter century, I have been challenged from time to time by followers of Major Douglas to answer the good major. While I have discussed his writings occasionally, I have never published a book-length refutation of his system. This has not been because my problem in refuting Social Credit – an accusation made in a recent newsletter published by a Social Credit author (see Appendix B). No, my previous refusal to write this book was based on the inescapable reality of scarcity: time. I try to write at least one serious book every six months, and I did not regard the Social Credit movement as sufficiently large, sufficiently well-funded, or sufficiently influential to take time out of my schedule to write a full-length book on the topic. I wrote a great many books and published many books written by other authors before I finally decided to write this book.

We are creatures. We do not have unlimited resources. The only truly irreplaceable resource is time. I guard my time very carefully. Thus, the reader should not imagine that my previous hesitation in writing this book was in any way intellectual. It was a time-constrained hesitation. I had many far more important things to write. But several advocates of Social Credit kept goading me, implying in print that I am intellectually incapable of refuting Major Douglas. Suggestion: never deliberately bait an author who runs a publishing organization.

My Topic is Major Douglas

In this book, I focus on the writings of Major Douglas. I have not dealt with his followers. There are several reasons for this. First and foremost, I am dealing with a movement that cloaks itself in one man's name. Professor Finlay has commented on this aspect of the Social Credit movement.

> Other movements generally manage to establish a body of belief and of believers who can stand apart from the parent, drawing strength from an already widely known tradition. With Social Credit this never happened. Douglas always retained too crucial a position, and independent Social Credit developments never acquired a healthy life of their own.[4]

This practice of founder-worship is more common among religious movements than it is in professional or academic circles. A man can be a Keynesian economist and not worry in the slightest about the discovery of specific errors in the original writings of John Maynard Keynes. The founder of Keynesian economics is not regarded by his disciples as the equivalent of the founder of a religion. Keynes' academic disciples do not seek to defend his name and his words with all of their heart,

---

4. John L. Finlay, *Social Credit: The English Origins* (London: McGill-Queen's University Press, 1972), p. 88.

mind, and soul. Such is not the case with Social Credit. To refute Major Douglas is to refute all of his disciples. So, I do not need to refute them one by one. I merely need to refute Major Douglas.

Furthermore, to refute one or two of his disciples is hardly worth anyone's time, especially mine. In any case, in the period since 1939, there have been very few published disciples to refute. There is no college-level textbook or treatise by a Social Credit economist, over seven decades after its creation. It is never sufficient to present a peculiar – even bizarre – theory of money and capital, as Major Douglas did. You must also show how the whole of economic theory is re-shaped by your theory of money and capital, how your proposed alteration fits all the parts of economics in an integrated whole. This is what Major Douglas never did, nor have his disciples done. The old rule is true: "You can't change just one thing." When you change one thing, you change many things. If you cannot show how your recommended change affects everything else, your work has barely begun. This has never been done by any promoter of Social Credit, yet Major Douglas offered his reform scheme in 1917. Neither he nor his defenders ever completed stage one.

It is as if Major Douglas had offered the world a theory of jet propulsion, but never recommended anything more aerodynamically sophisticated than a World War I biplane. This, in and of itself, would not refute his theory of jet propulsion, but I wouldn't want to be the first pilot to "take the plane up for a spin." It may come down in a spin a great deal faster than it went up.

Typical of the leadership of the Social Credit movement is the statement by Maurice Colbourne, author of *The Meaning of Social Credit*, published in Canada by the Social Credit Board of Edmonton. In the book's Preface, he offered this opinion of himself: "The second advantage I have is that I am not an economic expert. Thank goodness for that too. . . . No, I am a much more important person than a professional economist. I am a Consumer."[5] It is all well and good for a political movement to enlist the skills of amateurs to write tracts, but if during its entire history spanning seven decades the movement has been unable to attract or train up a single professional economist to defend what is explicitly a program of economic reform, then that political movement is not in a strong position. It is unlikely ever to be taken seriously by a majority of voters. It will have to content itself with attracting people who are interested in devoting their time and their emotional reserves to hopelessly lost causes. This cause was lost by 1939. Its name lingers on in a Canadian political party, but its original idea no longer has a significant audience. My view is that life is too short to pursue a lost cause that was lost for a good reason.

Competing Groups Without an Integrated System

There is another reason for my refusal to deal with the later disciples of Major Douglas. I am not sure which ones are the important ones. Some are in Canada. Others are in Australia. There are Social Credit leaders in New Zealand, South Africa, and England. None of these organizations has much political power. There is no single Social Credit organization that can offer a believable claim to be the best representative of the Social Credit tradition. I never shoot at a blurry target.

Men claiming to be the heirs of Major Douglas' vision have offered many interpretations of what Major Douglas *really* meant. Problem: they do not agree with each other about this "true meaning." (Perhaps they will all now be able to agree on one point: that my book is simply terrible. The question is: Will they agree on the specific economic reasons why my book is terrible? Who knows, maybe my book will at last bring a little unity to the fragmented Social Credit organizations!)

---

5. Maurice Colbourne, *The Meaning of Social Credit* (4th revised edition; Edmonton, Alberta: Social Credit Board, 1935), pp. 9, 10.

What is an outsider to do? More to the point, what are *you* to do? You are the reader. Presumably, you want to know whether Social Credit is true or false. How can you find out? The best way is to read all of his books and articles and then decide for yourself. This is not easy. Major Douglas' books are not all in print. They are not easily available. There is no set called *The Complete Works of C. H. Douglas*. His disciples have not kept his writings in print in the way that Marxists have kept Marx's works in print and Keynesians have kept Keynes' works in print. How are you going to figure out whether Douglas was right or wrong?

I have done my very best to summarize his ideas. I have quoted him word for word in this book. I provide footnote references so that you can go to a large library and verify what I have said that he wrote. While I do not agree with Douglas, I am interested in refuting what he said, not what his later disciples claim that he said. I do my best to state his case clearly and fairly, quoting his writings to prove my case, as I offer my criticisms. This is what a trained scholar is expected to do. It is my opinion that his disciples, not being formally trained in economics, have not previously done this. But what they have not done is beside the point. I want you to understand Douglas' system. Then I want you to understand why it is wrong.

Why Scholars Have Ignored Social Credit

Major Douglas' disciples will correctly regard this book as the first book-length criticism of Social Credit in many years – decades, in fact – written by a professionally trained scholar. In the past, scholars have paid little or no attention to the details of the economics of Social Credit except for historians who specialize in the history of obscure political movements. In 1955, Louis Spadaro submitted a Ph.D. dissertation at New York University's Graduate School of Business Administration which analyzed Douglas and two other promoters of social transformation through monetary reform: Pierre-Joseph Proudhon and Ernest Solvay. He called his dissertation, "Salvation Through Credit Reform." This is the only doctoral dissertation I am aware of which studies the economics of Major Douglas.[6]

Historians and social commentators would be wise to understand that ever since the death of Major Douglas, and probably a good deal before his death, Social Credit has been primarily a religious movement. I did not say *Christian*; I said *religious*: intense, committed, dogmatic, intolerant of criticism, and resistant to modification through rational discussion. Social Credit's defenders regard Major Douglas' **A + B Theorem** (see Appendix A) almost as reverently as liturgically minded Christians regard the Apostles' Creed. The reader should understand from the beginning that *Social Credit never has been a scientific movement*. No economist has ever written a book-length defense of its reform proposals.[7] Its early leaders were poets, literary critics, and mystics – virtually all of them committed to guild socialism. Its defenders today may believe themselves to be part of an economic movement, but in fact Social Credit is more like a church or a sect.

Scholars interact with scholars. Social Credit has successfully recruited no scholars since the late 1930's. Scholars therefore have had little interest in Social Credit except as a fringe political phenomenon in Canada and Australia. This movement has no power and very little influence. Social Credit is of interest only to a handful of historians who specialize in political movements; it is of no interest to economists. So, post-World War II economists have not bothered to refute Social Credit.

People Are Being Misled

The reason why I am no longer ignoring it is because decent people are being misled. They have been assured that the

---

6. If you know of another one, please contact me.

7. At best, there has been a single 29-page pamphlet written by a man who may have had a Ph.D. in economics, *Social Credit and Catholicism* (1936).

writings of Major Douglas promote the free market, economic productivity, and sound money. Social Credit economics, as originally formulated by Major Douglas, does nothing of the kind. After you read this book, you will better understand why I am so adamant about this. I am writing this book in order to warn conservative people who have been misled about the true message of Major Douglas.

There will, of course, be attempted refutations of my book, mostly in the form of lengthy book reviews in low-circulation newsletters. Once again, let me remind the reader (and my future critics) that I am responding to Major Douglas, not to his well-meaning but economically untrained disciples. This may displease certain of my critics who feel slighted because I have paid no attention to them, but my strategy is deliberate. If Major Douglas was wrong, they surely are wrong. I do not have to refute any of them if I can refute him. (Still, if one of the movement's leaders responds with a book, and if he has the blessings of his peers, I shall respond: see Appendix B.)

More to the point, *I do not have to persuade them if I can persuade you*. Martin Luther did not persuade a single Pope to join the Protestant Reformation, but he did persuade many followers of many popes. We should not expect the "popes" of any movement to be persuaded by their movement's critics. Leaders of a movement have too much to lose psychologically for them to be persuaded by critics, no matter how tiny their movement is. My failure to persuade them is neither here nor there; my failure to persuade you, however, would be most unfortunate.

The Emperor's New Clothes

When you read refutations of my book written by this or that representative of Social Credit, please keep in mind the story of the emperor who had no clothes. Although he insisted that he was well-dressed, and the clothing makers also insisted that he was well-dressed, and all the people except one small boy insisted that he was well-dressed, he was not well-dressed.

He was not dressed at all. Be sure that those defenders who insist that Major Douglas was well-dressed are not themselves like all those people along the highway when the emperor paraded by: self-deceived.

To defend yourself against economic nonsense disguised as a refutation of this book, ask yourself the following questions when you read my book and also the refutations:

> "Does the author extensively quote Major Douglas?"
> "If he doesn't, why not?"
> "Do the quotations prove the author's case (pro or con)?"
> "Does the author make sense?"
> "Does Major Douglas make sense?"
> "Do I really understand all this?"
> "If not, is this my fault or the author's?"
> "Might it be Major Douglas' fault?"
> "Is the author using verbiage – gobbledygook – instead of rational arguments?"
> "Did Major Douglas use gobbledygook?"
> "Am I being subjected to a 'snow job'?"

Here is my suggestion: *do not believe anything that is not crystal clear*. Suspend judgment until you understand exactly what you are being told. If you cannot summarize an author's arguments in your own words, then do not become his disciple until you can. Do not become a vocal critic, either. *You must be sure of what you believe*. When you can verbally summarize your opinion to someone who knows nothing about Social Credit, you have a grasp of the topic. If you can't, you don't.

The fact that one or two of Major Douglas' disciples may write a book responding to mine is irrelevant if the response is not clear. If a book does not answer my arguments in a clear, logical fashion, quoting word for word the writings of Major Douglas in order to prove the case against me, then pay no attention to it. Do not be deceived by big words and lots of assertions. Do not be taken in by the old debater's trick: "If your case is weak, shout. If it is really weak, pound the podium, too." If the arguments you read – mine or my critics – are not clear, or if they are not substantiated by word-for-word quotations from Major Douglas, suspend judgment.

Let me put it bluntly: *like the emperor, Major Douglas wore no clothes*. His disciples are equally naked. But you should not take my word for this yet. You should read this book carefully. If you are persuaded that I am correct, then you should also read any responses. Remember what the Bible teaches about deciding whose story is correct:

> He that is first in his own cause seemeth just; but his neighbour cometh and searcheth him (Proverbs 18:17).

Listen carefully to both sides. Then make your own decision. But bear this in mind as you read: if one of those who pleads his case is clear, quotes from the original sources, and does not exaggerate his claims, while his opponent uses convoluted language, doesn't cite the original sources, and substitutes accusations for simple logic, believe the first person.

If defenders of Social Credit write that I should have considered the writings of Disciple A or Disciple B, my response is simple: if they still defend the ideas of Major Douglas as originally presented by him, then I do not need to refute any disciple. If, on the other hand, he made a lot of mistakes, let the disciple identify them, correct them, and present a restructured version of Social Credit. I will respond to him. But the fact is, Social Credit is like a religious sect. The disciples quote only the master. I have followed their lead.

Conclusion

Let me ask you a question: *Are you committed to a search for truth?* If you are, do not become upset with anything in this book until you have finished reading all of it. Do not pre-judge this book. You can and should post-judge it. You can and should draw conclusions. But before you do, you should finish reading all of the book. Heed my warning: just because Social Credit sounds quite bizarre – anti-Establishment – this is not a sufficient reason to assume that Social Credit is correct. Just because its leaders challenge Establishment enemies who really do need challenging is no proof that their challenge is on target. Just because a few of its defenders say that Social Credit's economic theory is Christian[8] is no reason to assume that it really is Christian. Just because the world economy may look shaky is not a sufficient reason to believe that Social Credit's proposed reforms will produce spectacular economic growth, which is what Major Douglas promised.

If I am successful with this book, you will understand its arguments as you read it, and you will understand its thesis when you finish it. You may not agree with it, but you will understand it. Let me warn you one more time: if you do not understand an author when he deliberately writes a book aimed at the average reader, you can be fairly confident that the problem is with the author, not you. Either the author is incapable of expressing himself clearly or else his theory is wrong, and he is using a lot of jargon or technobabble to cover up the fact that his theory does not hold water. Always be suspicious of articles or books addressed to laymen if these articles and books are filled with jargon, and especially if they are attempted refutations of a clear, understandable criticism of a particular position or idea. Whenever you read that sort of article or book, think to yourself, "You may be right, mate, but don't expect me to climb on board your bandwagon until I understand exactly what you're talking about."

It is time to take a closer look at the bandwagon.

---

8. For example, Eric D. Butler, *Social Credit and Christian Philosophy* (Melbourne: New Times Limited, 1956); Charles Pinwill, *The North-South Dialogue on Christian Principles of Money and Banking* (Cranbrook, W.A., Australia: Veritas, 1990).

INTRODUCTION

> But the affinity between conservative and radical went further. It extended to hatred of a certain type of property: large-scale industrial property, but more especially the abstract and impersonal type of property that was represented by shares bought and sold on the market. . . . In the nineteenth century conservative and radical alike distrusted industrial and finance capital.
>
> Robert A. Nisbet (1966)[1]

Nisbet, a conservative sociologist – a rare species, I assure you – has identified the existence of an unstated yet functional alliance between conservatives and radicals throughout the nineteenth century. This alliance was not organizational; rather, it was ideological and emotional: shared hatreds. Both sides indicted capitalism, especially finance capitalism.

This unstated alliance extended into the twentieth century. This book is a study of one small phase of this alliance, the Social Credit movement. In the mid-1930's, it reached its peak in England and Alberta, Canada. The movement still exists, though just barely. While the Canadian branch, being political, has from the beginning departed from the teachings of the

---

1. Robert A. Nisbet, *The Sociological Tradition* (New York: Basic Books, 1966), p. 27.

founder, it has retained the original name. This has produced considerable confusion over the years, both inside and outside the Social Credit Party. Conservative voters have turned to this party in Canada over the last several decades, unaware that the founder of the Social Credit movement was not a conservative, nor were many of his early disciples, such as socialist G. D. H. Cole, fascist Ezra Pound, and communist Hewlett Johnson.

This is evidence of the long-term problem: what is regarded as a conservative critique of the economy is all too often inherently socialistic in its policy prescriptions. Conservatives retain their allegiance to the name and the rhetoric of the original critique, despite the fact that a consistent application of the proposed solution would produce results foreign to everything conservatives claim they stand for. A study of the Social Credit Party in Canada would, I believe, verify my thesis. It is a conservative movement that officially relies on what was originally a left-wing critique of capitalism.

Hostility to the Free Market

It is my contention that there is today an underlying hostility to certain aspects of free market capitalism, a hostility shared by conservatives, radicals, and modern liberals. All three have come to the same conclusion, namely, that without intervention from the national government in the field of monetary policy, capitalism will collapse.

In the early nineteenth century, capitalism was regarded as evil by conservatives and radicals because it supposedly exploits labor. In the twentieth century, this complaint shifted. Capitalism has been seen as insufficiently exploitative – not of men but of resources. Without the State's ability to create fiat money at will, the critics assure us, the free market will be strangled by underconsumption. In other words, the free market needs the State to provide the central institution in any highly developed division-of-labor economy: money.

After 1965, this "slow-growth" criticism of capitalism was

abandoned by a small group of anti-capitalist radicals who began to preach the benefits of a zero-growth economy. Economic growth was seen by these critics as a great evil: the exploitation of nature. A "back to nature" movement began among upper-middle-class people who lived in urban comfort.[2] While this outlook has steadily grown in influence since 1965, culminating in the "Green" movement of the 1980's, it has not yet gained widespread academic respectability, nor has it reversed national economic policy, especially during recessions. Today, the fundamental criticism of capitalism among liberals and radicals is still that it does not "deliver the goods" without monetary manipulation. The debate centers only on which elite group ought to have the authority to do the manipulating: quasi-private central bankers or government bureaucrats. As we shall see in this book, this is a debate that goes back to the late eighteenth century. As we shall also see, it is a debate that refuses to consider a third possibility: *free market money* through (a) the abolition of the government-licensed monopolies of central banking and commercial banking, i.e., a system of free banking,[3] or (b) civil laws abolishing fractional reserve banking because of the inherently fraudulent nature of its promise to depositors: the right to withdraw their funds on demand, when in fact the money has been loaned out.[4] This third possibility is considered as the ultimate fringe position by radicals, liberals,

---

2. The most cogent critique of this movement is William Tucker, *Progress and Privilege: America in the Age of Environmentalism* (Garden City, New York: Anchor Press/Doubleday, 1982).

3. Ludwig von Mises, *Human Action: A Treatise on Economics* (New Haven, Connecticut: Yale University Press, 1949), pp. 441-45. See also George A. Selgin, *The Theory of Free Banking: Money Supply Under Competitive Note Issue* (Totowa, New Jersey: Rowman & Littlefield, 1988).

4. Murray N. Rothbard, "100 Per Cent Reserve Banking," in Leland B. Yeager (ed.), *In Search of a Monetary Constitution* (Cambridge, Massachusetts: Harvard University Press, 1962); Rothbard, *What Has Government Done to Our Money?* (Auburn, Alabama: Ludwig von Mises Institute, [1963] 1990). For a detailed study of the history of this viewpoint, see Mark Skousen, *Economics of a Pure Gold Standard* (Auburn, Alabama: Praxeology Press of the Ludwig von Mises Institute, [1977] 1988).

and conservatives. This happens to be my view – specifically, point b.[5]

What are the main features of this conservative-radical alliance in our day? I cover several of them in this book. In subsequent chapters, I will show that these features appear in the writings of Major Douglas. One aspect of this shared worldview is a shared hatred of conspiracies – specifically, a bankers' conspiracy. Thus, we must consider briefly what is sometimes called the conspiracy view of history.

The Revival of a Conspiracy View of History

Those who believe in conspiracies behind events believe in personalism. History is not shaped merely by impersonal forces, such as the dialectical spirit (Hegel), dialectical materialism (Marxism), the *volk* (Nazism), or economic forces. It is shaped by persons. Christianity sees history as an outworking of the struggle between Christ and Satan: good vs. evil, angels vs. demons, covenant-keepers vs. covenant-breakers. This viewpoint can easily be corrupted, and has been. The incarnation of good and evil – especially evil – is identified with a particular group. Those who are good are "the people," or "the average guy": the amorphous group with whom one's followers prefer to identify themselves. The average person is seen as the victim; the elite Insider group is the villain. Problem: there is no agreement about which organization this ultimate Insider group is, but the most popular group to hate in the West, century after century, has been the Jews. In part, this is a religious identification; in part it is occupational: money-lending. Those who make money by lending money at interest are seen as the exploiters: getting paid something for nothing. The hostility to interest payments is fused with hostility toward bankers, and this often means Jews. Even Karl Marx, himself a Jew, with

5. Gary North, *Honest Money: The Biblical Blueprint for Money and Banking* (Ft. Worth, Texas: Dominion Press; Nashville: Thomas Nelson Sons, 1986).

rabbis on both his mother's side and his father's side, indulged in this kind of anti-Semitic rhetoric in his 1843 essay, "On the Jewish Question."[6] Marx spent much of his adult life in debt to pawnbrokers.[7]

Fringe conservatives, fringe radicals, most libertarians (all of whom these days are regarded as being on the fringe), and a handful of academically trained liberals believe in the existence of a clandestine conspiracy of international bankers and large-scale multinational business organizations. This belief is then used by most of its adherents to criticize today's system of State-manipulated capitalism. The practical question is: What should replace the present system? On this there is no agreement.

In June, 1964, Robert Welch, the founder of the six-year-old John Birch Society, a conservative anti-Communist organization, gave a speech, *More Stately Mansions*.[8] With this, he launched the organization's shift in focus from anticommunism to anti-conspiratorialism. The organization's monthly magazine, *American Opinion*, soon reflected this change in emphasis. In 1967, the Birch Society's publishing arm, Western Islands, reprinted John Robison's 1798 exposé of the Bavarian Illuminati, *Proofs of a Conspiracy*.

This shift from concern over Communism to concern over conspiracy was accelerated after 1964 by two factors. First, in November of 1964, Barry Goldwater was defeated overwhelmingly by Lyndon Johnson in the race for President of the United States. Goldwater had been the candidate of the fast-growing conservative wing of the Republican Party. His nomination had

---

6. Karl Marx, "On the Jewish Question" (1843), in Karl Marx and Frederick Engels, *Collected Works*, Vol. 3 (New York: International Publishers, 1975), pp. 146-74.

7. Robert Payne, *Marx* (New York: Simon & Schuster, 1968), p. 342. See Marx's desperate plea for money in a letter to Dr. Kugelmann, 13 Oct. 1866, in *Letters to Kugelmann* (New York: International Publishers, 1934), p. 42. He claimed that he was paying 20% to 30% per annum.

8. Reprinted in Robert Welch, *The New Americanism and Other Speeches and Essays* (Belmont, Massachusetts: Western Islands, 1966), pp. 115-52.

been heavily opposed by what soon became known as the Eastern Establishment wing of the Party, whose titular head was Governor Nelson Rockefeller of New York. Rockefeller, son of John D. Rockefeller, Jr., was the most prominent member of the most prominent family of millionaires in the U.S. Like his father and his brothers, he was a political liberal. It was clear that this wing of the Party favored the election of President Johnson, the Democratic Party's candidate, who had automatically replaced John F. Kennedy as President on November 22, 1963, the day Kennedy was assassinated.

This Eastern wing in 1952 had also opposed the nomination of conservative Robert A. Taft and had chosen General Dwight D. Eisenhower to run as the Party's presidential candidate. Taft was himself a member of a powerful Eastern Establishment family – his father had been elected President in 1908 – and was himself a member of the then-little known Yale University secret society, Skull & Bones, just as his father had been. The conservatives who supported him knew nothing of this longstanding family connection. These dedicated people had been under the domination of the Eastern wing of the Party since at least the Presidential election of 1928 (Herbert Hoover), and many of them had become totally fed up after Goldwater's loss.

Quigley Verifies the Story

The second factor appeared in 1966, when the Macmillan Company published politically liberal historian Carroll Quigley's 1,300-page history of the twentieth century, *Tragedy and Hope*. Quigley was a professor of history at Georgetown University, where many of America's foreign service officers are trained. He was also the author of an unpublished manuscript, completed in 1949, *The Anglo-American Establishment: From Rhodes to Clivedon*, but the editors at Macmillan almost certainly were unaware of its existence. This manuscript did not appear in print until 1981, five years after his death and a decade after Macmillan had pulled *Tragedy and Hope* out of print. It was published by an obscure company, Books In Focus.

Tragedy and Hope reflected Quigley's specialties: diplomatic history and military history. It included a brief section (pp. 945-56) on the British Round Table group, founded in 1891 by Cecil Rhodes and extended by Alfred Milner in the early twentieth century. Quigley pointed out that the Round Table had an American branch, the Council on Foreign Relations, begun in 1921. "The chief aims of this elaborate, semisecret organization were largely commendable," Quigley editorialized.[9]

This was the first time that any prominent historian – or any historian, as far as I am aware – had publicly exposed this crucial Anglo-American connection. I also believe that the book's editors were initially unaware of just how important this brief section was. Within two years they knew. Quigley claimed in 1975 that his book had been deliberately suppressed by Macmillan in 1968, after having sold 8,800 copies, with sales rising. He went after Macmillan with a lawyer. The company, he said, claimed that the book was out of stock, not out of print, which by law meant that ownership of the book would not revert to the author. Only out of print books revert to their authors. Meanwhile, the company replied to book stores which had ordered copies, telling them that the book was out of print. He said he had photocopies of such letters. Quigley wrote in 1975: "Powerful influences in this country want me, or at least my work, suppressed."[10] Only in the late 1970's, after Quigley's death, did a "pirate" edition become available again.

(The same thing had happened to Cleon Skousen's book, *The Naked Communist*, in the late 1950's. A prominent publishing firm had agreed to publish it, but the book never appeared. All copies were being stored secretly in a warehouse. Skousen then learned that the firm's president was a Communist. Only by

---

9. Carroll Quigley, *Tragedy and Hope: A History of the World in Our Time* (New York: Macmillan, 1966), p. 954.

10. Letter to Peter Sutherland, Dec. 9, 1975; reprinted in *Conspiracy Digest* (Summer 1976); reprinted again in *American Opinion* (April 1983), p. 29.

negotiating with a corporate vice president when the president was out of the country did Skousen receive back the rights to his book. As he later told me, he thinks the vice president was inebriated when he signed back the publishing rights.)

Almost immediately after the book's appearance, conservative Christian newsletter writer Don Bell reported on its crucial dozen pages, and the news spread rapidly throughout the American conservative movement, especially the "fringe" conservative movement that had few contacts in Washington, D.C. In 1970, Cleon Skousen wrote *The Naked Capitalist*, a 143-page book based heavily on Quigley's dozen pages. By this time, *Tragedy and Hope* was unavailable in book stores. Skousen had the well-deserved reputation of being a staunch anti-Communist. His new book included a section, "How the Secret Society Formed a Coalition With the Communist-Socialist Conspiracy Groups." Because the *Naked Capitalist* proposed the existence of a capitalist-Communist connection, rather than the familiar conservative complaint of a liberal-Communist connection, it created a minor sensation. Then, a year later, *American Opinion* regular feature writer Gary Allen published *None Dare Call It Conspiracy*. The paperback version of the book sold several million copies. It, too, relied on Quigley's *Tragedy and Hope*, using it as a springboard. Two features of this book were important in its success. First, it relied on conventional academic historians to prove its case. Second, it avoided the familiar thesis of the IJBC: the international Jewish banker's conspiracy. (An update by Larry Abraham, *Call It Conspiracy*, appeared in 1986. I wrote the Prologue and the Epilogue to the first edition.)[11]

In 1962, the American conservative commentator Dan Smoot had published *The Invisible Government*, a critique of the Council on Foreign Relations. He exposed its connections with tax-

---

11. Also published separately: Gary North, *Conspiracy: A Biblical View* (Ft. Worth, Texas: Dominion Press, 1986), co-published by Crossway Books, Westchester, Illinois.

exempt foundations and liberal internationalism in foreign policy. But he had not seen its connection to the Round Table group, with the latter's connections throughout the Anglo-American world. Smoot's book sold over a million copies, mostly by mail order. Most educated Americans had never heard of the CFR in 1962, including the vast majority of conservatives. The CFR had successfully hidden in plain sight since 1921. When Skousen and Allen identified the tight connections among the CFR, high-level American banking, American foreign policy, and an international conspiracy originating in London, the "troops" of the conservative movement responded positively. The leadership, however, reacted negatively.

Antony Sutton was the author of a massive three-volume study of the almost total reliance of the Soviet Union on imports of Western technology, *Western Technology and Soviet Economic Development* (1968-1973) published by the prestigious and well-funded anti-Communist foundation, the Hoover Institution. In 1973, he wrote *National Suicide: Military Aid to the Soviet Union*. This book merely extended his thesis regarding the transfer of technology to the USSR, but it was too close for comfort in the view of the directors of the Hoover Institution. They fired him. Arlington House, a small conservative publishing company, published the book. (He extended this thesis in *The Best Enemy Money Can Buy*, published in 1986. I wrote the book's Foreword.) In 1974, he shifted his focus from the fact of this massive transfer of technology to the politics that preceeded it: *Wall Street and the Bolshevik Revolution* (Arlington House). The next year came *Wall Street and FDR* (Arlington House), a study of President Franklin D. Roosevelt's connections to the New York banking establishment. But the next year Sutton went too far even for Arlington House: *Wall Street and Hitler*, published by '76 Press, which had published *None Dare Call It Conspiracy*. Sutton kept going: *Trilaterals Over Washington I* (1978) and *Trilaterals Over Washington II* (1982). Finally came *America's Secret Establishment: An Introduction to the Order of Skull*

& Bones (1986), a report on Yale University's secret society, founded in 1833. In 1988, George Bush, a Skull & Bones member and former CFR and Trilateral officer (he had resigned in 1980 when he became the Republican Party's nominee for Vice President), was elected President of the United States.

Liberals and Radicals Begin to Catch On

The capitalist-Communist conspiracy thesis began to move to the fringe of liberalism in the late 1970's. A labor union official, Dr. Charles Levinson, wrote *Vodka Cola*, a study of the USSR-Western capitalist connections, published by the small English firm of Gorden & Cremonesi in 1978. Joseph Finder, a careful, Harvard-trained journalist told the story of the USSR-Western capitalist connection in *Red Carpet*, published by Holt, Rinehart & Winston in 1980. (My firm, the American Bureau of Economic Research, Inc., picked up the paperback rights to this book in 1986 when the book was allowed by its original publisher to go out of print.) In 1983, Charles Higham's book appeared, published by a conventional but minor New York City publisher, Delacorte: *Trading With the Enemy: An Exposé of The Nazi-American Money Plot, 1933-1949.*

In the early 1980's, the fringe of the far left in Europe and the U.S. also began to study these connections. A European perspective was presented by Professor Kees van der Pijl of the University of Amsterdam, *The Making of an Atlantic Ruling Class* (1984).[12] Holly Sklar edited *Trilateralism: The Trilateral Commission and Elite Planning for World Management* (1990), published by the obscure South End Press, located in Boston. The Trilateral Commission is a sister organization to the CFR, begun in 1973. Its name stems from what its founders believe are the three world trade blocs: Europe, North America, and Asia.

12. London: Verso, 1984.

Older Conspiracy Theses

Why should I devote so much space to reviewing the history of books dealing with the topic of a capitalist-Communist conspiracy? Because it was a revival of a long tradition of conspiracy theories stretching back to the anti-masonic, anti-French Revolution theories of the 1790's. John Robison's book, *Proofs of a Conspiracy* (1798), circulated widely in both Great Britain and the United States. In the hands of Rev. Jedediah Morse (whose son Samuel later invented the telegraph), this book helped to accelerate the new nation's political division between Federalists (President John Adams, Alexander Hamilton) and Republicans (Jefferson and Madison).[13] This anti-Masonic conspiracy thesis faded in popularity after the War of 1812.

In 1816, the Second Bank of the U.S. was established. This was a federally chartered, privately owned central bank modeled after the Bank of England. In the early 1830's, President Andrew Jackson's battle against the Second Bank produced a wider acceptance of the idea of a banker's conspiracy against the commonweal.[14] The willingness of the bank's director, Nicholas Biddle, to shrink the money supply and thereby create a depression in order to break Jackson's political power base, only augmented this belief.[15] But Jackson was a gold standard man, not a fiat money advocate. He had begun his political career in the aftermath of the panic of 1819, America's first depression. During the panic, Jackson had opposed the sus-

---

13. Vernon Stauffer, *New England and the Bavarian Illuminati* (New York: Russell & Russell, [1918] 1967).

14. Gary North, "Greenback Dollars and Federal Sovereignty, 1861-1865," in Hans F. Sennholz (ed.), *Gold Is Money* (Westport, Connecticut: Greenwood Press, 1975), pp. 125-32.

15. Bray Hammond, *Banks and Politics in America: From the Revolution to the Civil War* (Princeton, New Jersey: Princeton University Press, 1957), chaps. 11-15. Thomas Payne Govan, *Nicholas Biddle: Nationalist and Public Banker, 1786-1844* (Chicago: University of Chicago Press, 1959), chaps. 17-36; James Roger Sharp, *The Jacksonians versus the Banks: Politics and the States after the Panic of 1837* (New York: Columbia University Press, 1970).

pension of gold and silver payments by the banks.[16]

In the late nineteenth century, American critics of what was called an Eastern bankers' conspiracy again began to gain converts. Very often, these critics were members of what became known as the Populist movement. The critics began to appear around 1867, two years after the American Civil War (1861-65) ended.[17] A bank run against gold had begun very early in the war. Banks suspended payment in gold, and this decision was supported by the governments of both the North and the South. Both governments also suspended payment. Both governments continually issued fiat money to pay for the war.[18]

After the Civil War, the victorious Northern government decided to return to stable money conditions and to re-establish a gold standard, which was achieved in 1879.[19] This was the Greenback era, a "greenback" being green-colored paper money which offered no redeemability in gold coin.[20] The era really began in 1861, when the northern banks suspended specie redemption.[21] This long and erratic process of withdrawal from wartime fiat money policies led to a series of recessions, beginning in 1867 and continuing through the late 1890's. It is impossible to halt the expansion of a prior period of fiat money expansion without causing a recession,[22] a pain-

---

16. Murray N. Rothbard, *The Panic of 1819: Reactions and Policies* (New York: Columbia University Press, 1962), pp. 94-96.

17. Allen Weinstein, *Prelude to Populism: Origins of the Silver Issue, 1867-1878* (New Haven, Connecticut: Yale University Press, 1970).

18. North, "Greenback Dollars," pp. 132-47. See also Bray Hammond, *Sovereignty and an Empty Purse: Banks and Politics in the Civil War* (Princeton, New Jersey: Princeton University Press, 1970); Richard Cecil Todd, *Confederate Finance* (Athens: University of Georgia Press, 1954).

19. Walter T. K. Nugent, *The Money Question During Reconstruction* (New York: Norton, 1967).

20. Irwin Unger, *The Greenback Era: A Social and Political History of American Finance, 1865-1879* (Princeton, New Jersey: Princeton University Press, 1964).

21. Wesley Clair Mitchell, *A History of the Greenbacks* (Chicago: University of Chicago Press, [1903] 1968).

22. Mises, *Human Action*, ch. 20.

ful political and economic fact which often thwarts the establishment of long-term policies of monetary stability. This tight-money policy created cries for debt relief from debtors who had borrowed during the war. Critics blamed the banking system. These cries persisted for the next three decades. The most effective means of debt relief, the critics insisted, was an expansion of money: first through a silver standard, then through a fiat money standard.

Thus, a connection was established between conspiracy theories regarding bankers and the idea that capitalism requires infusions of fiat money from the national government in order to bring prosperity. This idea was not unique to Social Credit. It had been common for half a century prior to the first public appearance of Major C. H. Douglas in 1917. (I offer a brief bibliography on this point in Appendix C: "A Bibliography of Fiat Money Reforms.")

Strange Bedfellows

Major Douglas was the heir of two generations of conspiracy theories regarding bankers and fiat money ideas. First, he promoted the familiar thesis of an international bankers' conspiracy, and he suggested that Jews were probably behind it to a great extent.[23] Second, he promoted an underconsumptionist theory and called for a government monopoly over money and credit. I have written this book in order to focus readers' attention on the errors associated with the doctrine of underconsumption and its policy proposal, fiat money.

Major Douglas offered his followers a complex and highly confusing version of underconsumptionism, but its very complexity aided its acceptance among non-economists. The economists of that era would soon rally behind John Maynard Keynes, whose theories were even more complex and confused than Douglas' theories, but which were expressed in profession-

23. See Chapter 11, below.

al jargon at least vaguely familiar to academic economists of an earlier generation. But few laymen read Keynes' *General Theory*. In contrast, Douglas provided a reform program whose slogans, though not the details of its proposed reform, could be easily picked up by economically untrained critics of capitalism, critics of banking, and, after 1929, critics of the Great Depression.

What the reader needs to understand is that Social Credit is merely one variant of a whole series of proposed monetary reforms, all claiming scientific validity, all blaming capitalism for its supposed tendency toward underconsumption, all proclaiming fiat money as the solution, and all suggesting a bankers' conspiracy. Two decades ago, I identified the fundamental conceptual and practical flaws in these analyses. I focused on the writings of Gertrude Coogan, a contemporary of Major Douglas, but a critic who had become far more popular within the fringes of America's right wing than Major Douglas had ever been.[24] Her influence has now faded. It is time for me to devote an entire book to Social Credit, for the influence of Social Credit in Canada and Australia is still present, especially among evangelical Christians.

Nevertheless, I deal with Social Credit only as an example. There were many other fiat money inflationists before Douglas, contemporary with him, and long after him. As Mises wrote in 1949, virtually the entire economics profession and all governments have adopted some version of underconsumptionism, and they have proposed or adopted one or another scheme of scientific fiat money management by central bankers.[25] I have collected three shelves of books by popular inflationists, and I own only a small fraction of those ever published. Louis Spadaro traced these ideas back to Karl Marx's socialist rival, Pierre-Joseph Proudhon.[26] Proudhon (1809-1865) was a socialist

---

24. Gary North, "Gertrude Coogan and the Myth Of Social Credit," in North, *Introduction to Christian Economics* (Nutley, New Jersey: Craig Press, 1973), ch. 11.

25. Mises, *Human Action*, p, 186.

26. Spadaro, "Salvation Through Credit Reform," unpublished Ph.D. disserta-

whose slogan, "property is theft," has echoed down through the decades, yet his monetary ideas have been promoted ever since by conservatives. If politics makes strange bedfellows, then monetary theory makes them even stranger. The strangest bedfellow of all was Keynes. As we shall see, in several significant respects, Major Douglas and his disciples were under the covers with him.[27]

Conclusion

There has been an operational alliance between critics of the free market. Since the days of Proudhon, this alliance has produced a standard criticism of capitalism based on the idea that there is an inherent tendency toward underconsumption in capitalism. The recommended cure is a program of fiat money inflation directed by the national government.

Each of the defenders of these schemes always claims that his recommended reform will produce price inflation. None of them ever demonstrates that his system has a built-in regulator comparable to the free market's system of redemption on demand: either open-entry free banking (high reserves) or else a government-mandated 100% reserve banking system: no right of withdrawal of a bank deposit until the agreed-upon maturity date of the loan made with the deposit.

Thus, when I argue that Social Credit has never been conservative, I am not arguing that conservatives have not again and again promoted monetary reform schemes comparable to the one recommended by Social Credit. What I am saying is that these reform schemes are inherently hostile to the stated goals of conservatism: limited civil government, personal economic responsibility, the rule of law, the decentralization of power, consumer sovereignty, the reduction of bureaucratic management by the State, and steadily falling prices as the

---

tion, Graduate School of Business, New York University 1955.

27. See Chapters 7 and 10, below.

economy's output increases. I am also saying that these reform schemes are all in opposition to the biblical view of money.

Social Credit's recommended reform is unique only in its degree of linguistic complexity – nothing compared to Keynes' *General Theory*, however – and in the amount of public support it received in the mid-1930's. It was once quite popular. My basic criticism against it applies equally well to all the other fiat money systems: (1) the danger of entrusting such power to the State, which is always tempted to impose an inflation tax; (2) the inability of bureaucrats to determine a "scientific" method of optimum monetary creation, since no such method exists. In short, those who promote Social Credit are statists parading as conservatives and amateurs parading as scientists. So are the Keynesians and all other economists who defend the same view of State authority and monetary science.

Politicians have a built-in preference for the State to borrow money rather than raise taxes. They have a preference for low interest rates. They authorize central banking because central bankers appear to be able to provide money at rates lower than the free market otherwise would provide. That is, politicians prefer monetary inflation to (1) raising taxes openly and (2) borrowing from interest-seeking investors. Central banks return to their national treasuries most of the interest payments received from the government IOU's they hold. This also pleases the politicians. This is why they tolerate central banking.

It is no solution to the problem of price inflation to turn the power of money creation over to the politicians rather than the central bankers. The politicians of the French Revolution destroyed the value of France's currency in a matter of months. The Bank of England has done a far better job in preserving the value of the British pound, 1694 to the present. But neither the politicians nor the central bankers are as reliable as the free market is. Better to leave money creation to gold miners, silver miners, and copper miners; they face expensive geological barriers. People with printing presses, paper, and ink do not.

1

TESTING THE PROPHETS

> Beloved, believe not every spirit, but try the spirits whether they are of God: because many false prophets are gone out into the world (1 John 4:1).

Put every spirit on trial: this is easier said than done. What does this ethical command mean? There are no longer prophets in New Testament times. (While a few groups may claim that there are still prophets in our day, I wonder if these prophets would be willing to undergo the fate of the Old Testament prophet, namely, execution if their predictions turn out to be false: Deuteronomy 18:20-22.) There are, however, Christian leaders who claim that they have discovered authoritative biblical truths about certain topics. Those who come in the name of Jesus Christ, proclaiming some truth, especially a new truth, must be examined carefully by the listeners. Question: Examined in terms of what standard?[1] The Christian ought to respond, "The Bible."[2] The problem is, for almost two thou-

---

1. R. J. Rushdoony, *By What Standard?* (Tyler, Texas: Thoburn Press, [1959] 1983).

2. Greg L. Bahnsen, *By This Standard: The Authority of God's Law Today* (Tyler, Texas: Institute for Christian Economics, 1985); Bahnsen, *No Other Standard: Theonomy and Its Critics* (Tyler, Texas: Institute for Christian Economics, 1991).

sand years, Christians have responded, "The Bible plus something else." That "something else" has generally been some version of Greek philosophy: either the rationalist side (most common) or the irrationalist side (increasingly common in the twentieth century).[3]

The Four Traditional Approaches

The Christian who seeks to try a modern "spirit" in the court of biblical truth has a great responsibility: to master the text of Scripture generally, and also the specific area in which the supposed prophet is speaking authoritatively. There are problems enough when the person is making authoritative public pronouncements about strictly theological matters. But what if he is speaking on some area of applied theology? What if he is seeking to apply the Bible to a specific area of life generally thought of as being part of "the things of this world"? How should this speaker be examined? There have been four approaches to this problem in the history of the Church. We need to consider all four.

1. Things Indifferent

Many Christian cross-examiners assume that all pronouncements outside the narrow range of what is called *theology proper* are inherently neutral religiously, and should be examined on their own terms. That is, these pronouncements are *adiaphora*: things indifferent to the faith. A representative example of a thing supposedly indifferent to the faith would be molecular chemistry. The Bible is understood as having nothing to say about chemistry. The truths of chemistry should be allowed to go their own way without interference from Christians. While the examiner would probably have a strong opinion regarding

3. Cornelius Van Til, *A Christian Theory of Knowledge* (Presbyterian & Reformed Publishing Co., 1969).

the uses of chemistry, such as the manufacture or mind-altering drugs, he would remain silent regarding a particular theory of molecular bonding.

But there is a problem here. Jesus turned water into wine. What chemical formula did He use to accomplish this feat? The Christian tends to argue that this transformation was a miracle, that Jesus did not necessarily use a chemical formula. The non-Christian chemist is unimpressed with this argument. He sees it as a challenge to the universal laws of chemistry. But at least the Christian affirms the existence of miracles irrespective of the hypothetical universal laws of chemistry.

There is another problem here. A chemist's theory of molecular bonding rests on the assumptions of quantum mechanics. Are these assumptions religiously neutral? They involve a theory of cause and effect, namely, that at the subatomic level, there is no physical cause and effect, only statistical probabilities.[4] Should this assumption be automatically dismissed as indifferent to the faith?

This "things indifferent" approach may appear to work in cases as seemingly peripheral to the Christian faith as chemistry. But what about historical geology? What about biology? Here we find problems. These areas are not so easily relegated to the supposed realm of the things indifferent.

2. *Separate Realms: External and Internal*

There are Christian geologists who accept the evolutionary timetable of historical geology. They agree with – or refuse to challenge – the standard estimate of a 4.6 billion-year-old earth.[5] They are perfectly willing to accept such "neutral" sci-

4. Gary North, *Is the World Running Down? Crisis in the Christian Worldview* (Tyler, Texas: Institute for Christian Economics, 1988), pp. 20-31.

5. See, for example, Davis Young, *Creation and the Flood: An Alternative to Flood Geology and Theistic Evolution* (Grand Rapids, Michigan: Baker Book House, 1977), p. 87.

entific conclusions. This is just another example of neutral science, they say, analogous to chemistry. They are committed to a philosophy of neutralism, for this allows them to be local church members in good standing and state university faculty members in good standing. Problem: when your bread is buttered by the spiritual heirs of Charles Darwin, you are sorely tempted to proclaim the nutritional value of the meal.

Other Christians immediately recognize the threat to their faith that such a time table represents, for the Bible clearly indicates that the creation took place about 4,000 years before the birth of Jesus. They are willing to test the geologic prophets by means of the Bible's time frame. For their trouble they are dismissed as theological neanderthals by academically inclined Christians. Why? Because at this point they have refused to take the familiar strategy of the "things indifferent." They have judged this brand of science by the Bible and have found the former defective. They have tried the spirit of Darwinism and have concluded: "Thou art weighed in the balances, and art found wanting" (Daniel 5:27).

Christian Darwinians have pronounced the same judgment against the creationists. The Darwinians have weighed biblical chronology in the balance of the evolutionary time scale and have found biblical chronology wanting. So, there can be no reconciliation between the two views. One of the two kingdoms must fall: the Bible's or Darwin's.

The governing presupposition of the historical geologist or Darwinian biologist who claims to be a Christian is that there are two kinds of truth. There is scientific truth, which governs the external affairs of men – economic, professional, and intellectual – and there is also mythic or symbolic truth, which governs Christians on Sunday morning. It is clear which truth takes priority: the one which generates a monthly paycheck, meaning the one which is consistent with one's formal academic certification, i.e., humanist-approved truth. The Bible teaches that the earth was created before the sun, moon, and stars.

"Poetry!" says the Christian geologist employed by a state university. But he is not employed to teach poetry. He is employed to teach evolution through impersonal natural selection, and this is what he does. He forgets Jesus' fearful warning: "But I say unto you, That every idle word that men shall speak, they shall give account thereof in the day of judgment. For by thy words thou shalt be justified, and by thy words thou shalt be condemned" (Matthew 12:36-37).

3. The Unity of Truth: Biblical Law

The governing principle of the Christian creationist is that the Bible is true; therefore, Darwinian science must be incorrect. This is his operating presupposition. It governs his search for evidence. He begins with God's Bible-revealed word, not with the supposedly neutral mind of man. Truth is one, the Christian presuppositionalist says; thus, science must be restructured to conform to biblical truth. There is a hierarchy of truth. The Bible is at the top of this hierarchy. Men are required by God to pronounce judgment in terms of the Bible.

This places the Bible above all other supposed truths. There are no things indifferent. There are many things that are not yet understood to be biblically relevant, but this is a matter of our poor understanding, not the Bible's lack of jurisdiction. What we know is that everything is relevant to Christian faith because everything is under God's judgment. There is nothing outside of God's judgment. God brings judgment in terms of His revealed law; thus, everything must be under God's law. The truths of science must be sifted and rearranged, or perhaps discarded, in terms of biblical revelation. Bible-rejecting people may discover things that are true, but they can do this only because they are not being consistent with their God-denying religion's presuppositions. They make these discoveries only because they first steal a concept of cause and effect that comes only from God's creation and God's revelation of himself in history. Whatever they say that is true is a gift of God: common grace.[6] This is my operating presupposition.

4. The Unity of Truth: Natural Law

The final approach also assumes that there is only one system of truth in this world, but with this difference: the unity of truth is based on man's mind, not biblical revelation. If "science" says that something is true – that is, if some scientist publicly announces it – and this proposed truth does appear rational or logical to the Christian observer, he concludes that this scientific truth must be consistent with the Bible. After all, we must not proclaim two different kinds of truth. So, he begins to search for any kind of connection between the Bible and the newly discovered truth. He seeks to validate his rationally derived truth by an appeal to the Bible. In other words, he seeks to baptize his scientific truth with the Bible. Sometimes this baptism is achieved by sprinkling; in other cases it requires full immersion.

The presupposition of intellectual and moral consistency governs this quest, but the quest is governed by the presumption that the scientific discovery must govern our interpretation of the Bible. It is not that the Bible is seen as false, or that it is seen as not speaking to the issues raised by the scientific discovery. The investigator does not relegate biblical revelation to the realm of things indifferent or things internal. Rather, he assumes that the Bible's truth is subordinate to science. There is a hierarchy of unified truth, but natural law (science) is at the top. The truth-searcher assumes that the Bible speaks with less precision than science or philosophy. This has been the approach of most Christian intellectuals throughout history. This is the approach of those Christians who call themselves political pluralists.[7]

---

6. Gary North, *Dominion and Common Grace: The Biblical Basis of Progress* (Tyler, Texas: Institute for Christian Economics, 1987).

7. For a critique of this position, see Gary North, *Political Polytheism: The Myth of*

This, I contend, has been the approach of those Christians who have come to other Christians in the name of Social Credit.

Is Social Credit in Some Way Christian?

When Major Douglas proposed the economic reform known as Social Credit, this question did not concern him. As he forthrightly announced in a 1937 speech, "I am not here as a protagonist of Christianity, I am looking at this from a very different point of view. . . ."[8] But in the 1930's, he attracted an important follower in Canada, William Aberhart, a radio evangelist and politician who ran a successful campaign to elect a Social Credit government in the province of Alberta. From that day until now, Christians have adopted Social Credit as an ideal supposedly consistent with Christianity. Major Douglas did not embrace Mr. Aberhart's theology; Mr. Aberhart embraced the rhetoric (though not the policies) of Major Douglas' economic system. Major Douglas recognized the hierarchical nature of his proposed reform: Social Credit must be on top. Any of his disciples who wanted to promote some other reform had to be willing to place it at the foot of Social Credit's altar.

This book is addressed primarily to Christians who have read something about Social Credit, or who may even have publicly embraced some of its ideas. I have not written to convert the leaders of the Social Credit movement to a systematically and self-consciously biblical economic point of view. People who have invested many years of their lives and their reputations in a defense of any doctrine are unlikely to abandon this doctrine late in life. To do so would be an open admission that they have wasted the best years of their lives in piling up what the Bible calls wood, hay, and stubble. People are generally

---

Pluralism (Tyler, Texas: Institute for Christian Economics, 1989).

8. C. H. Douglas, *The Policy of a Philosophy* (Liverpool: K.R.P. Publications, 1937), p. 5.

unwilling even to face this possibility, let alone admit it in public. I do not expect defections by Social Credit leaders.

I am far more interested in persuading people who may be loosely connected to the modern Social Credit movement, but who have not yet committed themselves to it psychologically. I want them carefully to think through exactly what Major Douglas taught rather than what his recent disciples claim that he taught. I also want people to think through the inevitable economic implications of what he taught. These implications are neither conservative nor Christian, as we shall see. In short, those who have become interested in the Social Credit movement should study Major Douglas' writings very carefully before they commit themselves to it – a movement claiming to be scientific but also, in the opinion of several leaders of the movement, ethically Christian. My book will help introduce readers to what Major Douglas *really* taught.

His disciples will probably argue that he taught nothing like this, so I offer readers this challenge: compare my citations with the original sources. Also, examine the literature of modern Social Credit to see whether these passages are dealt with in a scientific manner. See if the responses to my book offered by present-day defenders of Social Credit are thorough, clear, well-documented, and dispassionate, as befits a scientific movement. See if they address the issues raised in this book. If you discover that their responses do not meet these criteria of rigorous scientific discourse, then you will be ready to answer my next question:

Is Social Credit Scientific or Utopian?

My answer is straightforward: utopian. There are very few traces of science in the writings of Major Douglas. For one thing, his books contain almost no footnotes to other men's books. There are no references to professional economics journals. There are no references to technical journals. There are very few statistics, and nothing of an integrated nature: economic facts in the light of scientific economic theory. There was no attempt by Douglas to integrate his theory of pricing and distribution with overall economic theory: capital theory, international trade theory, business cycle theory, interest rate theory, value theory, and so forth. There are few references to economic history in his books. Let the reader understand in advance that the marks of scientific economics are generally absent in the writings of Major Douglas.

Utopianism

What about utopianism? This is far easier to demonstrate. The utopian nature of his thought is best seen in his denial of the economic limit known as scarcity, i.e., the fact that for most things in history, at zero price there is greater demand for them than supply of them. A denial of scarcity is *the* mark of utopianism in economics. Note: I am not saying that some of the effects of scarcity cannot be overcome through progressive social sanctification and its predictable result, economic growth. What I am saying is that the mark of the utopian is his denial that scarcity serves as a significant limit today, and will continue to do so whether or not his suggested reforms are tried.

The utopian regards scarcity as merely a temporary technical limit, the result of society's unwillingness to adopt the utopian's recommended reform. The utopian assumes that nature is inherently bountiful; human institutions are the cause of scarcity. In Chapter I of Part II of Major Douglas' book, *Social Credit*, he announced his rejection of the idea of scarcity. He went beyond this astounding assertion; he also rejected the system of positive and negative sanctions known as punishment and reward. He made himself quite clear in this regard: he accepted the permanent reality of neither scarcity nor sanctions.

> If the considerations thus far advanced are accepted as valid, certain conclusions seem inescapable. A system of Society which depends for its structure on the theory of material rewards and

> punishments, seems to involve, fundamentally, a general condition of scarcity and discontent. You cannot reward an individual with something of which he has already sufficient for his needs and desires, nor can you easily find a punishment which will be effective in a world in which there is no incentive to crime. We might legitimately expect, in such a Society, a mechanism which would ensure a continual, and, if rendered necessary by the advancement of science, an artificial disparity between demand and supply of material goods and services, together with an organisation which would prevent any infringement of the rules by which this disparity is maintained.
>
> We do, in fact, find exactly such a state of affairs in the world to-day. The exact methods by which the financial organisation produces the illusion of scarcity will demand our attention almost at once, and at some length; the organisation by which these arrangements are enforced is, of course, familiar in the form of the Common Law.[9]

Social Credit rejects "the illusion of scarcity." It also rejects the necessity of economic sanctions in a post-reform world. This means that there should be neither profit nor loss in a decent economy. But there is a problem here: *profit and loss are sanctions that guide production*. As Ludwig von Mises argued, such a zero-profit world would be populated only by omniscient beings. *Profit and loss result from men's lack of perfect knowledge regarding the future*. If every person perfectly knew the economic future, there would be neither profits nor losses.[10]

In such a world, there would also be no need for money.[11] If I knew perfectly the future condition of supply and demand, I would not need money. Money is a means of hedging myself against what I do not know about the future. I keep cash in my wallet because I never know when I may want to buy some-

9. *Social Credit* (3rd ed.; London: Eyre & Spottiswoode, 1933), pp. 78-79.

10. Ludwig von Mises, *Human Action: A Treatise on Economics* (New Haven Connecticut: Yale University Press, 1949), p. 291.

11. *Ibid.*, p. 250.

thing. Money allows people to make these snap decisions because money is the most marketable commodity.[12] But if I knew the future state of the market perfectly, I would not need a highly marketable commodity. I would need only that commodity which exchanges perfectly with whatever commodity or service I want to buy at that time.

Because Major Douglas denied that scarcity is anything more than a temporary technical factor in life, I regard Social Credit as a utopian movement. I also contend that Social Credit, if enacted by law, would work very poorly because it is utopian. I do not ask the reader to take my word for this. I offer this book as supporting evidence. Readers should decide whether this book proves my case.

Questions the Reader Should Keep in Mind

As you read this book, keep thinking about the idea of scarcity. Keep asking yourself this question: "What is in short supply: goods and services or pieces of paper called money?" This is the fundamental issue raised by all economic reform schemes that promise exceptional prosperity through a monetary reconstruction involving the creation of money by the government. Social Credit is one such scheme.

Second, consider this question: "If capitalism is as inefficient as Major Douglas said it is, where did the West's wealth come from after 1700, and especially after 1933, when the third edition of *Social Credit* was published?"

Third: "Is it safe to trust government bureaucrats to regulate the supply of anything as important as credit?"

Fourth: "Did Major Douglas supply us with scientific monetary guidelines which, if enforced by law, would surely keep the economy from becoming inflationary?"

Fifth: "How clear are the writings of Major Douglas?"

Sixth: "Why has no professionally trained economist ever

---

12. *Ibid.*, p. 398.

defended Social Credit?"

Seventh: "Why have the disciples of Major Douglas not kept all of his writings in print?"

Eighth: "Have the present-day defenders of Social Credit addressed the issues Gary North raises in his book?"

Ninth: "How would Social Credit's primary reform – the abolition of bank credit – be implemented without destroying the economy during the transition?"

Tenth: "Why did the Social Credit government of Alberta, Canada, refuse to impose any of Social Credit's recommended reforms in the years of uncontested dominance, 1935-39?"

Eleventh: "If Social Credit is Christian, why were so many of its original defenders anti-Christian?"

Conclusion

Social philosophies are not mere abstractions. They are calls to action. A philosophy must produce specific policies. Major Douglas knew this: "If there is one thing which seems to me beyond dispute, it is that you cannot have a policy . . . the policy of a country, policy of a race, or of a nation, without having a philosophy behind it."[13] He warned against what he called the perils of abstractionism.[14] He believed that his philosophy was so radical in its policy prescriptions that it was in fact revolutionary. He offered mankind the possibility of transforming the world in short order:

> Our new philosophy will change the run of the universe at once. It will enable you to have a new conception. So if you can do that, and in my opinion you can do it systematically, you will, in an incredibly short time, become the most formidable force that the world holds, because you will have, in my opinion, the sounder philosophy, and you would have, in that philosophy, a

13. *Philosophy of a Policy*, p. 4.

14. *Ibid.*, p. 5.

better policy.[15]

We cannot separate Major Douglas' philosophy from his policy. He insisted that the two were a consistent system. He warned his followers against trying to separate the two. Then he called them to something like revolutionary action. He praised the participants in English Civil War (1640-1649) and condemned his own followers in Alberta, who after two years in power had not implemented any of his suggestions. He could not have made himself any clearer: "[W]e have to get the scale of this thing more into the scale which was behind those people in the days of the Civil War, when they were not going to work, but were going to stick their enemy in the gizzard. There is no doubt about it, this thing is not going to be done by soft measures. We have had a demonstration in Alberta of the fallacy of imagining that you can make an omelette without breaking eggs. . . ."[16] Note the traditional revolutionary cliché regarding omelettes and broken eggs.

Founders of movements are far more likely to be forthright regarding their goals and methods than bureaucrats and armchair critics are. I believe we should take founders at their words unless we have strong evidence to the contrary. Had all Germans taken Hitler's *Mein Kampf* seriously in 1924, they might have avoided 1933-45. Similarly with the writings of Major Douglas: let us take them seriously, so that we might better understand the policy implications of his philosophy.

His philosophy, as I hope to show, was not Christian, nor can it be conformed to, or assimilated into, conservative Christianity. His economic analysis, as I also hope to show, was not coherent. It is my self-appointed task in this book to prove both of these statements.

Because I am critical of Major Douglas' proposed economic

---

15. *Ibid.*, p. 11.

16. *Ibid.*, p. 17.

reform, I have quoted him at considerable length in this book. The critic must not create stick men to destroy in place of real men. The reader needs to be confident that I am not distorting what Major Douglas wrote. If we are to take him at his word, we need to know what his words were. While this strategy of extensive citation has made this book longer than I would have preferred, I think it will make the book more believable, even though it will take longer to read.

2

THE ORIGINS OF SOCIAL CREDIT

> That we henceforth be no more children, tossed to and fro, and carried about with every wind of doctrine, by the sleight of men, and cunning craftiness, whereby they lie in wait to deceive (Eph. 4:14).

Major Clifford Hugh Douglas (1879-1952) is presented by some of his recent disciples as a man who offered an inherently Christian reform of capitalism. They insist that he was not a socialist and that his economic system does not produce anything like socialism. We need to test these claims. We must begin with a brief study of the man and his early disciples.

Douglas launched Social Credit in 1917. He served as an engineer in the Royal Flying Corps during World War I. Social Credit eventually became a political movement. It attracted some remarkable people during its first two decades – some of the oddest remarkable people in England. With only one possible exception, none of them was an economist.[1]

1. The exception may have been Georges Henri-Levesque. He wrote a 29-page pamphlet, *Social Credit and Catholicism*, in 1936. According to Eric Butler, who wrote a later introduction which was published in the 1967 reprint by Omni Publications, Hawthorne, California, the author was a graduate of the School of Social and Political Sciences in Lille, France, and served as Professor of Economics at Laval and Montreal Universities.

Social Credit on the surface appears to be a movement that rests on a particular economic doctrine. But at least one of its early adherents believed Social Credit to be much more than an economic program. Ezra Pound, the legendary modern poet, was a disciple of Douglas' economic views and the author of a book, *Social Credit*. Pound wrote in 1936 in the *New English Weekly* (2 April): "The surprise on Re-reading is that Douglas seems . . . to deal so little with economics and so greatly and generally with the philosophy of politics."[2] This is an exaggeration – a common weakness of poets (and also of Fascists) – but it indicates that Douglas' contemporaries and fellow-workers saw him as more than just a man with a mysterious past with an even more mysterious economic program.

(Because of Pound's wartime collaboration with the Mussolini government – making English-language short-wave radio broadcasts on poetry, monetary theory, the evils of Jewish bankers, and the treason of Franklin Roosevelt – the United States government claimed he had committed treason. The government's transcripts of these broadcasts were never shown to his lawyer.[3] Pound wrote to one law firm in 1945, invoking the economic theories of Major Douglas.[4] He was never brought to trial on treason charges. Instead, the government declared him insane and therefore mentally incapable of standing trial. He was placed in a mental hospital for an indefinite period in late 1945. It was here that Eustace Mullins visited him daily and became his disciple and his biographer.[5] In 1949,

2. Cited by John L. Finlay, *Social Credit: The English Origins* (London: McGill-Queen's University Press, 1972), p. 2.

3. Julien Cornell, *The Trial of Ezra Pound: A Documented Account of the Treason Case by the Defendant's Lawyer* (New York: Day, 1966), p. 2. Cornell received transcripts from the British Information Service (p. 3). For the text of a representative diatribe, see the April 23, 1942 broadcast (pp. 139-41).

4. *Ibid.*, p. 8.

5. Mullins, *The Federal Reserve Conspiracy* (Union, New Jersey: The Christian Educational Association, 1954); Mullins, *This Difficult Individual, Ezra Pound* (reprint; Hollywood, California: Angriff, [1961]).

while he was still legally insane, a committee of American poets and literary figures awarded him the prestigious Bollingen Prize of $1,000 for the best poetry published in 1948, a privately funded award made through the auspices of the Library of Congress, a U.S. government institution.[6] Pound was released in 1958. Poet Robert Frost was instrumental in pressuring the government to release him, as was Dag Hammarskjold, Secretary-General of the United Nations.[7] Pound returned to Italy, where he died in 1972. Pound's 1930 book, *What Is Money For?*, was re-published by the politically conservative American publishing company Devin-Adair in 1959.)

Douglas in 1937 encouraged his followers to extend their conception of his work beyond the range of monetary reform. He wrote: "In a great many people's minds, Social Credit is a scheme of monetary reform. . . . But, in my opinion, it is a very superficial definition of Social Credit that it is merely a scheme of monetary reform; . . . Social Credit is the policy of a philosophy."[8] The questions are: What kind of philosophy? With what premises? Leading to what conclusions?

His writings were mainly concerned with two things: (1) a criticism of capitalism and (2) a specific set of reforms – mainly monetary – which supposedly will overcome what he said is the root cause of capitalism's failure. Because he concentrated on economic policies rather than philosophy, it is not easy to identify his philosophy, but he made it clear that there was an underlying philosophy. In Chapter 11, I deal with his philosophy. The fundamental unstated premise of his philosophy is that there will be no final judgment by God at the end of history. His conclusion (stated very clearly): there should be neither rewards nor punishments in a sound economy.

---

6. *Ibid.*, p. 119.

7. Henry M. Meacham, *The Caged Panther: Ezra Pound at St. Elizabeths* (Schenectady, New York: Twayne, 1968).

8. *The Policy of a Philosophy* (Edinburgh: K.R.P. Publishers, 1937), pp. 3-4.

Who Was Major Douglas?

Little is known about his life. He had a passion for secrecy. He insisted that nothing be written about him by his disciples. His only child, a daughter, continued this tradition of silence. There is no published biography.[9] This makes it impossible to give a reliable account of exactly how he came to believe what he believed about economics. We know too little about him.

He entered Pembroke College at Cambridge University in 1910 when he was in his early thirties. He remained for only four terms and did not graduate.[10] There is very little trace of his engineering background. He did not graduate from any engineering institute, as far as the records indicate. He worked in 1914 as (at best) a mid-level engineer in the construction of London's Post Office tube or subway. He later claimed to have worked for British Westinghouse, but there is no record of such employment in the Westinghouse files.[11] He did work with the Royal Aircraft Establishment during World War I.[12] In the first two years of its existence, 1920-22, the *Engineering Who's Who* did not list his name; only after he began to gain notoriety for his ideas on Social Credit did the editor include him.[13]

What we should conclude, based on the available evidence, is that the career of Clifford Hugh Douglas (his birth certificate listed only Clifford) was undistinguished except in his role as the developer of the reform program known as Social Credit. There is nothing wrong with being undistinguished, with little formal education and no traceable professional career, but those who still defend his teachings ought to be willing to acknowledge that in 1917 he was, at best, an amateur economist – skilled perhaps, innovative perhaps, but an amateur.

---

9. Finlay, *Social Credit*, p. 88.
10. *Ibid.*, p. 90.
11. *Ibid.*, p. 91.
12. *Ibid.*, p. 92.
13. *Ibid.*, p. 89.

One question the reader needs to get answered is this: Did Major Douglas advance beyond the stage of "untrained amateur economist" after 1917? His economic ideas must stand on their own. His defenders cannot legitimately appeal to his supposed engineering skills as in some way validating the scientific nature of his economics. Why not? First, because there is no record of his engineering work. Second, and far more important, because engineering is a completely different science from economics. It deals with inanimate objects, not human action. Human action involves personal responsibility before God and man. If men were machines, the two sciences might be linked, but man is not a machine. We should not speak of the "mechanics of society" except in the loosest metaphorical sense.

Douglas presented his first essay on economics in an engineering journal, the *Organizer*, in 1917. This was an obscure, limited-circulation journal. The editor of this journal, Holbrook Jackson, then introduced Douglas to his old friend, A. R. Orage, editor of *New Age*. Meanwhile, Douglas had two articles published in the *English Review* in 1918 and two more in 1919. In January, 1919, Orage republished Douglas' December *English Review* article. *New Age* delivered a far larger audience to Douglas than he had previously enjoyed.[14] *New Age* continued to publish Douglas' articles during the 1920's. This journal was his primary outlet in the initial period of Social Credit.

Who Was A. R. Orage?

New Age had begun in 1894, when it was distinctively Christian in tone. Its circulation rose to 56,000. A new editor took over in 1898, a socialist, Joseph Clayton. Circulation then fell. He sold it in 1907.[15] Orage immediately took over as editor of the weekly journal. Its circulation continued to fall: from 23,500

---

14. *Ibid.*, p. 62.
15. *Ibid.*, p. 63.

a week in 1907 to 2,250 in 1918.[16] Yet it gained considerable influence. Why? Because of the influence of Orage.

Orage was a disciple of the atheist philosopher Friedrich Nietzsche. Nietzsche's philosophy has been described as follows by Cambridge University historian David Thomson: ". . . an anti-intellectual revival of paganism, a frontal attack on the teachings of Christianity."[17] Holbrook Jackson had introduced Orage to Nietzsche's writings. Orage wrote two books on Nietzsche in 1906 and 1907, introducing British readers to the man who called for a new world order governed by supermen. It was in 1907 that Jackson and Orage persuaded the Fabian socialist and atheist playwright George Bernard Shaw to put up the money to buy *New Age*.[18] Jackson departed from the project in 1908, leaving Orage as the dominant force. For fifteen years until he left the magazine, Orage attracted some of the most talented authors in Britain to write for *New Age*, although he paid them little or nothing for the privilege.

Orage was intellectually a socialist, but his commitment to Nietzsche made him anti-democratic and intolerant of the poor.[19] From 1912 on, Orage was a syndicalist: a defender of the need for revolutionary violence by trade unions.[20] He became a disciple of his old friend A. J. Penty, who preached the necessity of a restoration of medieval guild socialism. Orage called for "a new epoch, new not only in social and economic structure but new spiritually."[21] This "new spirit" was Eastern mysticism, not Christianity.

Because of Douglas' influence, Orage came to believe that the manipulation of the national currency was the principal

16. *Ibid.*, p. 64.

17. David Thomson, *Europe Since Napoleon* (2nd ed.; New York: Knopf, 1965), p. 405.

18. Finlay, *Social Credit*, p. 66.

19. *Ibid.*, p. 69.

20. *Ibid.*, p. 74.

21. *Ibid.*, p. 75.

cause of economic hardship. It was this idea that also stirred Ezra Pound, a frequent contributor to *New Age*.[22] They both regarded Social Credit as a means of destroying the power of the credit-manipulators.

Orage was not merely a disciple of Douglas; he was a collaborator. Douglas included a 60-page commentary on his ideas, written by Orage, in his second book, *Credit-Power and Democracy* (1920).

Philip Mairet was one of the early partisans of Social Credit. He compiled *The Douglas Manual* in 1934. He was one of the four founders of the Chandos Group, named after a local restaurant, which was begun in 1926 to discuss social and political affairs from the point of view of Social Credit.[23] This group occasionally attracted such luminaries as the socialist G. D. H. Cole, Lewis Mumford, and the poet T. S. Eliot.[24] Mairet wrote *A. R. Orage: A Memoir* in 1936. He was not a hostile witness against Orage. The book was reprinted in 1966 by University Books, an American firm specializing in academically oriented studies of the occult. It was distributed through the Mystic Arts Book Club, which was the mail-order outlet for University Books. University Books published it because Orage was a dedicated mystic, a senior disciple of the occultist Gurdjieff.

In 1922, Orage resigned as editor of *New Age* to become, in Mairet's words, "a missionary of the gospel according to G. I. Gurdjieff."[25] In New York City, he became – again, in Mairet's words – "Gurdjieff's right-hand man. . . ."[26] This was not a major theological break from his past. By the time he took over as editor of *New Age* in 1907, he had become a Theosophist. He

---

22. "Review of *Ezra Pound and Italian Fascism*," *The Economist* (17 Aug. 1991), p. 83.

23. Finlay, *Social Credit*, pp. 168-70.

24. *Ibid.*, p. 170.

25. Philip Mairet, "Reintroduction," *A. R. Orage: A Memoir* (New Hyde Park, New York: University Books, 1966), p. vi.

26. *Ibid.*, p. vi.

was also a disciple of Mahayana Buddhism. He lectured widely on these topics.[27]

Orage remained a disciple of Gurdjieff until 1930. When the Great Depression began, Orage began to re-read economics. He also began giving lectures on Major Douglas' system.[28] In 1931, he broke permanently with Gurdjieff and returned permanently to England.[29] He launched a magazine, *New English Weekly*, in 1932. His goal was to create a new outlet for Social Credit ideas.[30] On the dust jacket of the American edition of E. S. Coulter's book, *The ABC of Social Credit* (1934), we read: "She has worked on the New English Weekly, the official organ of the movement in England. . . ." Mairet worked with Orage during this period. The journal published articles by Cole, Pound, and other friends from Orage's *New Age* years.[31] Orage discovered the youthful (age 18) Dylan Thomas.[32] Orage died in 1934, a few hours after having presented a radio broadcast defending Social Credit.[33] His reputation was so great by that time that the funeral service was conducted by the Dean of Canterbury. As Mairet says, very few of those in 1934 who paid tribute to his career "knew anything about the unorthodox faith in which he died."[34]

The Red Dean of Canterbury

Why would the Dean of Canterbury, one of the most influential clerics in the Church of England, preach at the funeral of someone like Orage? Because of who this particular dean was: Hewlett Johnson, public defender of the Soviet Union, known

27. *Ibid.*, p. 16.
28. *Ibid.*, p. 105.
29. *Ibid.*, p. 106.
30. *Ibid.*, pp. 108-9.
31. *Ibid.*, p. 113.
32. *Ibid.*, p. 128.
33. *Ibid.*, p. 119.
34. *Ibid.*, p. 129.

to his critics as the Red Dean of Canterbury. He served as Dean of Canterbury for over three decades, 1931-1963. He was on the Board of *The Daily Worker*, the Communist newspaper. He wrote a series of defenses of Communism, including *Soviet Success* (1947) and *China's New Creative Age* (1953). A few years after he preached at Orage's funeral he was hired by the Fabian socialist publisher Victor Gollancz to be the general editor of the Christian Book Club.[35] This was the follow-up to Gollancz's hugely successful Left Book Club, begun in 1936.[36] Dean Johnson's own book, *The Socialist Sixth of the World* (1939), went through a remarkable twenty printings by 1944. In that book, he reminisced about the influence of Major Douglas in his life:

> It was at this time [the early 1920's], with these new interests, that I came across Major Douglas and the Social Credit Movement, perceiving at once what appeared to me to be the essential correctness of his analysis and its bearing on social problems. If later I have moved on to other solutions, it has been on moral and practical rather than technical grounds, and because a wider horizon had, in the meantime, opened up. Social reformers will always owe a debt to Douglas.[37]

This praise came from the most notorious clerical sympathizer of Stalin in the West during the twentieth century. It makes a conservative wonder just how conservative Social Credit really is. It makes a Bible-believing Christian wonder just how Christian Social Credit really is. If Social Credit is Christian in the way that Hewlett Johnson was Christian, then Bible-believing Christians will have problems with Social Credit. A word to the wise is sufficient.

---

35. Rose L. Martin, *Fabian Freeway* (Chicago: Heritage Foundation, 1966), p. 55.

36. Paul Johnson, *Intellectuals* (New York: Harper & Row, 1988), p. 279.

37. Hewlett Johnson, *The Socialist Sixth of the World* (London: Victor Gollancz Ltd., 1944), p. 40.

Conclusion

My point by now should be clear. I ask: If Major Douglas did in fact suggest a Christian and conservative reform of capitalism, why was he promoted in 1919 by an editor who was a disciple of Nietzsche, a guild socialist, and an Eastern mystic – a man who returned to England to promote Douglas' system during the major period of his popularity, the early 1930's? If Social Credit appealed to such men as A. R. Orage and Ezra Pound, let alone the Red Dean of Canterbury, in what way is it Christian?

His Christian disciples owe it to their followers to answer this question. They also need to answer this one: Is there any statement in Douglas' writings in which he identified himself as a Christian – not just as a person who appreciated this or that aspect of the teachings of Jesus, but as a believer in the unique divinity of Jesus the Messiah? If they cannot do this, their followers need to question the theological origins of Social Credit.

3

SCARCITY AND WEALTH

And unto Adam he said, Because thou hast hearkened unto the voice of thy wife, and hast eaten of the tree, of which I commanded thee, saying, Thou shalt not eat of it: cursed is the ground for thy sake; in sorrow shalt thou eat of it all the days of thy life; Thorns also and thistles shall it bring forth to thee; and thou shalt eat the herb of the field; In the sweat of thy face shalt thou eat bread, till thou return unto the ground; for out of it wast thou taken: for dust thou art, and unto dust shalt thou return (Genesis 3:17-19).

And thou say in thine heart, My power and the might of mine hand hath gotten me this wealth. But thou shalt remember the LORD thy God: for it is he that giveth thee power to get wealth, that he may establish his covenant which he sware unto thy fathers, as it is this day (Deuteronomy 8:17-18).

Basic to any economic theory is an explanation of how wealth is created and distributed. Consider the full title of Adam Smith's famous book, *The Wealth of Nations* (1776): *An Inquiry into the Nature and Causes of the Wealth of Nations*. Smith wanted to know why some societies possess greater wealth than others. He asked, among many other questions: What are the policies of civil government that lead to greater wealth in society? He answered: above all, allow the voluntary exchange of goods and services without coercive interference from civil magistrates. He concluded that it was the economics of mercantilism – State control over the terms of trade – that hampered economic growth. The solution is to reduce the authority of politicians and bureaucrats to set the terms of trade: tariffs, quotas, prices, and so forth.

The Critics of Capitalism

This conclusion has not satisfied many generations of critics of free market capitalism. They begin as Smith did, by asking the same question: What are the policies of civil government that lead to greater wealth in society? They conclude something entirely different: additional government controls over the economy. They blame poverty on capitalism's policy of placing ownership in the hands of individuals and then leaving them free to buy and sell from each other. Some critics of capitalism call for a return to a version of mercantilism: controls over the terms of trade. National socialism (Nazism) and Fascism are examples of this type of thinking: the "corporate state" which proclaims the "partnership between business and government." Other critics call for full socialism: the State's ownership of the means of production. Still others call for a reform in the monetary system. This was the heart of Major Douglas' recommended reform.

This is not to say that anyone and everyone who calls for a reform of the monetary system is necessarily a hostile critic of free market capitalism. Some are, some aren't. Marx surely was. In the *Communist Manifesto* (1848), Marx and Engels recommended "Centralisation of credit in the hands of the State, by means of a national bank with State capital and an exclusive monopoly."[1] This was point five in their ten-point program to

1. Karl Marx and Frederick Engels, *Collected Works* (New York: International Publishers, 1976), VI, p. 505.

replace capitalism with socialism. The questions we must answer are these: Which kind of monetary reform did Major Douglas propose? Was his a socialist solution? Mercantilist-Fascist? Was he a free market reformer? Or was he something else?

To evaluate the wisdom of any reformer's proposals, we need a standard. I have declared in Chapter 1 that this standard must be the Bible. We need to survey what the Bible teaches on wealth and money before we examine the details of Social Credit. Those who claim that Social Credit is consistent with the Bible must prove their case from the Bible. They have not accomplished this task, as of early 1993. I intend in this book to prove the opposite: Social Credit is inconsistent with the Bible, as well as inconsistent with the logic of economics.

The Biblical View of Wealth

The Bible begins with the doctrine of creation: God created the world (Genesis 1). This means that everything that mankind possesses is a gift of God. Christianity calls such gifts *grace*. So, each person begins life as an heir of the grace of God, what is sometimes called *common grace*. Jesus said of God the Father in heaven: "He maketh his sun to rise on the evil and on the good, and sendeth rain on the just and on the unjust" (Matthew 5:45b). Men do not earn these blessings.

Ownership-Stewardship

God gave to Adam and Eve the ownership of the world: "And God said, Let us make man in our image, after our likeness: and let them have dominion over the fish of the sea, and over the fowl of the air, and over the cattle, and over all the earth, and over every creeping thing that creepeth upon the earth. So God created man in his own image, in the image of God created he him; male and female created he them. And God blessed them, and God said unto them, Be fruitful, and multiply, and replenish the earth, and subdue it: and have dominion over the fish of the sea, and over the fowl of the air, and over every living thing that moveth upon the earth" (Genesis 1:26-28). This placed mankind in authority over the world but under God's authority.[2] This also gave to man the power to create wealth as God's stewards – not original creativity but subordinate creativity.

Man's authority was never absolute. There were limits on it. "And the LORD God commanded the man, saying, Of every tree of the garden thou mayest freely eat: But of the tree of the knowledge of good and evil, thou shalt not eat of it: for in the day that thou eatest thereof thou shalt surely die" (Genesis 2:16-17). God in effect placed a "No Trespassing" sign in front of one tree: His declaration of private property. This sovereign declaration becomes the model for all ownership.[3]

Adam and Eve disobeyed God. They crossed the boundary and ate from that tree. God therefore punished Adam, as head of his household, for this trespass:

> And unto Adam he said, Because thou hast hearkened unto the voice of thy wife, and hast eaten of the tree, of which I commanded thee, saying, Thou shalt not eat of it: cursed is the ground for thy sake; in sorrow shalt thou eat of it all the days of thy life; Thorns also and thistles shall it bring forth to thee; and thou shalt eat the herb of the field; In the sweat of thy face shalt thou eat bread, till thou return unto the ground; for out of it wast thou taken: for dust thou art, and unto dust shalt thou return (Genesis 3:17-19).

From now on, mankind would face *scarcity*: thorns and weeds in man's "gardens." In short, *there are negative economic sanctions in history*. The primary one we call scarcity.

---

2. Gary North, *The Dominion Covenant: Genesis* (2nd ed.; Tyler, Texas: Institute for Christian Economics, 1987).

3. Gary North, *Boundaries and Dominion: The Economics of Leviticus* (Tyler, Texas: Institute for Christian Economics, 1993).

Scarcity

What do we mean by the word "scarcity"? Biblically, scarcity means that nature, which had not thwarted mankind before the curse, now thwarts the entire human race. Men must sweat in order to obtain what they want. That is, they must suffer unpleasantness in order to gain benefits. While air conditioning has reduced the burden of sweating for modern workers in wealthy societies, people now "sweat" internally. They suffer stress. They get ulcers. There is no escape in history from the curse on man's labor.

The economist offers a different definition of scarcity: "At zero price there is greater demand for something than there is available supply to meet all the demand." Thus, men must make bids in order to obtain a scarce resource. They enter a kind of auction. They must give up one scarce good or service in order to obtain another good or service. So, the economist describes the *effect* of scarcity. The Bible tells us *why* we face scarcity.

The earth was cursed by God because Adam was cursed. The earth was like a military man whose commanding officer rebels, fights the wrong battle, and gets everyone killed, wounded, or captured. Nature suffered a penalty because of the rebellion of man.

I have said that there is no full escape from the curse on the ground in history, but this does not mean that there cannot be a progressive reduction in scarcity and its oppressive effects. Economic growth is proof of this. A very good definition of economic growth is this one: "An increase in the number of our options." We have more choices because we can *afford* more choices.

The Bible teaches that as we progressively obey God and overcome our sin and rebellion, He will reward us with greater external blessings. We read of this promise in the Book of Deuteronomy, chapter 28, verses 1-14. On the other hand, if we disobey, we will be cursed: Deuteronomy 28:15-69. So, the

Bible teaches, our external prosperity is related to our external obedience to God's law.

The Grace of God

How can we obey God? Only through God's grace. The Bible is very clear about this: *grace always precedes obedience.* We do not earn our way into heaven. We do not earn God's favor. God graciously grants us saving faith, and He also grants us opportunities to obey him by performing good works: "For by grace are ye saved through faith; and that not of yourselves: it is the gift of God: Not of works, lest any man should boast. For we are his workmanship, created in Christ Jesus unto good works, which God hath before ordained that we should walk in them" (Ephesians 2:8-10). In short, the Bible teaches that grace precedes obedience. We are always in debt to God. We are always paying off our obligations to Him.

The only reason we are granted the grace to continue to pay is because Jesus Christ, the Son of God, died on the cross in order to pay God full price for our sins. "But God commendeth his love toward us, in that, while we were yet sinners, Christ died for us" (Romans 5:8). "For the wages of sin is death; but the gift of God is eternal life through Jesus Christ our Lord" (Romans 6:23).

This means that while there can be no full escape in history from the painful effects of the curse on us and on the earth, there can and should be a progressive escape from the most burdensome of these curses.[4] Why is it impossible to escape fully from the curse of God in history? Because there cannot be moral perfection in history, other than the moral perfection of Jesus Christ. "If we say that we have no sin, we deceive ourselves, and the truth is not in us" (I John 1:8).

Nevertheless, "If we confess our sins, he is faithful and just

---

4. Gary North, *Is the World Running Down? Crisis in the Christian Worldview* (Tyler, Texas: Institute for Christian Economics, 1988).

to forgive us our sins, and to cleanse us from all unrighteousness" (I John 1:9). This is why there is legitimate hope for the future. This is why there is economic growth. But we have been warned not to enjoy the gifts of God – grace – and then forget the Giver. Beware, God warns, that "thou say in thine heart, My power and the might of mine hand hath gotten me this wealth. But thou shalt remember the LORD thy God: for it is he that giveth thee power to get wealth, that he may establish his covenant which he sware unto thy fathers, as it is this day" (Deuteronomy 8:17-18).

The Biblical View of Money

The Bible offers considerable information about how money functions in a society, and also about how monetary policy should be conducted. The most famous statement in the Bible about money is Paul's warning: "For the love of money is the root of all evil: which while some coveted after, they have erred from the faith, and pierced themselves through with many sorrows" (1 Timothy 6:10).

Why should the love of money be the root of all evil? Why not the love of something else? Because money is the representative example of all the earth's goods. Money is the representative example because *money is the most marketable commodity*: the material good which money-loving people imagine can buy all the other desirable things in this world. It can legitimately be regarded as the economic incarnation of the world's goods. Money is the incarnation of wealth.

Gold and Silver

Gold and silver have functioned as money in history. So have other commodities. Economists usually identify the following features of those commodities that have historically functioned as money: recognizability, divisibility, durability, transportability, and high value in relation to weight.

Wealth is equated in the Bible with silver and gold: "And Abram was very rich in cattle, in silver, and in gold" (Genesis 13:2). Anyone who claims to believe in the Bible and who also refuses to acknowledge that money is a form of wealth has to conclude that gold and silver can never be money. But the Bible makes it clear that gold and silver have functioned as money, from the days of the famine in Egypt through Christ's payment of taxes: the coin inside the fish (Matthew 17:27).

The Bible does not teach that money must always be gold or silver. The Bible does not specify any commodity that should always be money. That is, the Bible does not identify "true money." This means that whatever people decide they want to use as money is legitimate, so long as the biblical law against counterfeiting is obeyed.

What the Bible does teach is that righteousness is analogous to the precious metals: silver and gold. For God's people, righteousness and wisdom should be more desirable than silver or gold, but silver and gold are thereby identified as among mankind's most dcsirable goods.

> The words of the LORD are pure words: as silver tried in a furnace of earth, purified seven times (Psalm 12:6).

> The fear of the LORD is clean, enduring for ever: the judgments of the LORD are true and righteous altogether. More to be desired are they than gold, yea, than much fine gold: sweeter also than honey and the honeycomb (Psalm 19:9-10).

> For thou, O God, hast proved us: thou hast tried us, as silver is tried (Psalm 66:10).

> The law of thy mouth is better unto me than thousands of gold and silver (Psalm 119:72).

> Therefore I love thy commandments above gold; yea, above fine gold (Psalm 119:127).

> Riches and honour are with me; yea, durable riches and righteousness. My fruit is better than gold, yea, than fine gold; and my revenue than choice silver. I lead in the way of righteousness, in the midst of the paths of judgment: That I may cause those that love me to inherit substance; and I will fill their treasures (Proverbs 8:18-21).

> The tongue of the just is as choice silver: the heart of the wicked is little worth (Proverbs 10:20).

> How much better is it to get wisdom than gold! and to get understanding rather to be chosen than silver! (Proverbs 16:16).

> A word fitly spoken is like apples of gold in pictures of silver (Proverbs 25:11).

Historically, individuals have chosen gold and silver as money. These metals are rare. They are expensive to mine. They are attractive physically. Coins of pure or nearly pure gold or silver cannot be mass produced. This controls the money supply. One of the attributes of money is high value in relation to weight. Gold and silver possess this attribute.

False Mixtures, False Weights

The Bible identifies debasement as an evil: "Thy silver is become dross, thy wine mixed with water" (Isaiah 1:22). Isaiah equated the mixing of dross (cheap) metals with silver and then calling the finished product silver as a form of moral debasement. He prophesied a coming judgment against Judah, and he described it as a metallurgist's fire:

> And I will turn my hand upon thee, and purely purge away thy dross, and take away all thy tin: And I will restore thy judges as at the first, and thy counsellors as at the beginning: afterward thou shalt be called, The city of righteousness, the faithful city. Zion shall be redeemed with judgment, and her converts with

> righteousness. And the destruction of the transgressors and of the sinners shall be together, and they that forsake the LORD shall be consumed (Isaiah 1:25-28).

To debase a money metal is to counterfeit money. Counterfeiting is a form of deliberate deception: fooling sellers of goods and services into believing that the buyer has offered them a high quality coin. The counterfeiter takes a quantity of high-value metal and then mixes in a low-value metal. This increases the supply of molten metal. He pours this mixture into coin or ingot molds. This increases the number of seemingly high-value coins or ingots in his possession. He then goes out and spends these false coins. This is judicially the same as tampering with the scales, a practice prohibited repeatedly by God.

> Just balances, just weights, a just ephah, and a just hin, shall ye have: I am the LORD your God, which brought you out of the land of Egypt (Leviticus 19:36).

> Thou shalt not have in thy bag divers weights, a great and a small (Deuteronomy 25:13).

> A just weight and balance are the LORD'S: all the weights of the bag are his work (Proverbs 16:11).

> Divers weights, and divers measures, both of them are alike abomination to the LORD (Proverbs 20:10).

> Divers weights are an abomination unto the LORD; and a false balance is not good (Proverbs 20:23).

> Shall I count them pure with the wicked balances, and with the bag of deceitful weights? (Micah 6:11).

What the Bible requires is that those who produce gold or silver coins and then spend them on other goods and services must not debase their coinage. They must not manufacture coins that appear to be made of a specific percentage (fineness) of gold or silver when in fact the shiny metal coins contain a lower percentage than what has been promised or implied by tradition.

What is true of a counterfeit coin, which is relatively easy for someone to test by color, weight, or hardness (in the case of pure gold), is even more true of paper money and credit money. One piece of paper money looks like all the others of the same denomination. Thus, the paper money counterfeiter finds it quite easy to produce extra pieces of paper – far easier than the counterfeiter of metal coins. If the counterfeiter is the State, and has legal access to the specialized paper and ink that only the government is allowed to use (according to government law), then this is doubly evil. It is a misuse of a God-given delegation of sovereignty to the civil government. It is a betrayal of the nation's trust. It is theft.

Price Inflation

When a counterfeiter spends a few debased coins into circulation, he can buy today's goods at yesterday's prices. But if the counterfeiting continues, there will be more and more coins or pieces of paper being offered in the market. This means that money-denominated prices will be bid higher. In the case of coins, the public will find ways to identify the debased coins. Then a price differential will appear between the high-gold content coins and the fakes. But in the case of paper money, this differentiation is impossible. So, all pieces of paper money fall in value equally.

If the government passes a law that requires all coins of the same denomination to trade at the same price, then the high-gold content coins will be hoarded or exported outside the government's jurisdiction. This is Gresham's Law in action: "Bad coins drive good coins out of circulation." This only happens when the State imposes a unique price control: equal value for coins of unequal value. Thus, Gresham's Law should be stated as follows: "Coins that have been *artificially overvalued* by civil law will steadily drive out of circulation those coins that have been *artificially undervalued* by civil law."

Monetary inflation produces price inflation. That is, counterfeiting drives up the price of goods and services; hence, this process of money growth lowers the market value of the debased currency units. Those who hold onto money will see their wealth depleted when prices of other items rise. In the case of a government monopoly over money, those who trust the government when it inflates the money supply generally lose. Those who do not trust the government's money spend the money on goods whose value in money rises. They profit at the expense of those who trust the government. If commercial banks are licensed by the State to create credit money, the same process continues. The same is true of a State-licensed central bank.

Monetary inflation redistributes wealth to those who gain access early to the newly counterfeited money and spend it. Who pays? Those who do not spend it early or those who gain access to the money later in the process, after prices have risen. Those who trust the monetary unit lose; those who do not trust it win. This is an ethically perverse system. This is why the Bible prohibits monetary inflation, either by the State or private counterfeiters.

Conclusion

Any economic theory that begins with nature rather than God's sovereign creation of nature out of nothing cannot be Christian. Any economic theory that begins with man rather than God cannot be Christian. It may not directly attack Christianity, but it is not Christian. It may provide a great deal of good information about this or that, but it is not Christian.

Any monetary system that allows the State to create additional paper money or credit apart from an equal increase in whatever metal the paper receipts promise to pay – gold, silver, or copper – is opposed to what the Bible requires. The same holds true for central banks and commercial banks that issue more receipts to metal than they have in reserve, i.e., fractional reserve banking.[5]

Major Douglas did not begin with the Bible. He did not begin with the doctrine of creation. He did not begin with the idea that all of our wealth is the gift of God. He never mentioned the laws of God revealed in the Bible and God's promise of visible blessings to those societies that obey these laws. He recommended a monetary reform that would place the control over money in the hands of the State. He recommended that the State issue money and credit irrespective of any increase in the State's supply of gold or silver. Let me offer my book's conclusion in advance: *Social Credit requires what the Bible expressly prohibits.*

Summary

1. Economic theory is supposed to help us understand how wealth is created.
2. Adam Smith concluded that free societies with few government controls over the economy produce more wealth.
3. Critics of capitalism claim that more government controls are required to create more wealth.
4. Some critics of capitalism argue that monetary reform is the key to prosperity.
5. To evaluate a reformer's proposals, we need a standard.
6. The proper standard is the Bible.
7. To evaluate a proposed economic reform presumes that the Bible has something authoritative to say about economics.
8. The Bible teaches that wealth begins with God's creation: grace.

---

5. For a detailed discussion, see Gary North, *Honest Money: The Biblical Blueprint for Money and Banking* (Ft. Worth, Texas: Dominion Press; Nashville: Thomas Nelson Sons, 1986).

9. God gave Adam and Eve authority over creation.
10. He gave them power to create wealth as His stewards.
11. Man's authority is never absolute.
12. When Adam disobeyed, God cursed nature: a cursed form of scarcity imposing added costs on man.
13. The economist defines scarcity as "more demand than supply at zero price."
14. The Bible explains why this is the case: a curse by God on man and the asset entrusted to man, namely, the earth.
15. Because of sin, there is no final escape from the curse in history.
16. There is a progressive removal of the curse in history.
17. A society that obeys God will be blessed.
18. God's grace enables men to obey.
19. The Bible identifies gold and silver as wealth.
20. The Bible forbids the debasing of coins.
21. The same prohibition applies to receipts for money metals: no more receipts issued than metal held in reserve.
22. The Bible therefore prohibits anyone, including the State, from issuing paper money or credit that is not backed up by money metals or whatever asset the receipts promise to pay on demand.
23. Fractional reserve banking is also prohibited.
24. The Bible therefore prohibits monetary inflation beyond what gold mining or silver mining produces.

4

SOCIAL CREDIT'S BLUEPRINT

> Where there is no vision, the people perish: but he that keepeth the law, happy is he (Proverbs 29:18).

Vision is mandatory for the survival of God's people: an accurate view of this world and the world to come. God's law is equally mandatory: a concept of ethical cause and effect that connects the affairs of this world and God's judgments to come, both in this world[1] and the next. Why judgments, both positive and negative? Because there must always be personal motivation for reform, whether personal or social. Men always ask this question: "What's in it for me and those I love?" They recognize that there is no escape from sanctions,[2] and they prefer positive to negative sanctions.

Successful reform requires a blueprint. This blueprint sketches the details of the final goal: the vision. There must also be a program that links cause and effect with one's vision of the future. There must be a way to get from here to there over time. That is, there must be a map, or better put, a manual of

---

1. Kenneth L. Gentry, Jr., *He Shall Have Dominion: A Postmillennial Eschatology* (Tyler, Texas: Institute for Christian Economics, 1992), chaps. 6, 10.

2. Ray R. Sutton, *That You May Prosper: Dominion By Covenant* (2nd ed.; Tyler, Texas: Institute for Christian Economics, 1992), ch. 4.

action. Some might even call it a recipe, although this tends to equate an action manual with a transforming formula, which is not correct. We are not talking about a formula; we are talking about a program of progressive corporate sanctification. Without both a blueprint and a manual for action, our reform efforts will be wasted.

Whenever a reformer comes before those in need of reformation, he should be ready with a specific answer to the question: "What is to be done?" Whether the proposed reform is personal, institutional, or social, the reformer needs a blueprint for action which is consistent with the moral and technical content of his proposed reformation.

Reformers rarely offer such a blueprint. Think of Karl Marx and Frederick Engels, the co-founders of "scientific socialism," or Communism. Between them, their writings fill many book shelves. Yet when we search for specific answers to the question, "What is to be done?", there are not ten pages of advice. There is barely one page. There are the famous ten steps in the *Communist Manifesto* (1848), but these were steps to socialism, not pure communism, which somehow was supposed to follow socialism. There is also the terse slogan in Marx's 1875 pamphlet, *Critique of the Gotha Program*: "From each according to his abilities, to each according to his needs." That was hardly a blueprint for reconstruction. The two of them filled tens of thousands of pages with their criticism of capitalism and also detailed criticisms of their socialist opponents, but they never did offer a positive program. They did not have a blueprint.

The Opportunity of a Lifetime

In 1935, in the middle of the Great Depression, the Social Credit League won 89% of the seats in the legislature of the Western Canadian province of Alberta. This party was a breakaway organization from the United Farmers of Alberta, which had rejected Social Credit earlier in the year. For the next two years, it ran the government of Alberta without significant opposition. The party's leader, William Aberhart, had been a radio evangelist since the early 1920's, and had originally organized his followers under the Calgary Prophetic Bible Institute.[3]

Upon his election, he immediately wrote to Major Douglas and offered him the job of adviser. But when Douglas began sending letters of advice, Aberhart ignored them. He kept asking Douglas for a complete blueprint, but Douglas refused to provide one. Instead, he advised piecemeal reforms, none of which Aberhart accepted. Then Aberhart decided to go to the provincial banks for credit to keep the government afloat. This was exactly what Social Credit economics opposed: dependence on commercial banks. Douglas complained about this. Aberhart never hired Douglas, never brought him to Canada, and never instituted any of Douglas' recommendations.[4] Thus ended the first and most important political victory in the history of Social Credit.

Rarely does the founder of a reform movement get the opportunity to advise a victorious politician who has won the election in the name of the proposed reform. Nothing came of it. But what else could Douglas have expected? Earlier in the year, during the campaign, Aberhart had proposed a turnover tax or sales tax on commodity transactions. Douglas had complained about this in a letter to one of his followers. Aberhart, he wrote, had "made the common tactical mistake of elaborating his detail to a general audience to too great an extent."[5] In other words, a Social Credit politician was not supposed to tell the voters what he would do in office after an electoral victory. This should alert us to a fundamental problem with Social Credit. Its founder did not have a detailed, integrated program

3. C. B. Macpherson, *Democracy in Alberta: Social Credit and the Party System* (2nd ed.; Toronto: University of Toronto Press, 1962), p. 145.

4. *Ibid.*, pp. 163-65. See also *The Alberta Experiment: An Interim Survey* (London: Eyre & Spottiswoode, 1937). This book published the correspondence between them.

5. Douglas to J. F. Lymburn (June 1, 1935); cited in *ibid.*, p. 156.

– a blueprint, if you will – but the voters were supposed to vote for Social Credit politicians anyway. Thus, the first time a Social Credit politician rose to power, he turned out to be just another politician.

Such is the fate of reform movements that do not offer detailed blueprints in advance.[6] If its vocal representatives become politically successful on election day, no one can accurately predict what they will do.

Community Credit

Yet it is not the case that Major Douglas left the world with no blueprint. In 1933, he proposed a reform plan for Scotland. Although he lived until 1952, he never published another. This is all we have. I have decided to discuss the details of this blueprint before turning to Major Douglas' theories. I want the reader to consider the practical implications of Social Credit, since Major Douglas always insisted that his reform proposal was nothing if not practical. If the reader does not like what he finds in this blueprint, he will probably be more alert to the theoretical problems of Social Credit. If, on the other hand, he likes what he finds, I will have my work cut out for me in subsequent chapters.

A year prior to the 1935 election in Canada, Major Douglas wrote: "The community creates all the credit there is; there is nothing whatever to prevent the community entering into its own and dwelling therein except it shall be by sheer demonstrated inability to seize the opportunity which at this very moment lies open to it; and opportunity which if seized and used aright would within ten years reduce class-war to an absurdity and politics to the status of a disease."[7]

6. This is why I published the ten-volume Biblical Blueprint Series, 1986-87.

7. *Control and Distribution of Production* (2nd ed.; London: Stanley Nott, 1934), p. 44.

Yes, the community does create credit. But there are important questions that we need to get answered. What community? How does it create credit? In what way did Douglas believe the "community" creates credit? In what way should this "community" distribute the credit? The answers to these questions are at the heart of Social Credit's proposed reforms.

The Community

Let me describe a credit-creating "community." Let us say that you have some money that you are willing to lend. I want to borrow some money. You lend me money. I borrow it, promising in writing that by an agreed-upon date, I will repay you your principal plus a rate of interest. (I could also agree to pay interest quarterly or monthly rather than at the end of the loan.) This is surely a community action, albeit a rather small community. Without a borrower there is no credit; without a lender, there is no credit. *As a community of two, you and I have created credit.* Is there anything sinister in all this? If so, I do not see it.

Let me change the details. You want to lend some money. I want to borrow. You take your money to a bank. You believe the banker is more knowledgeable than you are regarding risky loans. I then go to the banker for a loan. He decides that I am not a high-risk borrower, so he lends me your money. He charges you a fraction of the interest I pay him. This pays him for his time and trouble. Is there anything sinister in all this? If so, I cannot see it.

If he should create money on the basis of your deposit, lending out more than you deposited, then there would be something sinister. That would be what is sometimes called *fractional reserve banking*. He would have issued more receipts to money than money in reserve. That would be an inflationary act: diluting the value of all the monetary units in the economy

– an act of theft.[8] But I am not talking about fractional reserve banking. I am talking about pure deposit banking.

We can see a community in this credit-debt transaction between you and me, or among you, the banker, and me. What has any other community got to do with it? More to the point, what have the politicians got to do with it? Where do they come in? Remember that old phrase: "I'm from the government, and I'm here to help you." When you hear it, hide your valuables.

The Government's Elite Credit Masters

Major Douglas proposed the creation by the State of an elite group of credit masters, as we shall see.[9] These people would have the authority of the State behind them. They would possess the authority to distribute community's credit. They would have the power to issue credit to private businesses and government projects. They would regulate prices, imposing by law what Major Douglas elsewhere called the **Just Price.**[10] They would also declare what Douglas called a **National Dividend.** The State would send checks to most citizens. These checks would serve as money. The Just Price and the National Dividend are the twin pillars of Major Douglas' blueprint for reform. This was a monetary reform, but it was much more than monetary reform, as he said on at least one occasion.

The government can of course print pieces of paper. We need to ask: What makes one piece of paper money and another piece of paper worthless? Not the paper. Not the ink. We know that sometimes when governments print lots of pieces of paper called money, the result is a lot of worthless paper. We

8. Murray N. Rothbard, *What Has Government Done to Our Money?* (Auburn, Alabama: Ludwig von Mises Institute, [1963] 1990).

9. See Chapter 10, below.

10. *Economic Democracy* (2nd ed.; London: Cecil Palmer, 1921), p. 112. He also referred to this as "The Just Price and the Price Factor": *The New and the Old Economics* (Edinburgh: Scots Free Press, 1936), p. 26. See *The Douglas Manual*, edited by Philip Mairet (London: Stanley Nott, 1934), Part IV, "The Just Price."

also need to ask: What converts what had once been money into worthless paper? These are crucial questions to ask anyone who proposes a monetary reform. If you don't have answers to these two questions, you will not ask the crucial question: *What legal and institutional safeguards does the proposed reform establish to guarantee voters that the post-reform currency will not become worthless?* My advice: get a very clear answer to this question before you turn a government printing press over to the reformer.

The Source of the Capital

If I borrow money from you, I know where the money came from: you. You have given up whatever the money will buy today in order to receive back this money plus interest later on. You have forfeited present assets – the purchasing power of money – for the sake of future assets: the purchasing power of even more money at a later date. All this is easy to understand, or should be.

But if an elite State bureaucracy of credit masters is to gain access to capital, where will this capital come from? What kind of capital is it? Major Douglas was never very precise about this, but in his Appendix to the third edition of *Social Credit* (1933), we can see the outline of his answer. This Appendix is titled, "Draft Social Credit Scheme for Scotland."

Major Douglas' One Blueprint

Major Douglas called for the creation of a fact-collecting program to compile a national inventory of goods. He called this part of his scheme **clause 1**. This information should be obtained from "company balance-sheets, land registration offices, and insurance companies. . . ." This, of course, was long before the days of computers. What would be included in this gigantic inventory? Such things as "land, roads, bridges, railways, canals, buildings, drainage and water schemes, minerals, semi-manufactured materials." Now get this: "No distinction between public and private property."[11]

Printing Money

But he did not stop there. We human beings are also a form of capital. So, he said, "Add to this the sum representing the present commercial capitalised value of the population."[12] What are *you* worth, my friend? How would any government agency estimate what you are worth? More to the point, once estimated, what use will the agency make of this estimation? Douglas recommended the following use:

> From the grand total thus obtained a figure representing the price value of the Scottish capital account could be obtained. Financial credit to any equivalent can be created by any agency such as a Scottish Treasury empowered by the Scottish people.[13]

Understand what this means. Douglas recommended the *monetization of the nation's estimated capital.* That is, the government should create spendable money on the basis of this statistical estimate of the total wealth of the country. Some percentage of the total value of the nation's capital should then be used to authorize an issue of new money.

This was an old scheme by the time Douglas proposed it. Early in the French Revolution, the government confiscated all the land and buildings owned by the monasteries, and later it confiscated the estates of people who had fled France. Then the government issued paper money, with the confiscated property serving as collateral. This is not to say that these pieces of paper were redeemable in land. They were not. Frenchmen could not

---

11. *Social Credit* (3rd ed.; London: Eyre & Spottiswoode, 1933), p. 205.
12. *Ibid.*, p. 205.
13. *Ibid.*, pp. 205-6.

turn in paper money and obtain ownership of a specific property. But the land was said by the government to back new issues of paper money. What was the result? The government kept issuing more and more money, all based on the so-called collateral of the land. The result was mass inflation and the destruction of money.[14]

The problem was, the value of the land was measured by prices denominated in the paper money. Every time the government printed up new money, the monetary value of the land increased. So, the government could then issue even more money, since the value of its collateral had gone up since the last issue of money. This of course again raised the money value of the land. Up, up, up went land prices, but the printing presses went even faster. Up, up, up went all prices in France until the government declared price controls and chopped off the heads of any seller who violated the price laws. The result of this law was that sellers hoarded goods. This, too, became a capital crime. (I mean "capital" as in "head," which was chopped off, not "capital" as in money, even though it was capital crime in that sense, too.)

Here is the question we must ask every monetary reformer: *What, legally and economically, will keep the government from printing too much paper money or issuing too much credit?* The honesty of the politicians? The good judgment of the bureaucrats in charge of printing money? These are the very practical questions that Major Douglas never answered clearly, as we shall see in subsequent chapters.

You can see the problem. The statistical estimate of the nation's wealth is calculated in money. If the government issues paper money on the basis of this statistical number, the new money will raise prices. When prices rise, the value of the "community's" capital rises. This allows another issue of paper

---

14. Andrew Dickson White, *Fiat Money Inflation in France* (Irvington, New York: Foundation for Economic Education, [1912] 1959).

money. It is the same problem that the French Revolutionaries faced. The more money the government prints, the higher prices rise. The higher prices rise, the more money people need to make ends meet, and the more collateral for the issue of new money the government possesses. The government then prints more money. There is no theoretical limit to this.

If a bank issues a warehouse receipt to metal stored in its vault, someone can redeem the note and receive a fixed weight and fineness of gold, silver, copper, or whatever the warehouse receipt promises to pay. If the issuer prints up more receipts than he has in reserve, he can be forced into bankruptcy if more people show up to redeem their notes than he has items in reserve. This threat acts as a brake on the issue of unbacked warehouse receipts. (In a nation that outlaws fractional reserve banking, such unbacked warehouse receipts would become illegal.)[15] But there is no comparable brake for an issue of unbacked paper money, which is not a redeemable warehouse receipt.

Why is Social Credit regarded as conservative?

Shutting Down Private Markets

Major Douglas claimed in his 1937 lecture, "The Policy of a Philosophy," that Social Credit is more than a monetary reform. He was telling the truth. His recommended reform also involved the destruction of the markets for privately owned real estate. He made this clear in **clause 2**: "No transfer of real estate directly between either persons or business undertakings will be recognised. Persons or business undertakings desiring to relinquish the control of real immovable estate will do so to the Government, which will take any necessary steps to re-allot it to suitable applicants."[16]

15. Gary North, *Honest Money: The Biblical Blueprint for Money and Banking* (Ft. Worth, Texas: Dominion Press; Nashville: Thomas Nelson Sons, 1986), chaps. 8, 9.

16. *Social Credit*, p. 206.

This proposal does not say that the government will pay anything to those who relinquish control over their real estate. Perhaps this is to be left to the discretion of the politicians. However, the word "re-allot" indicates that the government will not sell the property. Thus, it would seem that the government will not pay for the property, either. If it does, it will pay the owner with fiat money, as we shall see. In any case, the language of the reform indicates that private owners will not be able to designate lawful heirs. The government will decide who is to gain ownership of real estate. Bureaucrats will "re-allot" the real estate to "suitable applicants." Suitable to whom? Not the original owners.

There is another crucial market arrangement that will be made illegal: retirement funds. A retirement plan is administered by a trustee or a holding company. Under Social Credit, this will become illegal. "As from the initiation of this scheme, the holding of any stock, share, or bond by a holding company or trustee will not be recognized."[17]

He did not offer any explanation for either of these two prohibitions. He expected his followers to take his word for it.

Why is Social Credit regarded as conservative?

The National Dividend

Having shut down the sale of privately owned real estate and having made mutual funds and pension funds illegal, the government then should announce a levy, Douglas said. Presumably, this will be strictly a statistical levy, not the actual confiscation of ownership rights. I say presumably; Douglas did not make this clear.

This levy seems to have been a statistical device for establishing how much new money would be created. Douglas used a 1% figure as an example, but nothing in his system ever estab-

17. *Ibid.*, p. 206.

lished a limit on this figure – no formula, no principle of law, nothing. But 1% sounds small. For public relations purposes, he no doubt thought this would do just fine. He called this "an arbitrary figure." Arbitrary it would be! This levy was part of a plan that he called "The Initial National Dividend," or **clause 3**. He explained:

> (3) For the purpose of the initial stages an arbitrary figure, such as 1 per cent of the capital sum ascertained by the methods outlined in clause (1), shall be taken, and a notice published that every man, woman, and child of Scottish birth and approved length of residence, with the exception mentioned in the paragraph that follows, is to be entitled to share equally in the dividend thus obtained. . . . The dividend to be paid monthly by a draft on the Scottish Government credit, through the Post Office and not through the banks.[18]

He insisted that "no interference with existing ownership, so called, is involved in such a proceeding."[19] We are back to the issuing of unbacked credit: fiat money.

He called this a dividend. What is a dividend? In the world of private enterprise, a dividend is a payment from a business to an owner of a share of corporate stock or other ownership claim. A business earns a return on the capital invested, and it pays out a portion of these earnings to investors. Instead of borrowing money from a bank, businessmen decide to sell a portion of the ownership to investors. A bank insists on payment. The payment of dividends, however, is left to the discretion of the business' owners. People buy shares for two reasons: receiving dividend payments and receiving capital gains. Capital gains are increases in the market value of the shares.

There are limits to dividends. The main one is the solvency of the company. There is a relationship between the investment

---

18. *Ibid.*, p. 207.
19. *Ibid.*, p. 207.

into the company and the income pulled out of the company. The investor forfeits the use of everything the money would buy when he turns the money over to the company (initial offering) or to another investor who is selling his share of ownership (secondary market). What the initial investor gives up constitutes the capital of the firm. There is no increase in the money supply; there is only a transfer of money from one entity (the investor) to another (the firm). The same is true of dividends: the money goes the other way. Paying corporate dividends creates neither monetary inflation nor price inflation.

Not so in Douglas' system. It is a reform based on the creation of new money and credit. Social Credit is not a direct tax scheme, he insisted. (I argue that because it is inherently inflationary, Social Credit can easily become an *inflation tax* scheme, paid for by those who hold cash or instruments of wealth that promise to pay money: bonds, cash-value life insurance, pension funds, mortgages, etc. The beneficiaries are those who spend the newly created money fast, go into debt, and pay off later with depreciated money.)

Under Social Credit's national dividend scheme, no citizen is required first to turn money over to the government, as a private investor would turn money over to the seller of ownership shares. On the contrary, the government sends out pieces of paper called money. These payments are not a dividend on money previously invested, i.e., money forfeited by the investor. These payments are made with fiat money: an additional injection of purchasing media into the economy. No one has stopped spending in order to enable another person to spend. Everyone continues to spend. This dividend is *monetary inflation*, and a similar scheme in France, 1789-94, produced vast price inflation.

How fair is Douglas' proposed system? Consider the fate of anyone with high income. This person is, in Douglas' words, "the exception mentioned in the paragraph that follows."

> No payments of the national dividend will be made except to individuals, and such payments will not be made where the net income of the individual for personal use, from other sources, is more than four times that receivable in respect of the national dividend.[20]

On what moral basis should any law-abiding citizen not benefit from this national dividend? His assets were counted in making the estimate of total national wealth. Why should he be left out of the "earnings," which of course are not earnings at all, but merely the government's successive issues of unbacked fiat money? Douglas always claimed not to be interested in morality in proposing his reforms. He was strictly practical, he said, as we shall see in Chapter 5. Apparently, this exclusion of the rich had to do with political pragmatism. As a Christian, I would call this proposal immoral: a form of political theft.

The State guarantees a national monthly income, "tax-free in perpetuity,"[21] for everyone except rich people. Would any honest person in his right mind call this system conservative? Or Christian?

Why is Social Credit regarded as conservative?

Nationalizing Credit in One Stroke

A bank lends money on assets owned by commercial borrowers. If a business expects to be paid a sum of money in a year, it can take the promissory note to a bank and ask to borrow money on the basis of the note, which serves as collateral for the loan. If the bank trusts the business, or at least the person who signed the promissory note, it makes the loan at a market rate of interest. This rate of interest is called the *discount rate.* We come now to **clause 4**:

---

20. *Ibid.*, pp. 207-8.

21. *Ibid.*, p. 208.

> Simultaneously with the publication of the foregoing notice a figure to be published known as the discount rate, to replace the existing bank discount rate, a suitable value of this for initial purposes being 25 per cent. It is important that the figure should not be less than 25 per cent, and it might reasonably be higher.[22]

This means that in 1933, the Scottish government, by decree, would have imposed on all banks a mandatory discount rate, meaning a commercial interest rate, of at least 25% per annum. What were interest rates in 1933? The world, then as now, had competitive rates across borders. A rate in any large commercial nation would be pretty close to the rate in any other nation of approximately the same risk, wealth, and monetary policy. Throughout the world in 1933, banks were failing, money supplies were dropping, and prices were falling. This put downward pressure on interest rates. Borrowers were afraid to borrow. For example, in the United States in 1933, a stock exchange loan was 1.1%. Prime commercial paper was paid 2.73%. Prime bankers' acceptances, 90 days, went for 0.63%. U.S. Treasury bills earned 0.5%. A year later, the rate was 0.25%. Two years later, in 1935, the rate was a minuscule 0.14%. Business interest rates in 1935 were in the 0.5% range.[23] Similar rates prevailed throughout the industrialized world.

Consider the owners of a Scottish business. Their competitors in the rest of the world could borrow money at anywhere from 1% to 0.5%. Can you imagine what a mandatory discount rate of 25% or more would have meant? Businesses would be required to pay 25 times to 50 times what their foreign competitors were paying. This would have bankrupted every company in Scotland that relied on bank debt unless it could borrow

22. *Ibid.*, p. 208.

23. *Historical Statistics of the United States: Colonial Times to 1970*, 2 vols. (Washington, D.C.: U. S. Government Printing Office, 1975), II, p. 1001.

from a bank in a nation not yet under a Social Credit government. It would have meant the bankruptcy of all Scottish banks, which would have had zero borrowers at this mandated interest rate. *It would have meant the nationalization of all Scottish banking.* The government would overnight have become the sole legal lender. This, of course, is the whole point of Social Credit: the nationalization of credit. Douglas knew exactly what he was recommending, but he never called it what it really was: the forced nationalization of banking and credit.

This is a program to destroy private property. A government places a price control – in this case, a price floor – on commercial interest rates, thereby bankrupting many businesses and all private banks within its borders. This is a system for destroying the capital invested in many businesses and all privately owned banks. It is the deliberate, systematic destruction of private wealth without compensation.

Why is Social Credit regarded as conservative?

Price Controls

Price controls are established by governments in order to thwart the decisions of buyers and sellers, i.e., to thwart consumer sovereignty. Price controls make private bargaining illegal. This is why the French Revolutionary government imposed them.

When a price ceiling is set below the price that would have prevailed on the free market, sellers start withholding supplies, while too many buyers show up. Shortages are the result. Similarly, when a price floor is set above the price at which exchanges would take place voluntarily, suppliers bring more goods to market than there is demand. Gluts are the result. Thus, only when prices are set by the government where the free market would have set them anyway does the economy avoid either shortages and gluts.

We come to **clause 5**: "Simultaneously, an announcement to be published that any or all business undertakings will be accepted for registration under an assisted price scheme."[24] These prices "shall, as far as practicable, be maintained at a figure to include such average profit, where this is agreed as equitable for the type of business concerned. . . ."[25] Average profit? Major Douglas completely misunderstood how profits arise and what their economic function is. Profits are residuals that remain after all expenses have been met. Except in government-regulated public utilities, no one guarantees profits. No one can; they are residuals. Innovative firms make large profits initially, while inefficient firms make low or no profits. Profits stem only from the ignorance among one's competitors. "Buy low, sell high" is the rule of profits, but this rule proves impossible to follow unless some entrepreneur spots a bargain and buys it for resale later. He must buy it before his competitors raise its price by bidding for it in the open market.

A Social Credit government is supposed to guarantee all firms an equitable rate of profit. Equitable? In whose eyes? We can guess: in the eyes of established, inefficient firms that are facing competition from innovators. This was a scheme to restructure Scotland's entire economy along the lines of a gigantic public utility: mandatory average profit, mandatory price controls.

What firm would voluntarily want to register to become part of such a bureaucratic regulatory nightmare? Only the nation's less profitable firms. So, Douglas added this incentive: *no registration, no credit from the government.* **Clause 7** establishes that all business credit must go through the banking system. But the private banking system will be forced to charge 25% on its loans. Registered firms will have access to government credit – "below cost"[26] – while unregistered firms will have to pay 25% per annum, minimum. "Unregistered firms will not be supplied

24. *Social Credit*, p. 208.
25. *Ibid.*, pp. 208-9.
26. *Credit-Power and Democracy*, p. 143.

with the necessary bill forms for treatment in this manner, with the result that their prices will be 25 per cent, at least, higher than those of registered firms. (It is obvious that the larger the discount rate can be made, the greater will be the handicap of the non-registered firms.)"[27]

This is coercion, pure and simple. It is a law against those individuals with money seeking out other individuals who want to borrow. This law monopolizes credit transactions inside the nation's banks, and then it bankrupts all private banks inside the nation. If passed and enforced, the nation's businesses would become totally dependent on either foreign lenders or the national government and its paid agents, State-employed credit masters.

Why is Social Credit regarded as conservative?

Make-Work Plans

Clause 8 specifies: "The hours of Government offices will be reduced to four hours per day. To meet the temporary congestion of work, additional staff will be employed. . . ."[28] This will be a second shift of workers doing identical work. In other words, it mandates the training of two or more sets of bureaucrats when only one set can accomplish the same task.

Why is Social Credit regarded as conservative?

Cutting Wages

Clause 9: "Wage rates in all organised industries will be reduced by 25 per cent where such reduction does not involve a loss to the wage-earner exceeding 20 percent of the sums received in the form of national dividend. . . . Any trade union violating a wage agreement to render its membership liable to suspension of national dividend, and any employers' organisa-

27. *Social Credit*, p. 209.
28. *Ibid.*, p. 210.

tion committing a similar offence, to be liable to suspension of price assistance or wage reduction."[29] Any person who quit work for the next five years forfeited his national dividend. He had to keep working "in whatever trade, business, or vocation he was classified in the last census. . . ."[30]

This scheme might be regarded by some as conservative because it is opposed to trade unions, but it is equally opposed to employers.

Taxes

Finally, **clause 10**: the abolition of property taxes. Only a non-graduated (flat) income tax or a sales tax was to be imposed.[31] Here is the only conservative recommendation in the proposed credit scheme. His book ends here.

In *Warning Democracy*, he announced: "Modern taxation is legalised robbery, and it is none the less robbery because it is effected through the medium of a political democracy which is made an accessory by giving it an insignificant share in the loot."[32] But what is to distinguish ethically between this kind of robbery through taxation and Social Credit's version, where the State, in order to gain a monopoly over credit, sets an interest rate floor that bankrupts many businesses and all private banks? I see no difference.

Guaranteed Income: The Dole

The heart of Social Credit's economic reform is its creation of a stream of lifetime income that does not require people to work or invest. *There is no relationship between risk and reward in Social Credit*: no extra reward to the investor for having invested wisely in a consumer-satisfying production process, and no

---

29. *Ibid.*, pp. 210-11.
30. *Ibid.*, p. 211.
31. *Ibid.*, pp. 211-12.
32. *Warning Democracy* (2nd ed.; London: Stanley Nott, 1934), p. 61.

penalty for having invested in a process that produced something that consumers did not want to buy. The rich receive no dividend payments. Everybody except the rich receives the same percentage of the national dividend just for being alive. Also, the larger this dividend payment is in relation to income from wages, the less the economic relevance of the reward for good work and the penalty for poor work. Here is the moral center of Social Credit: its rejection of sanctions.

> One method by which it is possible to visualise in a familiar form the embodiment of such a set of relationships is in the conception of, let us say, Great Britain, Limited. If we imagine a country to be organised in such a way that the whole of its natural born inhabitants are interested in it in their capacity as shareholders, holding the ordinary stock, which is inalienable and unsaleable, and such ordinary stock carries with it a dividend which collectively will purchase the whole of its products in excess of those required for the maintenance of the "producing" population, and whose appreciation in capital value (or dividend-earning capacity) is a direct function of the appreciation in the real credit of the community, we have a model, though not necessarily a very detailed model, of the relationships outlined. Under such conditions every individual would be possessed of purchasing-power which would be the reflection of his position as a "tenant-for-life" of the benefits of the cultural heritage handed down from generation to generation.[33]

A Social Credit economy supposedly will progressively remove economic inequality. There will be an equalization of income based on equal shares in the nation's capital: *one person, one share*. No one can be deprived of his claim to a share of everyone else's productivity (except, of course, when he violates a directive from the bureaucracy: see above, clause 9, on wage rates). Everyone is a *tenant for life*. This is a very good thing,

33. *Social Credit*, p. 185.

Douglas said. "It is both pragmatically and ethically undeniable that the ownership of these intangible factors vests in the members of the living community, without distinction, as tenants-for-life."[34] Social Credit would put all but the rich on the dole.

Why is Social Credit regarded as conservative?

The Premises of Socialism

Social Credit is socialistic in its basic philosophy. It begins with a false intellectual premise, namely, "the community" (society) owns all the capital within the State's borders. This means that *society is the same as the State*: the familiar assumption of all radicals and socialists. **Social Credit** proposes the establishment of a national system of compulsory **State credit**. When Douglas says "community," he means individuals who are members of a national *political* order. They exercise economic control through State coercion, not the free market. "If the community can use the plant it is clearly entitled to it. . . ."[35]

Douglas referred to the "real owners" in society: all members of the political order. They exercise their ownership through the threat of legal violence: the creation of the State's monopolistic credit masters. Douglas insisted that "*the power to draw on the collective potential capacity to do work*, is clearly subject to the control of its real owners through the agency of credit."[36] This is the essence of all socialism: collective ownership.

Douglas sometimes retained the language of free market individualism. "It is a fact inherent in the nature of the case that ownership must vest in an individual, and any attempt to get away from this law of nature results as a practical consequence in the appointment of an administrator whose power increases as the number of his appointers increases."[37] This is

34. *Ibid.*, p. 190.
35. *Economic Democracy*, p. 114.
36. *Ibid.*, p. 115.
37. *Warning Democracy*, p. 8.

quite true: ownership under God does "vest in the individual." But the problem for Douglas was that his system did not reconcile his view of communal ownership – no real estate sales, no private banking, price controls, etc. – with this rare defense of individual ownership.

Douglas began his economic analysis with a false socialistic premise: "Natural resources are common property, and the means for their exploitation should also be common property."[38] What are these means? Anything bought and sold through the use of credit, including human labor. Furthermore, Douglas maintained that improvements in economic productivity must be distributed to the entire community, not just to the innovator and those consumers who buy from him. In his first book, Douglas announced that "all improvements in process should be made to pay a dividend to the community."[39] This is the heart of economic error of Social Credit: it would put the nation on the dole. Entrepreneurship would die.

The free market rewards consumer-satisfying innovators with profits. Profit is a residual that remains after all costs have been paid for. Profit stems, as we have seen, from the fact that some entrepreneurs recognize that, in terms of future demand, certain producer goods are underpriced today. They buy these underpriced resources, produce consumer goods, and sell them to the highest-bidding consumers. This is the basis of economic progress: *the quest for profit forces producers to cut costs and find better ways of serving consumers*. Remove the profit motive, and you reduce the innovation motive. Also, you remove the "hammer" that the consumer holds over producers: the right to buy from someone else, thereby producing losses for the inefficient producer. Social Credit removes this hammer from the consumer and places it in the hands of the State's credit masters. Social Credit also removes savers' and investors' control over business

38. *Economic Democracy*, p. 112.

39. *Ibid.*, p. 103.

by monopolizing the supply of credit into the hands of the government. It removes capitalism's system of rewards and punishments. This is the heart, mind, and soul of Social Credit: not monetary reform, not government credit, and not price controls. At its core is a philosophy which denies the legitimacy of economic sanctions: rewards and punishments, carrots and sticks.[40]

Social Credit forbids men to buy and sell homes. It forbids them to change their occupations without permission, at least during the transition to Social Credit. It forbids them to borrow and lend except at interest rates at least 25 times higher than the rate which people voluntarily decide is reasonable. It centralizes banking and credit into the hands of a monopolistic State credit bureaucracy: the credit masters. It establishes price and wage controls on businesses, as well as profit limits on business. It allows the State to issue unbacked fiat money on the basis of a statistic: a monetary estimate of total national capital, including human capital. It issues these checks or paper money to everyone except the rich on a "one share, one check" basis. It forbids the buying and selling of these shares. It forbids parents to leave these shares to their heirs (**clause 3**: p. 208). And this is all justified in the name of private property: "It will be obvious that such a set of relationships does not impinge on what is commonly called the rights of property. . . ."[41]

This system does not reward the good investor, nor does it penalize the bad investor. No one is allowed to accumulate shares. Fiat money that is not sent to consumers as part of the National Dividend is invested in government-favored business firms by the government's monopoly credit masters as part of the Just Price system. That is, the investors are bureaucrats who are salaried by the government and therefore cannot personally profit from successful projects which their decisions have made

40. See Chapter 11, below.

41. *Social Credit*, p. 186.

possible. There is no reward for profitable investing, for there are only average profits. The enterprises of the nation are turned into one gigantic public utility: fixed rates, fixed prices, and average profits for all.

Finally, he wanted the part played by human labor, with its system of rewards and punishments, to fade away. He called for a system of State distribution of wealth in which "the distribution of cash credits to individuals shall be progressively less dependent on employment, that is to say that the dividend shall progressively displace wages and salaries as production keeps increasing per man hour."[42] *The whole nation goes on the dole!* If this cannot legitimately be called a welfare State, what can?

Why is Social Credit regarded as conservative?

Conclusion

What is the Social Credit economic system really all about? As we shall see in Chapter 11, it is about man's attempt to escape from God's negative sanctions in both history and eternity. Major Douglas, as a follower of Charles Darwin, rejected the biblical idea of heaven and hell, and he then constructed an economic system that reflected his theology.

Socialism comes in many forms, but they all boil down to the same thing: no special rewards to those producers who serve consumers as consumers pay to be served, and no special penalties for those producers who ignore consumers' demonstrated preferences in the market. Socialism denies what Jesus taught about the final judgment, namely, that from them to whom much is given, much is expected: "And that servant, which knew his lord's will, and prepared not himself, neither did according to his will, shall be beaten with many stripes. But he that knew not, and did commit things worthy of stripes, shall be beaten with few stripes. For unto whomsoever much is given, of him shall be much required: and to whom men have commit-

42. *Warning Democracy*, pp. 34-35.

ted much, of him they will ask the more" (Luke 12:47-48). In this crucial sense, as in many others, Social Credit is socialistic to the core.

I ask: Why would anyone who calls himself either a conservative or a Christian become an advocate of Social Credit? My answer: probably because he does not know what Major Douglas actually wrote. I believe this is one reason why leaders in the Social Credit movement have done so little to see to it that the complete writings of Major Douglas are easily available to the average Social Credit believer.

Today's Social Credit leaders, because they aim their appeal at conservatives and Christians, have been unwilling to use Major Douglas' proposed reform for Scotland as their model. Neither did William Aberhart in the 1930's in Alberta. There is little that is either conservative or Christian about that proposal.

Summary

1. A reformer should have a blueprint.
2. The founders of Communism did not have one.
3. When the Social Credit League won the 1935 election in Alberta, its leader had no blueprint.
4. When he contacted Major Douglas, the latter offered only piecemeal suggestions.
5. The government of Alberta never launched a Social Credit reform.
6. Social Credit rests on the idea of community capital.
7. This community capital is a statistical concept: the total value of all goods, private and public.
8. This statistic is then used to authorize the printing of money.
9. Social Credit proposes the creation of governmental, monopolistic credit masters.
10. These monopolistic credit masters issue credit to highly regulated private businesses (Just Price).
11. The government also sends monthly checks to every citizen except rich ones (National Dividend).

12. There is no scientific formula regulating the issuing of fiat money. The formula is "arbitrary."
13. During the French Revolution, a similar scheme led to mass inflation.
14. Social Credit makes it illegal to buy and sell real estate.
15. It also becomes illegal to invest in mutual funds or other trusts.
16. The government will hike bank interest rates by at least a factor of 25.
17. This will bankrupt all private banks.
18. This forces all businesses to borrow from foreign banks or from the government, for which they must register.
19. The credit masters will fix prices of all registered businesses.
20. They will fix an average profit for registered businesses.
21. Government workers will go on split work shifts of a few hours a day, but without pay reductions.
22. Everyone else's wages will be cut by law.
23. The National Dividend payments are a form of automatic income.
24. All payments will be equal.
25. Everyone becomes a tenant for life.
26. These shares cannot be sold or left to one's heirs.
27. Social Credit makes the assumption of all socialist systems: "community" equals "State."
28. Social Credit assumes that all natural resources are common property.
29. By limiting profits, Social Credit limits the consumers' control over producers.
30. By monopolizing credit, Social Credit removes savers' and investors' control over the use of credit.
31. There is no scientific way to control the money supply.
32. Social Credit prophesies an era in which human labor will not be a major source of people's income.

5

WHO REPRESENTS THE CONSUMERS?

And when the tempter came to him, he said, If thou be the Son of God, command that these stones be made bread. But he answered and said, It is written, Man shall not live by bread alone, but by every word that proceedeth out of the mouth of God (Matthew 4:3-4).

The idea of socialism was foreshadowed in Christ's first temptation. By "turning stones into bread," Christ would have become an earthly Messiah, who instead of overcoming the sinful condition of the world would have submitted to that condition. This temptation, to which a considerable part of modern mankind has yielded, constitutes the spiritual essence of socialism.

Igor Shafarevich (1975)[1]

Satan tempted Jesus to use His supernatural power to feed Himself after forty days of deliberately going without food. Satan was saying, in effect: "There is a shortcut to wealth in this world if you just use the wealth formula. Just say the magic

---

1. Igor Shafarevich, *The Socialist Phenomenon*, translated by William Tjalsma (New York: Harper & Row, [1975] 1980), p. 220.

word." But Jesus refused to say a "magic word." Instead, He reminded the tempter of God's ethical words. It is these that sustain men, not bread. Even after 40 days of going without food, Jesus had not become confused about God's priorities for man: *obedience first, then the rewards.* (As we saw in Chapter 3, both our obedience and God's rewards are aspects of God's grace to man: wealth-obedience-greater wealth.)

Jesus did not preach an other-worldly religion. He placed this request in what has become known as the Lord's prayer: "Give us this day our daily bread" (Matthew 6:11). But there is no doubt that in the religion of Jesus, God's word comes first. What God says matters most. It matters far more than mere bread.

Major Douglas began the Preface to his second book with a partial quotation from Jesus, but he immediately shifted the focus of Jesus' original words – the importance of God's word for human life – back to the goods of this world: "Man does not live by bread alone – but without a reasonable amount of food, clothes and shelter, his activities on this planet are both circumscribed in extent, and unduly limited in duration."[2]

Pragmatist or Moralist?

Major Douglas made it plain from the beginning of his career that he believed he was a pragmatist, pure and simple. In that one-page Preface to *Credit-Power and Democracy*, he set forth his public philosophy as clearly as might be desired: "In what is undoubtedly an attack on certain features of the so-called Capitalistic system, in this book, no attempt or desire to judge that system on any grounds but those of workability is made or implied. The business of an economic system is to deliver the right goods to the right users, and the private financing of public production is doomed because it is failing signally in delivering the goods." He then added six words, six words that

2. *Credit-Power and Democracy* (London: Cecil Palmer, 1920), p. vii.

summarize perfectly the essence of all pragmatism: "That is moral which works best." But is this statement true?

Had he had rearranged this sentence, the Christian social theorist could wholeheartedly agree: "That which is moral works best." But this restructured statement is not what Major Douglas was trying to convey, as his Preface so clearly reveals. In fact, my restructured statement is precisely what Douglas was doing his best to deny. He came before his readers dressed in the garb of a neutral scientist, a hands-on kind of fellow – *an engineer*, if you will. He said he was not going to burden the reader with a lot of moral ranting and raving. On the contrary, he said he intended to discuss only practical matters.

Elsewhere, he made it clear that what he really disliked was the kind of morality that is found in biblical law:

> It is my own opinion that until it is clearly recognised that the only sane objective of an industrial and productive system is to deliver goods as, when, and where desired with the minimum of trouble to anyone, and that the moment you begin to mix this clear-cut objective up with moral considerations, so called, including a strong dash of Mosaic law, you produce, maintain, and increase friction, inefficiency, and mental and physical distress, and that if you persist, as we are persisting, in this confusion of objective, you will eventually arrive at a situation involving the serious elements of breakdown.[3]

There is something we should understand about people who come to us with a proposed reform that supposedly is based entirely on practical concerns. These programs invariably sneak a disguised morality through the back door. While the reformer stands at the front door discussing practical reforms with you, his accomplice is in the back of your house going through your closets and cabinets. So, let us get one thing clear from the beginning: *there is no ethical neutrality*. Every reformer comes in

3. *Warning Democracy* (2nd ed.; London: Stanley Nott, 1934), p. 11.

the name of some god. This god, through the reformer, announces some system of ethical cause and effect. *Show me the source of a society's laws, and I'll show you its god.*[4]

Exposing the Hidden Thieves

Major Douglas, like all pragmatists, was a secret moralist. He offered an inescapably moral critique of capitalism to his followers, just as Karl Marx did, who also wrapped his critique of capitalism in the swaddling clothes of science. Douglas' lieutenants were neither engineers nor economists; they were moralists: editors, poets, mystics, and clerics. As was equally true of the appeal of Marxism, the appeal of Social Credit has always been a thick layer of moral judgment which undergirds a thin veneer of scientific objectivity and ethical neutrality.

Major Douglas argued throughout his career that if society ever legislated his proposed reform, wealth would no longer be siphoned off. Siphoned off by whom? Hidden thieves: those once described by Douglas as the Hidden Hand.[5] He identified this Hidden Hand or "Hidden Government."[6] This group controls national politics in the industrialized world. He warned us that "there are very few 'accidents' in the rise to power of public men."[7] This Hidden Government is finance capital. As he said, "Finance has the power to impose a policy on the public, even if that policy is demonstrably anti-public in character."[8] The Hand controls the media. We should be aware of "the distortion and suppression of facts by the Financial Hierarchy. . . ."[9] Douglas' goal was to throw the light of truth on

4. R. J. Rushdoony, *The Institutes of Biblical Law* (Nutley, New Jersey: Craig Press, 1973), p. 4.

5. *Warning Democracy*, p. 54.

6. *Ibid.*, p. 55.

7. *Ibid.*, p. 54.

8. *Ibid.*, p. 58.

9. *Credit-Power and Democracy*, p. 3.

these hidden thieves within the system. His technical economic analysis served as his spotlight – a distinctly moral spotlight.

Adam Smith used a metaphor, the "invisible hand" that guides the operations of the free market.[10] This was a metaphor for the free market's provision of social benefits despite each participant's intention to produce only an individual benefit for himself. In Douglas' case, however, the language was not metaphorical. He believed in the existence of a conspiracy that directs economic and political affairs. He asked his readers to follow the money in search of these conspirators. The problem is, he intended to replace this elite core of secret private conspirators – profit-seeking conspirators – with a government elite that would be almost equally immune to public criticism, but which would not use profit as its guide.

Douglas faced two overwhelming intellectual challenges: (1) to devise a system of judicial checks and balances on the enormous power which such State control over national finance necessarily brings; (2) to offer a substitute for profit and loss as a means of balancing economic supply and demand. To avoid political tyranny, he had to find an answer for the first challenge. To avoid economic breakdown, he had to find an answer for the second. He never addressed the first problem: constitutional and political. He provided only a few empty formulas for the second, with no suggestion as to how real-world numbers might be plugged into the formulas, day by day, decision by decision. This is why Social Credit has always been utopian rather than scientific. It is also why it has never been conservative, for it concentrates power at the top.

Who's in Charge Here?

Douglas repudiated the Marxist argument that all wealth comes from human labor. This denial was very important to his

10. Adam Smith, *The Wealth of Nations*, edited by Edwin Cannan (New York: Modern Library, [1776] 1937), p. 423.

system, since he wanted people to work much less and have much more. He therefore also repudiated the trade unions' claim that Labor – capital L – should control industry.[11] Who, then, should control industry?

To discover the answer, Douglas identified each claimant to this authority. The foreman controls the workshop, but he answers to the manager. The manager says that he is responsible to the chairman. The chairman says the shareholders are in control.[12] So, the age-old institutional question is still the same: Who's in charge here?

Can the shareholder make decisions for the corporation? No, Douglas answered: ". . . a shareholder in a trust-capitalistic manufacturing enterprise has no power to change the fundamental policy of the concern, *which is to pay its way as a means to the end of maintaining and increasing its financial credit with the banks*."[13] The shareholder is therefore institutionally impotent. Douglas did not mean the owner of one share of stock. He meant shareholders in general.

Douglas was incorrect about this. His error is widely shared, however.[14] Shareholders can and do remove managers who displease them. They do this in two ways. First, they sell their shares to different shareholders, who then appoint a new management team. As they sell, share prices fall on the stock market. This makes it less expensive for new owners to buy up additional shares and replace the old management team. Second, shareholders replace managers by giving new managers the right to vote their shares by proxy. Both approaches are common. The first approach is sometimes ridiculed by existing managers as "predatory" or "corporate raiding" or "vulture capital." They resent these corporate take-overs, for take-overs

11. *Credit-Power and Democracy*, pp. 3-5.

12. *Ibid.*, p. 4.

13. *Ibid.*, p. 6.

14. The classic statement of this error is Adolph A. Berle and Gardiner C. Means, *The Modern Corporation and Private Property* (New York: Macmillan, 1933).

threaten their power. Corporate take-overs are the means by which shareholders can exercise their authority over existing managers.[15] To ignore this process is to misunderstand the modern corporation.

The Locus of Sovereignty

Here we come to one of the least understood and most important aspects of modern capitalism: the locus of sovereignty. The confusion comes because men do not understand the *representative* character of all human authority. All authority is hierarchical and representative. The Bible teaches that Adam legally represented all men when he rebelled. Christianity teaches that Jesus Christ died on the cross as a legal representative, so that some people can receive eternal life (special grace) and all people can receive such gifts as life, sunshine, and rain (common grace).[16]

Where is the locus of sovereignty in capitalism? With the consumers. They decide which producers win and which lose. They vote with their money. They bring sanctions: positive (profits) and negative (losses).

The shareholders want profits. They vote for representatives who will hire senior managers to run the company profitably. These representatives represent the consumers to the shareholders and the shareholders to the consumers. This is analogous to the minister in a church who serves the Lord's Supper: he represents God before the congregation and the congregation before God. While the share owners do not directly enforce their will on management, just as voters do not directly enforce the laws of the land (except in rare cases of citizen's

15. Henry Manne, *Insider Trading and the Stock Market* (New York: Free Press, 1966), ch. 8. Manne [pronounced MANee] is the Dean of the George Mason University Law School in Fairfax, Virginia. He is one of the pioneers in the field called law and economics.

16. Gary North, *Dominion and Common Grace: The Biblical Basis of Progress* (Tyler, Texas: Institute for Christian Economics, 1987).

arrest), they do exercise control. How? By buying and selling the shares.

There are two kinds of voting in corporations: (1) legal voting by shareholders at shareholder meetings; (2) economic voting by shareholders in the stock market. The shareholder can sell his shares. If shareholders expect falling profits from senior management, many will sell their shares. As share prices fall, new owners buy them. This transfers legal authority to a different group of owners. The stock market is a giant *auction for control*: control over management and, ultimately, control over future profits (if any). The new owners can then "turn the rascals out," just as voters in civil elections do in civil government. The stock market serves as a continuous election.

The stock market is an extension of the free market. The stock market is a gigantic auction system because the free market is an even larger auction system. The reason why critics of the stock market do not understand it is that they do not understand the free market.

A Gigantic Auction

While economics can be a very complex subject, it always boils down to two simple themes: scarcity and price. Things command a price because they are scarce. At zero price there is more demand for them than supply of them. It would be as silly to expect a world without prices as it would be to expect auctions without bidding. The economy is in fact a giant auction. "I hear five. Do I hear six? Going once. Going twice. Gone for five!" If no one bids six, it will be sold for five. *High bid wins*. I don't care how complex an economist wants to make economics sound, it always comes down to the auction process. So, if you get confused by this book or any other, keep thinking: "Auction system. Auction system."

Anytime I get confused, here is what I do. I think of a parrot sitting on my right shoulder. He keeps squawking, "Supply and demand. Supply and demand." This is my *economic theory* parrot. On my left shoulder is another parrot. He keeps squawking, "High bid wins. High bid wins." This is my *economic policy* parrot. Between the two of them is my thick skull. When I can't figure out how to explain some aspect of trade or production, I listen to my two imaginary parrots. (Because they are imaginary, they require no bird seed and leave nothing on my shoulders.) I suggest that you pay attention to these two parrots.

The free market system offers consumers the legal right to buy or not buy. It also offers producers the legal right to compete for the money (ultimately, goods and services) of the consumers. The free market is a giant auction. *Consumers compete against consumers,* just as bargain-seeking attendees at an auction bid against each other. Meanwhile, *producers compete against producers,* just as profit-seeking auctioneers do when they schedule rival auctions on the same day.

The stock market places buyers of shares in competition against each other. It places managers of corporations in competition against each other. The investors do not compete against managers; they compete against other investors. Managers do not compete against investors; they compete against other managers. Investors hire managers as their legal representatives. When consumers veto the plans of managers, thereby producing losses for the companies they manage, investors learn that it may be time to replace today's managers with new managers who will serve consumers better. *The share owners are therefore the* **economic** *representatives of consumers.* If share owners fail to represent consumers well by hiring managers whose plans meet the demands of consumers, they will suffer capital losses. *Capital losses are economic sanctions imposed on shareholders by consumers.* The free market system is representative. Investors are the legal owners of their shares. They are represented economically by managers. But the investors are inescapably the economic representatives of consumers. Managers represent share owners both legally and economically. Share owners represent consumers economically.

Identifying the Thieves

Major Douglas never recognized this dual system of representative ownership: *legal* ownership but *economic* stewardship in the interest of the consumers. He instead identified the true owners in modern industrialism as the bankers, those who control the flow of capital. "Hence we see that the last word on *policy* is with finance, not with administration, and is concerned with the control of credit by the banks. . . ."[17] He never saw that in a free market economy without government-licensed central banks, *commercial bankers are the economic representatives of depositors*. He did not understand the biblical doctrine of representation: legal representation (the owners) and economic representation (the decision-makers). He did not understand the fundamental free market principle of *consumers' sovereignty*.

Social Credit is a proposed reform that targets the bankers, *meaning the banks' depositors*, in the name of restoring control over industry to the people. He called this process "the democratisation of the bank."[18] But this democratization did not mean rule by the political majority. "Democracy is frequently and falsely defined as the rule of the majority. . . . As so defined, it is a mere trap, set by knaves to catch simpletons; the *rule* of the majority never has existed, and, fortunately, never will."[19] He called for "real democracy."[20] What is this real democracy? It is the "freedom of an increasing majority of individuals to make use of the facilities provided for them, in the first place, by a number of persons who will always be, as they have always been, in the minority."[21] That is, only a minority can supply the majority with goods and services.

---

17. *Credit-Power and Democracy*, p. 6.
18. *Ibid.*, p. 6.
19. *Ibid.*, p. 7.
20. *Ibid.*, p. 8.
21. *Ibid.*, p. 8.

Who are these hidden minority providers? He did not say, at least not in this chapter. This is a shame. Since the moral and analytical heart of his criticism of existing capitalist society was the presumed all-powerful authority of private bankers, it certainly would have been useful if he had identified those hidden minority producers – the people he wanted to replace the bankers. It would have provided greater comfort to readers had he openly identified these true representatives of what he called "the ultimate Terror,"[22] meaning the democratic majority that can never be trusted.

The Green Shirts

We can now identify who the victims are, Douglas said: the little people who are being victimized by the financial thieves who hide inside the economic system. That such an appeal has been able to recruit followers to what is sometimes called the Populist fringe is well known. The Populist movement in the United States used just this sort of appeal in the late nineteenth century.[23] This was a farmer-based political movement, whose supporters were in debt and who wanted relief through monetary inflation, either through the substitution of a silver standard for the gold standard or the substitution of a fiat money standard.[24] Father Coughlin, a popular Roman Catholic radio preacher in the late 1930's, recruited millions of listeners with

22. *Ibid.*, p. 7.

23. Norman Pollack (ed.), *The Populist Mind* (Indianapolis, Indiana: Bobbs-Merrill, 1967).

24. Allen Weinstein, *Prelude to Populism: Origins of the Silver Issue, 1867-1878* (New Haven, Connecticut: Yale University Press, 1970); John D. Hicks, *The Populist Revolt: A History of the Farmer's Alliance and the People's Party* (Lincoln: University of Nebraska Press, [1931] 1959), ch. 18. The main publicist was William H. "Coin" Harvey, a defender of "free silver." The main politician was William Jennings Bryan, who was the unsuccessful Democratic Party nominee for President of the U.S. three times: 1896, 1900, 1908. See the monthly magazine, *Money*, published by the Money Publishing Company of New York, 1897-1900.

this sort of appeal: anti-financial conspiracy and pro-fiat money.[25] Major Douglas attracted them in the mid-1930's, most notably members of the movement called the Green Shirts, founded in 1933. Its weekly newspaper was not too subtly titled, *Attack! against the Bankers' Combine for the People's Credit.*

The founder of the Green Shirts, John Gordon Hargrave, had adopted Social Credit as early as 1924, and had made it the official ideology for an earlier organization of his, the "Kibbo Kift, the Woodcraft Kindred," a breakaway group from the Boy Scouts. Hargrave was anti-democratic and anti-Parliament. He created the Green Shirts by taking over another populist group that had adopted Social Credit, the Legion of the Unemployed. Its founder, George Hickling, later became the editor of *Social Credit.*

Initially, Douglas had welcomed the Green Shirts' efforts, but its stridency had alienated him by 1934. The group in 1935 constituted itself the Social Credit Party of Great Britain, but then faded away. In the meantime, the Green Shirts had achieved for Douglas what he had been unable to do for himself: attain national prominence.[26]

What was the political outlook of the Green Shirts? *Attack!* made it clear that democracy was the enemy. "We use an unarmed military technique that calls forth willing discipline under direct leadership – and allows of no sham Democratic committee 'wrangling.' "[27] Hargrave asserted in 1934: "Voting is useless. . . . The Bankers' Combine and its megaphone at Westminster is not afraid of voting papers or shouts of 'Work or Maintenance.' . . . *We must repudiate and fight those who would*

25. Charles E. Coughlin, *The New Deal in Money* (Royal Oak, Michigan: Radio League of the Little Flower, 1933); *Money! Questions and Answers* (Royal Oak, Michigan: National Union for Social Justice, 1936). See Sheldon Marcus, *Father Coughlin* (Boston: Little, Brown, 1973).

26. C. B. Macpherson, *Democracy in Alberta: Social Credit and the Party System* (2nd ed.; Toronto: University of Toronto Press, 1962), pp. 130-35.

27. *Attack!*, No. 24 (April 1924); cited in *ibid.*, p. 133.

mislead us by having us believe in the power of the vote. Our struggle must be fought outside Parliament, on the streets and wherever the enemy appears."[28]

That a would-be demagogue such as Hargrave would enthusiastically appropriate Social Credit to mix with his fascist-like Green Shirt movement points to the underlying problem for conservative defenders of Social Credit. First, why did Social Credit's proposed reform appeal to such a leader? Second, why didn't Douglas publicly repudiate Hargrave from the moment he learned about the Green Shirts' tactics?

Salvation by Technique

In Chapter 8 of *Credit-Power and Democracy*, Douglas revealed who should provide the necessary control over capital: technicians employed by the State. He proposed that society, through the State, turn control of the economy over to these technicians. Lest we forget, Major Douglas was such a technician. He recommended that we pass our sovereignty as consumers – which he denied that consumers possess – to members of his class. (Have we heard similar recommendations before?)

> If the public of this or any other country is really desirous of once and for ever freeing itself from the power of the economic machine, and using the immense heritage which science and industry have placed at its disposal, it has to throw up and place in positions of executive authority men who are technicians in so broad a sense that they understand that the very essence of perfect technology is to devise mechanism to meet the requirements, the policy of those who appointed them.[29]

Douglas' recommendation was first published in 1920. In the following year, an important book by Thorstein Veblen ap-

28. *Attack!*, No. 23 (Feb. 1934); cited in *ibid.*, p. 133.
29. *Credit-Power and Democracy*, p. 85.

peared: *The Engineers and the Price System*. Veblen had been the most radical academic economist in the United States, and after initial retirement from teaching in 1917 – he went back to teaching in 1919 at the newly formed and highly radical New School for Social Research – he grew even more radical. He once wrote an essay in *The Dial*, the radical periodical he edited, entitled, "Bolshevism Is a Menace – to Whom?" He argued that Soviet Communism was merely the principle of democracy carried into industry.[30] The essays he wrote in *The Dial* in 1919 became *The Engineers and the Price System* in 1921.

In that book Veblen argued that businessmen seek profits through restraining output. In the capitalist system, the investment banker becomes the key figure: the power behind the economic throne. Writes sociologist Daniel Bell: "Thus the tension between nonutilized capacity and restriction becomes the central motif of the book. . . ."[31] This was also the central motif of everything Major Douglas wrote. It was the theme of the Technocracy movement of the 1930's. The reader should be alert to the problem facing those defenders of Social Credit who claim that the system is essentially conservative: the most notorious American socialist author of the 1900-1929 period, Thorstein Veblen, advocated the same basic economic reform: a transfer of authority to the engineers. (Years later, Douglas cited Veblen's book, though he did not praise it much.)[32]

The Agents of Consumers

Basic to Douglas' analysis was his view of consumer sovereignty. He rejected the free market view that the consumer, through his decisions to buy from one producer rather than

---

30. Daniel Bell, "Introduction," Thorstein Veblen, *The Engineers and the Price System* (New Brunswick, New Jersey and London: Transaction Publishers, 1982), p. 13.

31. *Ibid.*, p. 28.

32. *Social Credit* (3rd ed.; London: Eyre & Spottiswoode, 1933), p. 49.

another, exercises sovereignty. He wrote that "the existing system does not distribute the control of intermediate production to individuals at all; and, secondly, gives them no say whatever as to the quantity, quality or variety of ultimate products."[33] Under capitalism, consumers have no say whatever!

No say whatever? But I *do* have a say. It's called, "I'll buy it." It's also called, "No, I won't buy it." You possess the same power. This is the heart of capitalism: *consumer sovereignty*.

Capitalists are the economic agents of future consumers. Those capitalists who guess wrong or plan wrong about what we consumers are willing and able to buy will suffer losses. This is the hammer that we consumers hold over producers. Because of the free market's system of profit and loss, consumers control producers. Economist Ludwig von Mises has described the relationship between producers and consumers: "In the capitalist system of society's economic organization the entrepreneurs determine the course of production. In the performance of this function they are unconditionally and totally subject to the sovereignty of the buying public, the consumers."[34] In other words, capitalist owners are legally sovereign over the production process, but they are not economically sovereign. Consumers are economically sovereign over the process.

Legally, producers represent themselves if they own the tools of production, but economically, they represent consumers. Understanding the difference between legal representation and economic representation is crucial for understanding capitalism. The link between the two kinds of representation is capitalism's system of profit and loss. By buying from producers who in the consumers' opinion serve them best, consumers reward certain

---

33. *Control and Distribution of Production* (2nd ed.; London: Stanley Nott, 1934), p. 10.

34. Ludwig von Mises, "Profit and Loss" (1951), in Mises, *Planning for Freedom* (4th ed.; South Holland, Illinois: Libertarian Press, 1980), p. 108. The publisher is now located in Grove City, Pennsylvania.

producers. Consumers thereby penalize other producers who do not serve them best. How? By not buying from them.

Real Confusion Over Real Credit

Major Douglas never discussed capitalism's profit system in the context of consumer sovereignty. Instead, he made the assumption that all socialists make, namely, that the State best represents consumers economically:

> Economically regarded, a nation is an association of people engaged in the production of Real Credit, and in this sense the State, as the custodian of the Real Credit of the community, may be said to represent the interests of Producer and Consumer equally, since both are equally necessary to the creation of Real Credit. Since, however, Producers and Consumers between them make up the whole community, we may conclude that Real Credit is social or communal in origin; that it belongs neither to the producer nor to the consumer, but to their *common* element, the community, of which they each form a part.[35]

Real Credit, as he called it, is social in origin, not individual. This is the familiar mind-set of the socialist: beginning with collective ownership rather than individual. The Christian view offers a third approach: begin with God as the original Owner. Then search the Bible to determine where God delegates ownership: to the State or to the individual.

What Is "Real Credit"?

Exactly what is this elusive thing, "Real Credit"? In 1920, he defined it as a measure of energy: "Now it cannot be too clearly emphasized *that real credit is a measure of the effective reserve of energy belonging to a community. . . .*"[36] He defined it another

---

35. *Credit-Power and Democracy*, pp. 157-58.

36. *Economic Democracy* (2nd ed.; London: Cecil Palmer, 1921), p. 122.

way in a speech before the London Socialist Forum in 1930: "In the first place it is necessary carefully to distinguish between real credit and financial credit. Real credit is a well-founded, that is to say, correct belief or estimate of the capacity of a person or community to materialise its desires."[37] One would be hard-pressed to come up with a less tangible, less measurable, and more mystical definition.

The estimator's problem is simple to state but impossible to solve by scientific, political, or bureaucratic action. No one besides God knows what these capacities are – even in his own soul, let alone in the entire community. This is the problem facing every system of State ownership: determining the total resources available – defined in the broadest sense possible – and matching this estimate with the seemingly infinite number of desires of individuals to attain their goals at zero price. Then the planners must design punishments and rewards to maximize output to meet the most important of these goals – something denied by Douglas. But who can determine which goals are most important to society in general? Not a committee, surely! The problem is incapable of any scientific solution, something the socialists at last admitted with the economic collapse of Communism in the late 1980's. But the theoretical case against socialism was over six decades old by then.[38]

In 1931, Douglas defined "Real Credit" somewhat differently: "Real credit may be defined as the rate at which goods and services can be delivered as, when, and where required. Financial credit may similarly be defined as the rate at which money can be delivered, as, when, and where required. The inclusion in both definitions of the word 'rate' is, of course,

37. *Warning Democracy*, p. 26.

38. Mises, *Economic Calculation in the Socialist Commonwealth* (1920), reprinted by the Mises Institute, Auburn, Alabama, in 1990. See also T. J. B. Hoff, *Economic Calculation in the Socialist Society* (London: William Hodge & Co., 1949), reprinted by Liberty Press, Indianapolis; Don Lavoie, *National Economic Planning: What Is Left?* (Cambridge, Massachusetts: Ballinger, 1985).

important."[39] Yet in his 1930 definition, he never mentioned *rate*. Why this became important in the interim, Douglas did not say. This second definition is present-oriented: actual delivery. The 1930 definition related to capacity: potential delivery. The two concepts are different.

Neither potential capacity nor actual capacity can be ascertained by a committee, government or private. Amazingly, Douglas admitted this: "Centralised *financial* credit is a technical possibility, but centralised *real* credit assumes that the desires and aspirations of humanity can be standardised, and ought to be standardised. . . . [N]o man, or body of men, however elected, can represent the detailed desires of any other man, or body of men."[40] This admission is crucial; it effectively destroys the theoretical possibility of a group of technicians who can coordinate Real Credit with State credit. *In short, this admission destroys Social Credit's number-one reform proposal, the technical heart of Douglas' system.* This admission left Douglas without any working definition of real credit. Yet the concept of Real Credit was crucial to his critique of capitalism, which he said results from a discrepancy between Real Credit and financial credit.

The Achilles Heel

From a practical standpoint, this failure of Douglas to specify exactly how Real Credit can be calculated scientifically is the Achilles heel of Social Credit. If the State's credit masters cannot identify exactly how much Real Credit there is in society, and then match exactly the issue of investment money and the national dividend so that the total money supply equals Real Credit, the proposed monetary reform collapses. It becomes nothing more than a slogan for scientifically unrestricted issues of fiat money. It places the power of money creation and capital investment into the hands of the State, but without providing a

39. *The Monopoly of Credit* (London: Chapman & Hall, 1931), p. 21.

40. *Credit-Power and Democracy*, p. 57.

legal, theoretical, or practical way to restrict the expansion of money other than political pressure. It substitutes the pressures of politics – almost always inflationist – for the gold standard's well-known pressure on bankers and government treasuries: the threat of a run on gold reserves. It does this in the name of monetary science – a science without the absolutely crucial definitions of Real Capital and Financial Capital and the statistical relationship between them.

Second, if Real Credit is not capable of bring defined in terms of something other than money, the issue of money by the State will raise the monetary value of Real Credit. This will make mandatory another issue of Just Price money and National Dividend money, to keep pace with rising Real Credit value, which will raise the monetary value of Real Credit. . . .

This is the fate of every monetary reform that relies on the issuing of money by the State. No fiat money reform proposal can separate the value of the collateral from the monetary effects of the credit on the collateral. In this respect, Social Credit is the representative example of all other fiat money credit reforms that attempt to issue sufficient currency to match the increase in output. The only way to estimate the increase in output in a money-based modern economy is by way of a system of statistical estimations of money prices received by producers. But this estimate is affected by the issue of money.

The Target of His Criticism

The failure of capitalism, Douglas said, is the failure of financial credit to match the output of Real Credit. The banks create financial credit. The banks supposedly extend credit only to producers, he said – conveniently overlooking the existence of modern consumer credit. The "result of these creations of credit granted to producers only, instead of to consumers" he insisted, "is to produce a rise of prices which nullifies the additional purchasing-power thus created."[41] Therefore, he concluded, "*The business of a modern and effective financial system is to issue credit to the consumer, up to the limit of the productive capacity of the producer, so that either the consumers' real demand is satiated, or the producers' capacity is exhausted, whichever happens first.*"[42]

This requires that someone – obviously not private bankers – estimate the absolute capacity of Real Credit to produce goods and services at any point in time. Then someone – again, not private bankers – must issue sufficient money to consumers to buy all of the output of Real Credit. The problem is, no one knows how to estimate Real Credit. So, no one knows how to balance Real Credit with financial credit. But neither does anyone know how to balance Real Credit and the National Dividend plus the Just Price program of producer credits.

Extinguishing Money

The problem with private banking, he said, is that it extinguishes credit when a producer's loan is repaid. This shrinks the money supply. That is, it shrinks the supply of financial credit. This is supposedly the central flaw of capitalism. This is what inevitably leads to underconsumption. He assumes that sellers in general cannot lower retail prices in order to sell off their inventories. Why can't they? Because this would produce universal losses. So, the banks must keep issuing new credit, but this merely creates the problem again: the extinction of money when the loan is paid off.

> Now this theorem that bank loans create bank deposits, and the deduction from it that the repayment of bank loans destroys deposits, is vital to an understanding of the process we have been discussing. The deficiency between purchasing-power, and goods with money prices attached to them, can be made up (at any rate

41. *Social Credit*, p. 100.

42. *Credit-Power and Democracy*, p. 106. Emphasis in original.

> to a large extent) by this process of creating bank money. This enables the business cycle to be carried through. And conversely, the refusal to create fresh money by banking methods or otherwise, whatever the cause of this refusal may be, is sufficient to paralyse both production and consumption.[43]

If he is incorrect here – and he is, as we shall see – his criticism of capitalism collapses.

Douglas vs. Christian Economics

As we have seen, Douglas did not want majority rule. He made clear something else he did not want: Christian legal standards, for "this desire to classify and pass sentence upon every variety of human effort has been the curse of the churches and codes of the so-called Christian era."[44]

While he does not cite Paul's injunction on the necessity of labor, he understood it, and he despised it. Paul wrote: "For even when we were with you, this we commanded you, that if any would not work, neither should he eat" (2 Thessalonians 3:10). Douglas wrote: ". . . the victims of this deadly habit of mind, both on the side of Capitalism and Labour, are still explaining that, unless a man do 'useful' work, neither shall he eat; . . ." Despite the fact that there is a glut of goods in England and America, "in both countries foodstuffs are allowed to rot, or are being actually destroyed, in order to keep up prices, the high-priests of industry cry for more and yet more production as a condition of existence, even though that production may be, as it often is, absolutely detrimental to society in general, and the worker in particular."[45]

In 1920, there was a major recession in the United States and England. The vast expansion of fiat money by the Federal

43. *Social Credit*, pp. 87-88.

44. *Credit-Power and Democracy*, p. 11.

45. *Ibid.*, p. 11.

Reserve System (America's newly created central bank: 1913) and the Bank of England (England's ancient central bank: 1694) during World War I stimulated production. This was made possible because both governments – indeed, governments all over Europe – suspended gold payments to their citizens. This was a form of theft. Then began a policy of taxation through monetary inflation and rising prices. The war ended in 1918. The two major central banks ceased inflating their money supplies. The previous calculations of producers had been based on the assumption of continued inflating. These plans were destroyed when inflation ended. This led to losses, 1919-21. But producers adjusted their plans to the new conditions. The recession ended in late 1921, less than two years after *Credit-Power and Democracy* was published.

The point is, producers make mistakes, especially when central bankers inflate and deflate. These mistakes are exposed when the goods can no longer be sold at the older, higher prices. Prices have to be lowered. In some cases, where storage costs and transportation costs are higher than the expected return from sales, the goods are destroyed. This visible destruction offends people because they do not see the losses that would result if the excess goods were kept in inventory.

Conclusion

The sovereignty of the consumer under capitalism is a powerful force. No producer is compelled by civil law to serve the consumer, but those people who can serve consumers yet who refuse to do so, or who try, yet fail to serve them efficiently, forfeit income and profits. The capitalist production and distribution system is voluntary, but it is not free from constraints. These constraints are overwhelmingly economic, not political.

Authority is always representative. Producers and capital owners represent the consumers. They represent them economically. They do not own consumers. They own the goods that produce goods and services for consumers.

Major Douglas, like virtually all of capitalism's critics, did not understand the doctrine of consumers' sovereignty. He honestly believed that producers dictate terms of sale to consumers. He wrote:

> Let me repeat – the only true, sane origin of production is the real need or desire of the individual consumer. If we are to continue to have co-operative production, then that productive system must be subject to one condition only – that it delivers the goods where they are demanded. If any men, or body of men, by reason of their fortuitous position in that system, attempt to dictate the terms on which they will deliver the goods (not, be it noted, the terms on which they will work), then that is a tyranny, and the world has never tolerated a tyranny for very long.[46]

There are indeed tyrants in the capitalist economy: the consumers. They are merciless. They keep asking producers this question: "What have you done for me lately?" And this question: "What can I expect from you tomorrow?" But Major Douglas saw the producers as the tyrants. He therefore failed utterly to understand capitalism's system of economic representation: the owners of capital must serve the consumers or suffer the consequences, namely losses or forfeited profits. It is the producer's opportunity to make a profit that serves the consumers as their hammer: share owners are pressured to elect managers who serve consumers well – with the least waste of scarce resources.

Because Major Douglas misidentified the bankers as the true masters of the economy, he misidentified them as the hidden thieves in the system. Central bankers – those who use the State to gain a monopoly over the control of money and credit – were indeed thieves, and remain thieves. But this is not because they are bankers – agents of private depositors who lend mon-

46. *Control and Distribution of Production*, p. 13.

ey. This is because the State has used its authority to create a private or semi-private monopoly over money. Douglas never understood the difference between commercial banking and central banking. He therefore never proposed a workable remedy for the evils he perceived. In the name of pragmatism – "workability," as he put it[47] – he offered a reform that could not possibly solve the problem he identified, as we shall see.

Summary

1. Jesus told Satan that man lives by the word of God.
2. Magic is not the way to wealth.
3. Obedience precedes rewards: the way to wealth.
4. Douglas focused on society's bread, not God's word.
5. He announced that he was not bringing a moral criticism of capitalism, merely a practical one: pragmatism.
6. Douglas said: "That is moral which works best."
7. Christianity teaches: "That which is moral works best."
8. There is no moral neutrality.
9. Pragmatists are secret moralists.
10. Someone has to be the boss.
11. Capitalism says that the consumers are the boss.
12. Corporations establish that shareholders are the legal owners.
13. Shareholders, in order to profit, must hire managers who serve consumers well.
14. Shareholders exercise control by voting: at shareholder meetings (legal control) and by selling their shares (economic control).
15. The stock market is a giant auction.
16. Producers compete against other producers.
17. Consumers compete against other consumers.
18. There are two forms of ownership: legal and economic (stewardship).

---

47. *Ibid.*, p. vii.

19. Douglas did not understand consumers' sovereignty.
20. He thought bankers are sovereign.
21. He did not believe in majority political rule.
22. He opposed Christian law in society.
23. He blamed the financial system for unsold goods.
24. He did not blame the 1920 recession on prior monetary inflation: sending false signals to producers.
25. When the monetary inflation ended, the recession began.
26. It ended less than two years after his book appeared.

6

WHO SHOULD CONTROL DISTRIBUTION?

> And he causeth all, both small and great, rich and poor, free and bond, to receive a mark in their right hand, or in their foreheads: And that no man might buy or sell, save he that had the mark, or the name of the beast, or the number of his name (Revelation 13:16-17).

Who should control distribution? This question has divided economists almost from the beginning. We need to ask ourselves several questions. Which people should we trust? State bureaucrats who can rarely be fired if they price things incorrectly? Or producers who lose their own money if they price their output incorrectly? Which group possesses greater power to coerce consumers, a monopolistic government bureaucracy or competing producers? Which group poses the greatest threat to our freedom? Which group is more likely to play God? In other words, who should be trusted by consumers: profit-seeking producers or Civil Service-protected bureaucrats?

The Unity of Production and Distribution

One of the most important errors in economics is to imagine that it is possible to separate free market production from distribution without affecting future production. Economist Murray Rothbard has said it well: under capitalism, production and distribution are an unbreakable process. They are two sides of the same coin.

> In the free market process, therefore, there is no separation between production and "distribution." There is no heap somewhere on which "products" are arbitrarily thrown and from which someone does or can arbitrarily "distribute" them among various people. On the contrary, individuals produce goods and sell them to consumers for money, which they in turn spend on consumption or on investment in order to increase future consumption. There is no separate "distribution"; there is only production and its corollary, exchange.[1]

If producers are not allowed to bargain with final consumers or middlemen regarding the terms of sale, there will be economic consequences on the production side of the process. Whatever producers decide to produce is heavily dependent on the nature of the distribution system. It is not possible, therefore, for thieves or government officials to confiscate private property, or exercise control over private property, especially capital goods, without affecting the entire production system. Producers will seek to escape these controls, even if they must cease producing. As the old slogan goes, "You can't redistribute it if there isn't any."

We ask: "Who owns this?" Here is the theoretical answer: "The person who has the legal right to *disown* it." If you cannot legally sell it, you do not legally own it.[2] At most, the so-called owner may be allowed to consume it. This kind of ownership

---

1. Murray N. Rothbard, *Man, Economy, and State: A Treatise on Economic Principles* (Princeton, New Jersey: Van Nostrand, 1962), pp. 408-9.

2. F. A. Harper writes: "The corollary of the right of ownership is the right of disownership." Harper, *Liberty: A Path to Its Recovery* (Irvington, New York: Foundation for Economic Education, 1949), p. 106.

subsidizes a particular kind of use: consumption, which is a restricted form of disownership.

We ask: "Who's in charge here?" The answer, in the field of economics, is: "The one who is legally authorized to make the sale." In most transactions, this means a seller of goods and a seller of money (called the "buyer").

When we begin a search to discover those who have economic control over any institution, a familiar rule of thumb is this one: *follow the money*. Those who collect the money (assets) and distribute it are the representatives of the legal owner or owners. In other words, the structure of institutional authority is intimately linked to lawful control over the use of the institution's assets.

Is Capitalism an Inefficient System?

As is so often the case with the critics of capitalism, Major Douglas' criticism was that today's capitalism cannot produce an abundance of goods and services. The failure of capitalism, he insisted, is the failure of its distribution system. Capitalism's industrial efficiency is potentially very high, but this efficiency cannot be attained through free market ownership, he maintained. The failure is supposedly on the distribution side. In other words, Social Credit rests on the argument that there is a separation between production and consumption under capitalism, and that the State has an obligation – not a moral obligation of course, as Douglas assured us repeatedly – to step in and correct the failure on the distribution side. This is the argument of every socialist and every defender of the "mixed economy," i.e., a mixture of private ownership and government control.

Where Is the Evidence?

Douglas never offered any statistical evidence supporting his argument that capitalism's productivity is being significantly hampered by its distribution system. He cited as economic fact a rumor regarding the opinion of H. L. Gantt, one of the disciples of scientific management pioneer Frederick Taylor. Taylor was the man who introduced time-and-motion studies in the 1880's. Gantt invented the famous Gantt chart for diagramming projects from start to finish. Douglas wrote: "The late Mr. H. L. Gantt, one of the most capable and enlightened industrial engineers that America has produced, is reported to have said that the industrial efficiency of the United States was about 5 per cent. in 1919."[3] Reported by whom? Reported where? Douglas never said.

On the face of it, Gantt's reported statement is preposterous. I have little doubt that Mr. Gantt never said anything like this. If he did, his observation has never been substantiated by any economic historian. Taylor and his disciples would spend hours, even weeks, studying the motions of a single worker, trying to locate tiny inefficiencies, and then retraining him to follow a new pattern. These refinements did produce increases in output, but nothing on the scale of twenty to one (5% efficiency to 100%). To reduce a nation to five percent of its industrial efficiency cannot be accomplished by anything short of full-scale nuclear war. Nevertheless, Douglas used this and other equally preposterous estimates of industrial inefficiency again and again in his critique of capitalism.

Douglas expected his readers to take his word for a series of inconsistent facts regarding the underlying, "untapped," productivity of modern capitalism. He refused to present evidence for his verbal estimates. His line of argumentation was anything but scientific. He had almost no information about the output of capitalism in his era. This seriously compromises his work.

In book after book, Douglas repeated something like the following: if the industrial system someday could operate at a mere 75 percent of its potential efficiency, today's level of pro-

3. *Credit-Power and Democracy* (London: Cecil Palmer, 1920), p. 16.

duction could be achieved by "the same number of persons working one-fifteenth of the time they now work – *i.e.*, about thirty minutes per day instead of about eight hours, or by one-fifteenth of the present number of persons working the same hours."[4] This means that the economic output of workers could be increased by a factor of 15 to one by operating the economy at only 75 percent of its present unused potential. This statement is an example of Douglas' totally unsubstantiated rhetoric. He offered no evidence of any kind. Yet his followers continue to regard him seriously as the pioneer of a theory of scientific pricing based on rigorous economic statistics.

He made similarly outrageous and unsubstantiated claims in his first book. "It has been estimated [by whom? – GN] that two hours per week of the time of every fit adult between the ages of 18 and 45 would provide for a uniformly high standard of physical welfare under existing conditions. . . ."[5] Only two hours per week! Well, perhaps just a bit more. A few pages later, he wrote: "The exact figures are beside the point, but something over three hours' work per head per day is ample for the purpose of meeting consumption and depreciation of all the factors of modern life under normal conditions and proper direction."[6] Either two hours a week or three hours a day.

"The Facts Are Irrelevant"

Notice his amazing admission. "The exact figures are beside the point." Beside the point? Exact figures were absolutely vital in proving his case that the free market is woefully inefficient. Without such evidence, he was an emperor with no clothes, a critic without proof. This from the man who proposed, as we

---

4. *Credit-Power and Democracy*, p. 17. ". . . the employment of not more than 25 per cent of the available labour, working, let us say, seven hours a day." The introduction of a horse-power-hour of energy could "displace at least ten man hours." *Social Credit* (3rd ed.; London: Eyre & Spottiswoode, 1933), p. 18.

5. *Economic Democracy* (2nd ed.; London: Cecil Palmer, [1920] 1921), pp. 86-87.

6. *Ibid.*, p. 105.

shall see, that accurate statistics are absolutely crucial for economic planning by the administrators of the nation's social credit/social dividend: the State's credit masters. Major Douglas was dressed in rhetoric, not science. His followers have never blinked an eye.

Why, then, has such a cornucopia of either leisure or material productivity not been attained under capitalism? He offered this answer: "As the economic distribution system stands at present, such a condition of affairs is impossible of attainment, because, although the goods would be produced, the purchasing-power to buy them would not be distributed."[7] So, it is a *lack of purchasing power in the hands of consumers* that is wholly to blame. He called this "sabotage," and labeled it "the outstanding feature of contemporary industry. . . ." He said this sabotage is "solely due to the blind effort to equate purchasing-power to production without altering the principles of price-fixing."[8] (Not a very clear statement, is it?)

The Real Cause of Economic Contraction: Government

This criticism of the free market's distribution system is at the technical heart of his proposal to reform capitalism. (The ethical heart is Douglas' denial of the legitimacy of economic sanctions.)[9] There supposedly is insufficient purchasing power within the capitalist economic system. This is a familiar criticism of capitalism in every era, but especially during periods of economic depression. The problem is, this criticism is wrong. It fails to identify the cause of low sales: *sellers' ignorance* about the proper price at which to sell their inventories.

The problem of distribution is not a system-wide lack of money or credit; the problem is a general lack of accurate

7. *Credit-Power and Democracy*, p. 17.

8. *Ibid.*, p. 17.

9. See Chapter 11, below.

information about consumer demand and sellers' competition,[10] coupled with personal bull-headedness against lowering selling prices. Economy-wide incorrect information is almost always the result of previous policies of fiat money inflation by a nation's central bank.[11] A second cause of the contraction is an increase in tariffs or import quotas.[12] A third cause is the government's decision to pressure businessmen not to lower selling prices and/or pressure not to lower wages.[13] A fourth cause of stagnation: the government raises taxes, especially taxes on profits and capital gains, discouraging entrepreneurs from creating new wealth and new jobs.

In 1929-38, all four factors were present: prior monetary inflation that came to a halt around 1929, plus a worldwide tariff war begun in 1930, plus government price floors, plus higher taxes (in the U.S., under President Franklin Roosevelt).[14] This is why the Great Depression was the worst in modern history. In all four cases, the root cause of the economic contraction is either civil government or its licensed monopolistic agent, the nation's central bank.

Shrunken Markets

The underlying cause of the visible economic crisis is the shrinking of markets, also known as a reduction in the division of labor. This reduces men's economic efficiency by reducing the specialization of production. Producers in the new conditions become less efficient and suffer temporary losses because

---

10. Fritz Machlup, *The Economics of Sellers' Competition* (Baltimore, Maryland: Johns Hopkins University Press, 1952).

11. Ludwig von Mises, *Human Action: A Treatise on Economics* (New Haven, Connecticut: Yale University Press, 1949), ch. 20.

12. Jude Wanniski, *The Way the World Works* (New York: Basic Books, 1978), pp. 125-42.

13. Murray N. Rothbard, *America's Great Depression* (Princeton, New Jersey: Van Nostrand, 1963), ch. 8.

14. Wanniski, *World Works*, p. 145.

the market has shrunk. In other words, *falling demand is caused by shrinking markets*. Let us put it another way: *falling output is caused by shrinking markets*. It is the same process.

This should not be difficult to understand. If some military saboteur were to find a way secretly to drug a nation's workers so that their output falls by half, what would happen to market demand in that nation (ignoring foreign bank credit and foreign trade)? It would fall by approximately half. Why? Because market demand stems from men's productivity. If a worker has less to offer for sale, his demand for goods is reduced. *Productivity determines demand.*

The same conditions of reduced productivity apply when markets shrink. When productivity falls, demand falls. Productivity falls because the division of labor falls. Specialization of production is reduced. The more specialized a business or a worker, the more painful the readjustment when markets shrink, except in those rare cases where demand stays high, such as brain surgery. (People who need brain surgery cut back spending in other parts of their budget.)

A free market economy is a gigantic auction. Like an auction in which many of the participants go home, and those buyers who remain become fearful of making bids at the older, higher price level, so are world markets. It takes time for sellers of goods and sellers of labor to adjust psychologically to the new conditions. We are all slow learners. Economic losses and unemployment help speed up our learning process.

Let's Make a Deal

Recall my suggestion: whenever you are confused about how the free market works, remember the two imaginary parrots. The economic theory parrot says, "Supply and demand." The economic policy parrot says, "High bid wins." With this in mind, consider the "no sale" problem.

If I want to sell you something at twice what you are willing to pay, is this the fault of capitalism? Put the other way round, if you want to buy something that I am selling, but for only half of what I am asking, is this the fault of capitalism? No, it is the fault of ignorance. Either I think it is worth too much or you think it is worth too little. Perhaps we are both correct.

When I say "You are offering to pay me too little," what do I mean? I mean that you have offered me *less than what I believe someone else besides you is willing to pay*. When you say "You are asking too much," you mean that I am asking *more than what you believe anyone besides me is willing to sell it*. It is a question of belief about the conditions of the market, i.e., belief about the next buyer or seller. A seller thinks there is another buyer just around the corner. A buyer thinks there is another seller just around the corner.

We may both believe incorrectly. In any case, I can't sell you the item at my asking price. So, I have six choices. (1) I can consume it myself. (2) I can pay to put it in storage. (3) I can spend money and advertise it. (4) I can lower its price. (5) I can give it away. (6) I can destroy it. The sixth choice may seem crazy, but if it costs me too much to store it or transport it, and if the law does not allow me to give it away (e.g., food that has not been approved by a public health inspector), then it may be sensible to destroy it. The choice, however, is legally mine. I am the legal owner.

Different people will choose different solutions to this "no deal yet" problem. But one thing is certain: the problem is not a lack of purchasing power in general. My problem is a lack of specific demand for my product or service, given the present array of prices in the economy. But this is not your problem as the potential buyer. Your problem is that I refuse to lower my selling price. Our problem is individual. It is not capitalism's problem in general.

If the government or the banks print up a lot of new money, this may or may not help me to sell my particular item, but it surely does not make everyone richer. Only one thing can make everyone richer: an increase in everyone's productivity.

This comes through increased thrift and increased capital formation, especially knowledge. Wealth does not come through a magic word or a magic pill. It does not come from printing up pieces of paper with pictures of officials on them.

The Problem According to Douglas

Douglas understood that productivity is crucial to prosperity. He believed that capitalism's low productivity – incredibly low compared with what supposedly could be produced with the same workers, raw materials, and machinery – is the result of a flawed system of credit. He wrote: "The industrial machine is a lever, continuously being lengthened by progress, which enables the burden of Atlas to be lifted with ever-increasing ease. As the number of men required to work the lever decreases, so the number set free to lengthen it increases."[15] What, then, is the economy's problem? Simple, he said: ". . . owing to the defective working of an outworn financial system, the lengthening of the lever has been largely offset by artificial obstacles to its beneficent employment. . . ."[16]

Douglas began with the example of a factory. A factory has two aspects, he said: (1) "a producer of goods"; (2) "a purely financial aspect."[17] It distributes purchasing power to individuals through "wages, salaries, and dividends"; it also serves as "a manufactory of prices – financial values."[18]

Manufactory of Prices?

How a factory manufactures prices is unclear. A factory sells goods to buyers. The selling price is initially established by the those in the factory who are assigned this task, but what they say is irrelevant if consumers refuse to buy. *A price is ratified or*

15. *Credit-Power and Democracy*, p. 20.
16. *Ibid.*, p. 20.
17. *Ibid.*, p. 21.
18. *Ibid.*, p. 21.

not ratified solely by the buyers. If the producer sets the price too high, he will see his profits reduced because of lost sales. If he sets the price too low, he will see his profits reduced because of lower total money income, since he will sell out his inventory, yet there will still be buyers waiting in line to buy more. A producer sets prices only as the economic agent of consumers. *Consumers can and will veto every price which they regard as unsatisfactory.*

Consider a simple example. A theater owner wants to make money by hiring a performer to perform on a particular date. At what price should he sell the tickets? At a price that will maximize his income. If he sells too low, there will be a line of disappointed ticket buyers. He loses the money they would have spent. If he sells too high, there will be empty seats that could have been sold if the price had been lower. He loses the money that he might have gained by lowering the price. So, the perfect price for seats is that price which fills every seat, gets the maximum price per seat, and leaves nobody waiting outside. This price structure *clears the market.*

The fact is, the theater owner is not a manufacturer of prices. He is "a seller of seats," meaning he is a provider of employment for performers and a provider of entertainment to consumers. He is a deal-maker, a "putter together" of buyers and sellers. So is a factory manager. He is a putter-together of workers, raw material owners, and buyers of products. He sets initial prices, but only as an economic agent of consumers. He is legally authorized to set prices, but the consumer is legally entitled to announce, "Not today, mate!"

Consumer Sovereignty: Economics

The consumer has the upper hand, economically speaking. There are lots of things he can buy with his money. He is flexible. How many things can a producer do, personally, with a pile of unsold inventory? *Money* is defined by free market economists as *the most marketable good.*[19] This highly marketable good is what the consumers own. This is not what producers own. Producers own highly specialized goods. These goods are valuable only in a limited market. Producers are more inflexible than consumers in the use of their assets because these assets are useful only in very narrow areas of consumer satisfaction. Consider a pair of custom-made shoes. What if the intended consumer decides not to buy? There is a very limited market for this specific pair of shoes. Because the consumer owns money, the most marketable commodity, he is economically sovereign, not the producer.

Factory managers do not control distribution. Consumers control it by buying from one producer and not another, or by saving money rather than buying from anyone. The consumer is sovereign in a free market economy. This is what Social Credit denies. It does so, as we shall see in Appendix A, on the basis of something called the A + B Theorem.

Conclusion

Major Douglas asserted without proof that today's capitalism is about 95 percent inefficient. He stated without proof that under Social Credit, families could live comfortably if the head of the household worked only three hours a day. Or perhaps two hours a week. This was total utopianism. He never offered a shred of statistical proof for all of this.

The cause of economic contraction is government intervention into the economy: prior intervention (increasing the money supply) and present intervention (raising taxes and tariffs, and establishing mandatory price floors). Goods and services will be exchanged when buyers and sellers voluntarily decide that the price is right. It may take time for buyers or sellers to persuade the others that the deal is a good one. This is because we do

19. Ludwig von Mises, *The Theory of Money and Credit* (new ed.; New Haven: Yale University Press, 1953), p. 32. This book was first published in 1912.

not have perfect knowledge. We may hesitate to buy or sell because we expect to get a better deal shortly. When this hope is thwarted long enough, we will usually make the deal.

Producers do not set prices except tentatively, to test the market. The consumers are sovereign. If consumers refuse to buy at listed prices, it does not matter that producers have the legal authority to set prices. A listed (i.e., hoped-for) price is an advertisement to sell; until a sale takes place at the legally announced price, this price is nothing more than an offer to sell. Only a consumer can translate this offer into a realized sale. Thus, the consumer is sovereign, not the producer. The consumer has the ability to say "no."

Summary

1. To discover economic control, follow the money.
2. Douglas claimed that capitalism operates at 5 percent of maximum efficiency.
3. There is no proof of any such estimate.
4. He blamed the distribution system for this failure.
5. The problem is a lack of purchasing power.
6. This criticism is wrong.
7. The reason goods do not sell is as follows: (1) buyers refuse to buy at the price asked by the sellers; (2) sellers refuse to lower the price. (Same argument, stated two ways.)
8. Government causes economic contractions: prior monetary inflation, tariffs and import quotas, price floors, and new taxes.
9. This shrinks markets and therefore shrinks productivity.
10. There are six things a seller can do when an item does not sell.
11. A permanent lack of sales has nothing to do with a lack of credit, but instead with a failure of sellers to lower prices.
12. Printing money will not increase everyone's wealth.

7

FALLING PRICES AND CAPITALIST PROFITS

Certain consequences, readily understood if it be remembered that wages, costs, and purchasing power are only different aspects of the same thing, accompany a continuous fall in *costs* under the existing financial system, and a fall in *prices*, while offsetting these consequences to some extent, involves the *entrepreneur* in a loss on the whole of his stocks, a loss which he is not usually willing, or indeed able, to take.

C. H. Douglas (1931)[1]

Falling prices and falling costs, argued Major Douglas, will inevitably produce losses for entrepreneurs. This is the crucial flaw of capitalism, he argued. Capitalism, because of a failure in the credit system, does not provide consumers with sufficient money to buy all the goods produced by capitalism. Prices therefore tend to fall. This produces losses for businessmen. Thus, he concluded, there is a chronic tendency toward underconsumption and business losses under capitalism.

If he was incorrect on this point, his criticism of capitalism

1. *The Monopoly of Credit* (London: Chapman & Hall, 1931), p. 28.

collapses. If his criticism collapses, there is no reason to pay any attention to his proposed solution, Social Credit, except as an example of fallacious reasoning. This is why we need to pay very close attention to what he says is the tendency of capitalism to self-destruct because of its permanent tendency to produce lower prices and therefore losses for businessmen.

Douglas quite correctly highlighted the effects of falling costs and falling prices on the one person in the economic system who makes capitalism work: *the entrepreneur*. If Douglas' assessment is correct, then he did indeed pinpoint the central flaw in free market capitalism. When a stable or slowly rising money supply is accompanied by increased production – which is what we all want – and perhaps even increased population, then entrepreneurs should expect to face an economy marked by steadily falling prices. Many prices will fall, some will stay the same, and a few will rise.

The question is: Is this bad? It is surely not bad for those consumers who possess money and who have access to consumer credit – a topic which Douglas rarely discussed. But is it bad for most consumers and most producers? Douglas said that a falling price level is bad for most people. The problem is, he never proved his point. He merely assumed it.

Another question is this: Were Major Douglas, John Maynard Keynes, and many other critics of capitalism correct when they argued some variation of Douglas' conclusion? Is the expansion of the nation's money supply necessary in order to keep the uncontrolled capitalist economy from falling into permanent economic depression? My answer is *no*. Their answer is *yes*. What these critics never recognize is that downward price flexibility is compatible with economic growth.[2] Anyone who has bought a microcomputer should know this. Their

2. Gary North, "Downward Price Flexibility and Economic Growth," *The Freeman* (May 1971); reprinted in Gary North, *An Introduction to Christian Economics* (Nutley, New Jersey: Craig Press, 1973), ch. 9.

prices keep falling, and the benefits to society keep increasing – except Communist society, of course, which was destroyed in the 1980's by the competition posed by the computer, both domestically (too much political freedom) and abroad (too much economic productivity).

Capital Goods

Capital goods lead to increased output per unit of resource input. That is to say, they produce greater wealth. They produce economic growth. Douglas believed in economic growth. He believed that there can be tremendous economic growth if society will adopt Social Credit, but he denied that the present capitalist economy can produce such growth without infusions of State monopoly credit. He argued that capitalist banking always fails to produce a sufficient quantity of money to clear the market of all goods and services. Because the economy fails to receive such injections of State credit, a crisis supposedly must ensue. If the output of goods and services should increase, he said, "the cycle would become unworkable in a very short period of time, since no one would be able to buy anything."[3] The question is: Was he correct?

Douglas believed in the policy of increasing an economy's productivity. *The progressive overcoming of scarcity in history is marked by falling prices.* Why, then, did he refuse to accept the desirability of falling prices? Because he assumed that retail prices in an expanding economy will not fall far enough to clear the market under capitalism because producers need to be repaid for production costs. So, the system needs new money.

Scarcity is defined by economists as follows: "Greater demand for resources than supply of resources at zero price." The higher the price relative to other goods or to other periods of history, the greater the degree of scarcity. Therefore, the lower the price relative to other goods or to other periods of history,

---

3. *Social Credit* (2nd ed.; London: Eyre & Spottiswoode, 1933), p. 85.

the less the degree of scarcity. Prices will never reach zero in history, the Bible teaches, for nature is under a curse, but it is a sign of God's blessing that prices approach zero as a theoretical limit.

We therefore need to ask: Why are falling prices inherently bad for the economy? Douglas said that falling prices are so bad that they threaten the survival of capitalism, but this assertion flies in the face of the reality he wanted: increased economic output.

The Alleged Problem of Depreciation

How Douglas would have explained the computer revolution is anyone's guess. I know from experience that a huge, filing cabinet-sized used computer that I bought in 1981 for over $38,000, with a $6,000 per year insurance contract, fell to zero value by 1988. By 1991 it was possible to buy a battery-powered portable computer with ten times my 1981 (used) computer's speed and memory capacity for about $2,500, and it weighed 6 pounds. Two years later, the next generation of laptop computers cost about $1,500 and weighed 3 pounds. So it goes and will continue to go. This is *high-speed depreciation*. We are all richer for these innovations which have produced rapid depreciation.

Yet Douglas wrote that depreciation under capitalism is a threat to the economy. Without "other factors" intervening, we would all starve. He wrote: "Depreciation alone would absorb the world's purchasing-power, although not seriously diminishing the world's true wealth, and if no other factors intervened, we should have starved in the midst of plenty many years ago."[4] Here is supposedly a major flaw in capitalism. The world's *true wealth* remains, yet depreciation threatens us all with starvation. What is true wealth? He never said. What are these "other factors" that somehow will be able to save the

4. *Ibid.*, pp. 85-86.

capitalist system? His answer: bank credit.

His argument was that those who bought capital goods are doomed to failure under capitalism unless there is a subsequent increase in the money supply. Even if there were no increase in the supply of goods and services, he said, the capitalist economy would still fail. Why? Because without a constantly increasing money supply, there cannot be profits: "Bearing this in mind, we can understand that it is impossible for a closed community to operate continuously on the profit system, if the amount of money inside this community is not increased, *even though the amount of goods and services available are not increased.*"[5]

Was he correct? No. Then what did he fail to understand? That all of a nation's money supply is always in someone's hand (cash), or his bank account (credit), or hidden under his mattress (cash). It does not mysteriously disappear. I therefore ask: Why is there an inherent shortage of money under capitalism?

Douglas' Attempted Answer

In the 1933 edition of *Social Credit*, Douglas responded to critics who had identified this flaw in his theory. He wrote that the "orthodox theory" of the economy "assumes that the money, equivalent to the price of every article which is produced, is in the pocket, or the bank pigeon-hole of somebody in the world."[6] This is exactly what orthodox monetary theory teaches, or at least taught until John Maynard Keynes' *General Theory of Employment, Interest, and Money* came along in 1936. After that, Keynesianism became the new orthodoxy.

Some people save part of their total holdings of money. In Douglas' day, orthodox economists taught that the money supply is sufficient to clear the market of consumer goods and services if prices remain flexible in a downward direction. This clearing will occur even if some people spend money on capital

5. *Monopoly of Credit*, p. 24.

6. *Social Credit*, p. 83.

goods. Why? Because those who are paid to produce capital goods receive money to buy consumer goods and services. This means that consumers can buy the economy's entire supply of consumer goods. But Douglas refused to accept this argument: ". . . even supposing at any given moment it were true, one week afterwards [i.e., one week after the employees of capital goods producers are paid – G.N.] it could no longer be true."[7] In effect, this money somehow disappears during the week.

This is a very odd conclusion. How could the money actually disappear? If I buy something from you with my money, you now have the money. It is true that if I buy a capital good (tool) from you, I do not use that tool directly for satisfying my own immediate personal consumption demands (assuming I am not using the tool to derive pleasure from my hobby). But the money I paid to you does not disappear. You can go out and buy whatever you can afford with the money I paid you. You can buy a consumer good because I didn't. The consumer goods that investors do not buy when they invest their money can be bought by the producers of capital goods who receive investors' money. Capitalist investment is productive, but not because investors give up ownership of pieces of paper with officials' pictures on them. Capitalist investment is productive because investors give up the use of consumer goods and services for a period of time for the sake of receiving a greater quantity of consumer goods and services in the future.

My point is simple: *there is nothing inherent in the free market economy that breaks the flow of funds*. Like Old Man River, the flow of funds just keeps rolling along.

Capitalism's Magnificent System of Falling Prices

The ultimate secret of capitalism is that it allows increased production from what seems to be a fixed supply of resources. This really is a secret. Very few capitalists understand it, let

7. *Ibid.*, p. 84.

alone capitalism's critics.

The first law of thermodynamics tells us that matter/energy is neither created nor destroyed. The second law tells us that in a closed system, the transformation of potential energy into kinetic energy is a one-way process: from order to disorder (entropy). This process of one-way transformation is sometimes called *time's arrow*. But economics tells us that men can increase their total wealth, even wealth per capita, through hard work, education, thrift, greater specialization, and above all, accurate forecasting of the future, i.e., entrepreneurship. Men continue to discover new resources and ever-more effective, less expensive ways to discover, use, and recycle old resources. Thus, we can *temporarily* offset the effects of the second law of thermodynamics. We produce increasing order out of the apparent disorder of our environment.[8] The standard physical explanation of this is that the earth is not a closed system; it draws energy from the sun. The less popular physical explanation is that life itself appears not to conform to the known laws of physics.[9]

There are at least two inescapable limits to growth: time and space. If any species multiplies itself long enough, no matter how low the compounding rate of growth is, the number of its members eventually approaches infinity as a limit. At some point long before this happens, the species' environment can no longer sustain all of its members. The Christian says (or should say) that this spatial limit on mankind points to the day of final judgment, when the human race becomes a host like the angels: no marriage, giving in marriage, or reproduction. But other than the dual limit of space and time, it is very, very difficult to identify a limit to growth which efficient planning and thrift cannot overcome.

---

8. Gary North, *Is the World Running Down? Crisis in the Christian Worldview* (Tyler, Texas: Institute for Christian Economics, 1988).

9. Erwin Schrödinger, *What Is Life? The Physical Aspects of the Living Cell* (Cambridge University Press, [1944] 1967), p. 75.

Henry Ford

I think it is safe to say that what Henry Ford did for the modern world was stupendous. He changed the face of the industrial world. How did he do this? By cutting the selling price of the Model T automobile to less than his *initial* costs of production.

Henry Ford stumbled into this pricing policy. He went into competition against Buick in 1908, which produced a full line of motor cars, with prices from $900 to $2,500 (when prices generally were a less than a tenth of what they are today). That was the year that William Durant created General Motors. Buick had 25 percent of market share in 1908.

In the first year, Ford lost money. He sold the Model T for $850, but the car was no match for the more dashing $900 Buick. To increase profits, Ford raised the price to $950 in 1909. This price hike increased corporate profits because the public was willing to buy lots of cars, but Ford's percentage of the automobile market declined. His advertisers advised him to raise prices another hundred dollars, but then Ford decided to shift his sales strategy. In 1910, Buick raised its entry-level car price to $1,150. Ford did the opposite: he lowered the price of the Model T by almost 20 percent, to $780. At this price, Ford could break even only if he vastly expanded sales or lowered production costs. Ford achieved both. The result was a 60 percent surge in Ford sales.

In the recession year of 1914, Henry Ford launched a revolution: doubling the wages of his workers to $5 a day. He was criticized by the *Wall Street Journal*. He was criticized by his shareholders. The result: low absenteeism, greater productivity. In the same year, Ford cut Model T prices twice. The result: huge sales. In 1916, despite the increase in general prices because of monetary policies of the recently created (in 1913) Federal Reserve System, the U.S. central bank, Ford lowered the price of the Model T to $360, increasing Ford's market share from 10 percent to 40 percent. Meanwhile, General Motors' share fell from 23 percent to 8 percent. In 1920, in the midst of the 1920-21 recession, Ford cut prices by an astounding 30 percent. This led to his capture of 60 percent of the market.

George Gilder writes: "During this entire period up to 1920, though his margins remained low, Ford's profits on net worth ranged between 20 and 300 percent and were by far the highest in the industry."[10] Here is how Gilder describes this strategy through 1927: "By 1927, he had sold 15 million cars, with a sales volume of $7 billion, and the company's net worth, with no new infusions of capital since the original $28,000, had risen to $715 million, including some $600 million in cash. By this same strategy, Ford also dominated the tractor market."[11]

A Familiar Process

This is the capitalist way of doing business: low prices, high wages, and high profits. The high profits come from innovation and accurate forecasting of consumer demand. The critics of capitalism, including Major Douglas, never grasp this fundamental strategy. It is inconceivable to them. The goal of a daring capitalist innovator is to cut selling prices below *existing* costs and allow the increased sales volume to enable his firm to buy raw materials and other production goods at a lower cost because of volume purchases.

The results of this production strategy have been studied in great detail. Gilder writes that "unit costs in the industry as a whole, adjusted for inflation, will tend to drop between 20 and 30 percent with every doubling of accumulated output. . . . Never is there a sign of long-run diminishing returns."[12] This remarkable and little-recognized rule of thumb applies to al-

10. .George Gilder, *The Spirit of Enterprise* (New York: Simon & Schuster, 1984), p. 158.

11. *Ibid.*, p. 157.

12. *Ibid.*, p. 158.

most every industry: computers, chicken broilers, kilowatt hours of electricity, and the value of insurance policies sold. "All drop in unit costs by the familiar 20 to 30 percent for each doubling of total volume."[13]

If every entrepreneur knew in advance that selling prices and costs would surely fall, and if every entrepreneur knew exactly how much selling prices and costs would fall, and if every entrepreneur could know in advance whether his revenues would be positive or negative in his niche in the market, then of course there would be no losses to any entrepreneur. *There would also be no profits*. But such a hypothetical world of perfect foreknowledge is impossible. It will never exist. Men are not God. They are not omniscient. So, the question is, can *some* entrepreneurs profit when prices are falling? Yes. Can the wealth of society *in general* increase under falling prices? Yes. Can the free market system survive? This is mainly a political question; economically, it can surely survive, and has.

Of course, a few industries do not enjoy such a degree of profit-maximization through cost-cutting. Consider the funeral industry. A sharp fall in the price of funeral services, industry-wide, will not lead to an even more spectacular increase in suicides and murders. Also, there are only so many people who will line up for brain surgery even if the price of this service falls sharply. But if we are talking about consumer goods that are not "life and death" goods, capitalism's law of price-cutting has held for a long time.

Major Douglas and the Underconsumption Theory

As with all defenders of an underconsumption theory of capitalist crises, Major Douglas did not understand this now-familiar capitalist rule of price-cutting. He believed that a firm cannot cut prices below its costs of production and still remain in business. This is true, but only if we are talking about costs

13. *Ibid.*, p. 158.

of production at the time of final sales. It is not true if we are talking about initial costs of production prior to increased output. Today's costs can be above today's revenues. The question is: What about tomorrow? The strategy is to reduce unit costs by increasing output dramatically to take advantage of what economists call *economies of scale*. This strategy never occurred to Douglas, nor does it occur to his present-day disciples. He wrote – with his typical lack of clarity – in 1933:

> Now any attempt, by current financial methods, to reduce prices (or even to stabilise them, as the phrase goes) is a mathematical absurdity unless the cost of this stabilisation, or lowering of prices, is met from some extraneous source. Or to put the matter another way, the margin of profit which makes it possible for a producer to go on producing, disappears unless the financial cost, and consequently the price of production, is allowed to rise steadily in relation to direct labour cost. As a result of this, if prices are forced down, production stops, and stocks are sold only at prices which mean loss, and ultimately bankruptcy, to the manufacturer and distributor. This is the situation produced by the fall of prices again initiated in 1928.
>
> To put the matter in a form of words which will be useful in our further consideration of the subject, *the consumer cannot possibly obtain the advantage of improved process in the form of correspondingly lower prices, nor can he expect stable prices under stationary processes of production, nor can he obtain any control over the programme of production, unless he is provided with a supply of purchasing-power which is not included in the price of the goods produced. If the producer or distributor sells at a loss, this loss forms such a supply of purchasing-power to the consumer; but if the producer and distributor are not to sell at a loss, this supply of purchasing-power must be derived from some other source. There is only one source from which it can be derived, and that is the same source which enables a bank to lend more money than it originally received. That is to say, the general credit.*[14]

14. *Social Credit*, pp. 98-99. Italics in original.

I will say it one more time: if you do not understand what a reformer is saying, do not become his disciple. He may not know what he is talking about, and so his writing is convoluted. I have no doubt that this was Major Douglas' problem.

Major Douglas did not understand the process of price competition under free market capitalism. He believed that there is an inherent deficiency of purchasing power in capitalism: a gap between costs (high) and revenues (low). This, he said, is why the banks must create fiat credit money: to close the gap. "The deficiency between purchasing-power, and goods with money prices attached to them, can be made up (at any rate to a large extent) by this process of creating bank money. . . . And conversely, the refusal to create fresh money by banking methods or otherwise, whatever the cause of this refusal may be, is sufficient to paralyse both production and consumption."[15] But his thesis was that the banks cannot create sufficient purchasing power; when business loans are repaid, this money somehow goes out of existence – how, he did not say exactly.

Douglas did not understand that price competition can and does close this gap. As prices fall, the purchasing power of money rises, yet Douglas was concerned about a decline in purchasing power. He did not understand purchasing power. This is because on this point he self-consciously and openly followed the monetary theory of the self-taught[16] economist, J. A. Hobson, who argued, as Douglas summarized him, for "the inadequacy of the money available in the hands of the public to buy the goods normally available. . . ."[17]

Douglas believed that supply and demand do not work to set prices that clear markets. "It is a widely spread delusion that

15. *Ibid.*, p. 88.

16. Joseph Schumpeter, *History of Economic Analysis* (New York: Oxford University Press, 1954), p. 832n.

17. *Social Credit*, p. 89. Elsewhere, Douglas said Hobson's theory was inadequate: *ibid.*, pp. 82ff.

price is simply a question of supply and demand," Douglas wrote in his first book.[18] He assured his readers that "it is frequently assumed that a mere glut of goods will bring down prices quite irrespective of any intrinsic economy involved in large scale production." This assumption is false, he said. "Unless these goods are all absorbed, the result may be exactly opposite. . . ."[19] In short, sellers will not lower their prices in order to clear their inventories. For some reason – he never explained what – sellers prefer to tie up their capital in unsold inventory instead of getting at least some money for the presently unsold goods. In this view of sellers' resistance, he shared a fundamental first principle with John Maynard Keynes.

John Maynard Keynes

Hobson was an underconsumptionist, just as Douglas was. He argued that capitalism is flawed by its inability to sell goods. He rejected the nineteenth century's orthodox economic theory of pricing: that there is no permanent gap between supply and demand. Keynes [pronounced CANES], the most influential economist of the twentieth century, favorably quoted Hobson in this regard.[20] But Keynes went far beyond mere quotation; he praised Hobson to the skies. Keynes wrote of Hobson's book, *The Physiology of Industry* (1889), that "Mr. Hobson has flung himself with unflagging, but almost unavailing, ardour and courage against the ranks of orthodoxy. Though it is so completely forgotten to-day, the publication of this book marks, in a sense, an epoch in economic thought."[21] I know of no economist and no economics book that Keynes praised more enthusiastically. He devoted six pages to analyzing Hobson's book.

18. *Economic Democracy* (2nd ed.; London: Cecil Palmer, 1921), p. 57.

19. *Ibid.*, p. 57.

20. John Maynard Keynes, *The General Theory of Employment, Interest, and Money* (New York: Macmillan, 1936), p. 129n.

21. *Ibid.*, pp. 364-65.

Why? Because Keynes was also an underconsumptionist. He also challenged the orthodox theory of competitive pricing. He also called for fiat money to revive a flagging economy.

Then, concluding his section on Hobson, Keynes discussed Major Douglas. Keynes did not accept Douglas' solution, but he insisted that "The strength of Major Douglas's advocacy has, of course, largely depended on orthodoxy having no valid reply to much of his destructive criticism."[22] Again, "Major Douglas is entitled to claim, as against some of his orthodox adversaries, that he at least has not been wholly oblivious of the outstanding problem of our economic system."[23] This grudging praise from the premier defender of government spending – the defender of the "mixed economy" – should alert conservative readers to the true nature of Major Douglas' theories. Douglas was not a conservative. He was a defender of State planning as a means of balancing the economy, just as Keynes was.

Douglas vs. Thrift

There was another close connection between Keynes and Douglas: their hostility to private thrift. "This idea of thrift, like that of economy, is an example of the perversion of an idea which has lost its original application."[24] Douglas adopted a version of what has become known as *the paradox of thrift.* Keynes offered a very similar analysis. The 1930's brought a fundamental shift in academic thinking with respect to thrift. Economist and investment advisor Mark Skousen is correct when he writes: "The Keynesian revolution in economic theory, which began in earnest in the 1930s, dramatically reversed the positive approach most economists and government leaders had taken toward savings and thrift. . . . Keynes and his followers lashed out at the hoarders and thrifty consumers. . . . By 1936,

22. *Ibid.*, pp. 370-71.
23. *Ibid.*, p. 371.
24. *Social Credit*, p. 121.

he referred to traditional views of savings as 'absurd.' He boldly wrote, 'The more virtuous we are, the more determinedly thrifty, the more obstinately orthodox in our national and personal finance, the more our incomes will fall. . . .' "[25]

Douglas was a pioneer in this hostility to personal thrift. He argued, as Keynes did, that thrift reduces present consumption, and therefore makes an economic slump worse. Instead of praising thrift because it increases the supply of consumer goods in the future, Douglas attacked thrift because it reduces the demand for present consumer goods. Like Keynes, he ignored the obvious fact that saving increases the demand for producer goods, and thereby increases income for those involved in the production of such goods. Douglas wrote:

> If I have an income of £500 per annum and I save, as the phrase goes, £100 per annum of this sum, either by the simple process of putting it in a bank, or by the investment of it in an insurance policy, I decrease my expenditure by 20 per cent., and I certainly provide myself with money for use at some future time. But there is no physical saving corresponding to this money saving. In fact, owing to the interconnection of the financial system with the producing system, there is probably an actual destruction of wealth due to the fact that I do not spend the whole of my income. More goods would have been drawn from the shops, more orders would have been given to the manufacturers to replace those goods, and consequently a real ability to produce more goods per unit of time would have been created, probably by an extension of manufacturing facilities, had I spent my income. But if I save my money, only one of two things can possibly happen in the world of actualities: either goods which have been produced will not be bought and will therefore be wasted, or in anticipation of the fact that I should not buy them they will never have been produced. That, I think, is an accurate description of the result of financial saving and insurance, so far

25. Mark Skousen, *The Structure of Production* (New York: New York University Press, 1990), pp. 244-24. He cited Keynes, *General Theory*, p. 111.

as it affects the production system.[26]

His language was remarkably similar to Keynes' with respect to the virtues of thrift, which they both denied. Douglas went beyond Keynes, however, when he labeled the praise of thrift as a form of idolatry:

> To explain what I mean, let us return for a moment to the recommendations of the Labour Party's Supplement. Consider as an example the remark that "the extension of banking facilities for workers would facilitate small savings." We have here a typical instance of idolatry. Saving is put forward as a virtue in itself, and we can only conclude that those responsible are either without any understanding of the true nature of money saving, or are influenced by that attribute of idolatry which makes it so dangerous that it delivers its victims bound hand and foot to any unscrupulous interest which sees through the delusion.[27]

Douglas escalated the rhetoric against thrift. He actually said that thrift might soon produce a catastrophe: "But so far from the financial economy and thrift, which is so constantly preached at the present day, representing either good management or sane progress, it is mathematically demonstrable that it can only result in unbalanced production and consequent catastrophe."[28]

Then how should we escape the paradox of thrift? Keynes' answer was more government spending, even if this meant unbalanced budgets. He also recommended the increase of fiat money, which would lower real wages by raising the money price of goods, thereby leading to increased hiring of laborers. (His supporters deny this, but this is what he wanted: higher employment through an inflationary lowering of the workers'

---

26. *Warning Democracy* (2nd ed.; London: Stanley Nott, 1934), pp. 56-57.
27. *Ibid.*, pp. 112-13.
28. *Social Credit*, p. 124.

real income.)[29] He also recommended using fiat money to lower the interest rate close to zero.[30]

Douglas' solution was similar but more direct: the Just Price system (zero-interest government capital to businesses) and the National Dividend (automatic monthly government checks to citizens), as we shall see in Chapter 9. This, too, involves the issuing of fiat money. In other words, the great evil of modern capitalism – its dependence on personal saving and investment – will end under Social Credit. The State's elite money-managers will replace the thrifty individual as the source of investment capital.

Purchasing Power

Major Douglas worried in 1920 about a loss of purchasing power: "The whole economic system is in ceaseless motion – purchasing-power is constantly flowing back from individuals into the credit system from whence it came, and if the outflow is less than the inflow, someone has to lose purchasing-power."[31] In other words, if the level of debt-credit does not constantly increase, some people's purchasing power will drop.

The economic facts are the very opposite. If new money – credit money or fiat money – ceases to be injected into the economy through the banks or the government, there will be an *increase* in the purchasing power of money. Why? Because capitalism's economic output is increasing while the total money supply remains constant. Thus, prices will tend to fall, meaning that *the purchasing power of money increases*. Like the computer

---

29. Keynes, *General Theory*, p. 268. He wrote: "Having regard to human nature and our institutions, it can only be a foolish person who would prefer a flexible wage policy to a flexible money policy. . . ." In short, the government should fool the workers by lowering their real incomes through price inflation. If they aren't fooled in this way, they will remain unemployed or underemployed, since they refuse to work for less money at today's price level.

30. *Ibid.*, pp. 220, 375-76.

31. *Credit-Power and Democracy*, p. 25.

that cost $50,000 in 1980 whose efficiency could be matched by a desktop computer costing $1,000 in 1990, so is the capitalist economy generally. The purchasing power of money in the computer market rose in the 1980's; it did not fall. This was also true of most raw materials in the 1980's.[32] While those companies that made expensive mini-computers in 1980 did experience a reduction of purchasing power, think of the hundreds of new micro-computer companies that experienced tremendous increases in purchasing power.

The Gold Standard and Economic Growth

Major Douglas faced a major problem: how to explain the historic productivity of capitalism, despite the fact that Social Credit policies had never been adopted. He argued on one page of *The Monopoly of Credit* (1931) that "one unit of human labor can on the average produce at least forty times as much as was the case up to the beginning of the nineteenth century."[33] While he offered no statistics to support this claim, let us accept it for the sake of argument. Yet two pages earlier he had written: "Bearing this in mind, we can understand that it is impossible for a closed community to operate continuously on the profit system, if the amount of money inside this community is not increased, *even though the amount of goods and services available are not increased*."[34] But this "closed community" called capitalism had been operating for over two centuries in 1920, multiplying men's wealth as nothing ever had in history. How was this possible?

The "Tyranny" of Gold

His problem is simple to state: because of his theory of free

32. See E. Calvin Beisner, *Prospects for Growth: A Biblical View of Population, Resources, and the Future* (Westchester, Illinois: Crossway, 1990).

33. *Monopoly of Credit*, p. 26.

34. *Ibid.*, p. 24.

market failure, he could not explain why there had been such tremendous economic growth during the period in which the gold standard constrained the increase of England's money supply. What he knew to be true in terms of economic growth his theory could not explain. During the period from 1700 to 1930, the price level in England had not changed very much except during wartime, when England went off the gold standard.

Professor Roy Jastram's book, *The Golden Constant* (1977), is a standard academic source on the history of English and American prices. He writes that "there are approximately 230 years of essentially stable prices, terminating in 1930, during most of which time England was on the gold standard."[35] That is to say, literally up until the year that *The Monopoly of Credit* was published, the history of English (and American) prices pointed to the opposite conclusion of Douglas' theory. The gold standard had kept the English money supply remarkably stable, 1700-1930, during which the English economy grew faster than any economy in the history of man, except possibly for the American economy after 1800, which was also tied to the international gold standard except during its Civil War (1861-65) and the immediate aftermath, called Reconstruction (1866-77).

Economic Growth

This is not to say that there had been no increase in the money supply under the free market and the gold standard. Increases in the supply of gold allowed the increase of money.[36] Also, fractional reserve banking was in effect after the establishment of the Bank of England in 1694. But there is no

35. Roy W. Jastram, *The Golden Constant: The English and American Experience, 1560-1976* (New York: Wiley, 1977). p. 39.

36. See "World Gold Production," Figure 8.2: Skousen, *Structure of Production*, p. 270, and "World Gold Stock and Gold Production, 1800-1932," Figure 8.1, *ibid.*, p. 268. His source for the latter chart is Refus S. Tucker, "Gold and the General Price Level," *Review of Economics and Statistics* (July 1934).

way to argue from the economic record that the gold standard seriously inhibited economic growth. The opposite is far easier to prove, namely, that *the gold standard created the monetary foundation of long-term economic growth.* What created the major economic crises were wars and the suspension of gold payments by the banks and the governments involved. This is not what Major Douglas wanted to prove, and more than John Maynard Keynes wanted. On this point, they were agreed – and equally wrong. But Keynes knew the history of English prices.[37] Major Douglas never mentioned it.

England went off the gold standard in 1931. The United States went off the gold standard domestically in 1933 and internationally in 1971. From 1931 until the present, price inflation has been with the West. The fact is, however, there was tremendous economic growth under the gold standard, as Douglas knew but refused to mention. What he had to explain was how this could be true if his economic theory is also true. His A+B Theorem was designed to explain why the profit system cannot work under capitalism. It failed.[38]

The trouble is, even in the depression conditions of 1930 or 1935, the international capitalist economy had made the West incredibly rich in comparison to the world of 1730 or 1830. It did so, according to Douglas' economic analysis, while laboring under the oppressive burden of the commercial banking system. Douglas never once addressed this anomaly. He should have.

Conclusion

Major Douglas, like so many critics of capitalism (and occasionally even friends), believed that capitalism could not deal with its inherent tendency toward falling prices. He insisted

37. Keynes, *A Tract on Monetary Reform* (London: Harcourt, Brace, 1923), pp. 11-12.

38. See Appendix A.

that injections of fiat money from a government credit agency are required to overcome this flaw in capitalism. He did not explain how capitalism had been able to prosper for centuries without the government program which Douglas recommended. He also did not discuss the role of the gold standard in inhibiting inflation and also providing liquidity to the system. Most of all, he did not deal with this crucial question: how entrepreneurs seek to profit by lowering prices below today's selling prices in order to profit from volume discounts in the future as a result of a significant increase in the volume of sales in the future.

Douglas shared his underconsumptionist views with John Maynard Keynes. Neither of them was willing to explain clearly why sellers supposedly refuse to sell inventories at any price, once they recognize that there will probably be very few buyers at today's price. It is irrelevant to the seller what he paid to produce the inventory. The only relevant question is this one: "How much will it cost me to hold onto this unsold inventory?"

Like Keynes, Douglas was hostile to individual thrift during an economic downturn. He argued that thrift reduces present consumption (true), thereby hurting the economy (not proven). He wrote that thrift under conditions of recession "can only result in unbalanced production and consequent catastrophe." He rejected any suggestion that thrift is a universal virtue. In this, he shared the view of Keynes and his successors. He failed to understand that the decision to save is the decision to seek a greater value of future goods by forfeiting present goods.

Summary

1. Douglas relied on Hobson's underconsumption theory.
2. Keynes praised Hobson's theory.
3. Keynes said that Douglas was closer to the truth than his free market critics were.
4. In a growing economy, prices should be falling (e.g., computer prices).

5. The economy does not need injections of fiat money or bank-created money.
6. There is no inherent need in capitalism of bank-created credit money to offset the money received by sellers of raw materials, land, and lenders.
7. There is no single central problem in capitalism for which there is a single solution ("magic pill").

8

A FALSE PRESCRIPTION

> Then he which had received the one talent came and said, Lord, I knew thee that thou art an hard man, reaping where thou hast not sown, and gathering where thou hast not strawed: And I was afraid, and went and hid thy talent in the earth: lo, there thou hast that is thine. His lord answered and said unto him, Thou wicked and slothful servant, thou knewest that I reap where I sowed not, and gather where I have not strawed: Thou oughtest therefore to have put my money to the exchangers, and then at my coming I should have received mine own with usury (Matthew 25:24-27).

In this parable, Jesus told of a lazy servant who sought to explain his failure to invest his master's money. The servant blamed the master, as if the master were evil. It was all the master's fault! The master was not impressed by this argument. He turned his envious, slothful servant's criticism against him. "Am I evil? Very well, then. At the very least, you should have placed the money into a local bank, so that I could have received some interest. " (The King James Version translates the Greek word as "usury," which in 1611 meant illegally or immorally high interest, but the Greek word meant interest, not high interest.)

Jesus used the parable to describe how much we owe to God for His grace to us. Jesus used an economic parable to drive home His point: on judgment day, God will expect much from us if He has given much to us. As He said elsewhere: "And that servant, which knew his lord's will, and prepared not himself, neither did according to his will, shall be beaten with many stripes. But he that knew not, and did commit things worthy of stripes, shall be beaten with few stripes. For unto whomsoever much is given, of him shall be much required: and to whom men have committed much, of him they will ask the more" (Luke 12:47-48).

Jesus was not opposed to money-lending as such. He was not opposed to banking and interest. He was not opposed to high profits. After all, the good servants in the parable had made 100% on their investment of the master's money (Matt. 25:20, 22). What He was opposed to was servants who do not increase the talents which God has entrusted to them.

A Bankers' Conspiracy!

Major Douglas warned that "if the population of this or any other country is willing to allow the mechanism of money to be controlled by the few, then, so long as inducement by money is the basis of credit, so long will the few control the many."[1] This was a major feature of his critique of capitalism: a system of money creation that places power in the hands of the few. This diagnosis appeals to those people who want to view history as a battleground between "the people" and "the conspiracy."

This view of history is at bottom false. There are always conspiracies competing for men's allegiance, but at the heart of any society is never a conspiracy. The heart of any society is the religious worldview of the people, whose allegiance is so important for conspirators. Some conspiracy or group of conspiracies may seek to represent the people. A conspiracy for a time may

1. *Credit-Power and Democracy* (London: Cecil Palmer, 1920), p. 62.

fool the people and manipulate them on specific issues, but the reality is this: *a conspiracy cannot operate unless it persuades men to obey*. It can do this by force for a while, but not indefinitely. To be successful in the long run, it must give the people what they want. It must do as Satan did in the garden: appeal to their spirit of rebellion.

When the elders of Israel came to the prophet Samuel and demanded a king, God was not fooled. He understood the lust of their hearts. They were rejecting Him. God decided to punish them by giving them exactly what they asked for. "And the LORD said unto Samuel, Hearken unto the voice of the people in all that they say unto thee: for they have not rejected thee, but they have rejected me, that I should not reign over them" (I Samuel 8:7). This is God's way of dealing with widespread moral rebellion. He curses them with their desires. "And he gave them their request; but sent leanness into their soul" (Psalm 106:15).

So, when any social or economic commentator points to a conspiracy as the central feature of a society, our initial response should not be to "throw the rascals out." Rather, it should be: "Let us cleanse the evil from our own hearts first, and then throw the rascals out." We must not confuse causes with effects. As James wrote, "From whence come wars and fightings among you? come they not hence, even of your lusts that war in your members?" (James 4:1). Wars do not come from a military-industrial complex or "merchants of death" or an international bankers' conspiracy. It comes from within. Jesus therefore warned men not to cast out demons until they have first placed God in the center of their lives. We should not clean up effects before we clean up causes:

> When the unclean spirit is gone out of a man, he walketh through dry places, seeking rest; and finding none, he saith, I will return unto my house whence I came out. And when he cometh, he findeth it swept and garnished. Then goeth he, and

> taketh to him seven other spirits more wicked than himself; and they enter in, and dwell there: and the last state of that man is worse than the first (Luke 11:24-26).

Major Douglas believed in a conspiracy of bankers. He called this "a hidden government."[2] Yet a few pages later, he admitted that "Even the leaders of a group are only leaders so long as they serve the interests of the group, and to that extent are as much slaves of it, as the humblest member of the rank and file; . . ."[3] It seems that the group is sovereign after all. The group's demands must be met by the leaders. But Douglas did not pursue this point. He should have.

The Need to Work

There was a second aspect of capitalism that Major Douglas opposed: labor. Social Credit economics is a system opposed to the idea that labor should be necessary for wealth. This is why Social Credit opposes the modern industrial system. He wrote: "Once again let it be repeated, the primary objective of the industrial system is *goods*, not employment. Once let it be arranged that the distribution of goods is not the 'reward' of employment, and there is some chance that the scientific intellects of the industrial world will achieve the end to which all their efforts are bent – the replacement of human labor by energy drawn directly from the source of all terrestrial energy, the sun. . . ."[4]

What does the Bible say? It says that God has placed a curse on man's labor (Genesis 3:17-19). We are required to work six days out of seven. "Six days shalt thou labour, and do all thy work" (Exodus 20:9). What God promises is that the curse on human labor will be reduced as sin is progressively removed

---

2. *Social Credit* (3rd ed.; London: Eyre & Spottiswoode, 1933), p. 25.
3. *Ibid.*, p. 35.
4. *Credit-Power and Democracy*, pp. 77-78.

from our lives through God's grace. Any movement that promises to increase our personal wealth and simultaneously reduce our need to labor must also suggest a program of ethical restoration as its foundation, not merely some promised magic pill: a one-shot restructuring of ownership or some other revolutionary piece of government legislation. There is no escape from the requirement that we work for our dinner. "For even when we were with you, this we commanded you, that if any would not work, neither should he eat" (2 Thessalonians 3:10).

Again, we see that the basic premise of Social Credit is that the Bible's view of man, labor, and rewards in history is a false view. Social Credit would substitute a legislative magic pill instead of God's grace, a single restructuring of the system of ownership instead of widespread ethical sanctification.

Consumer Sovereignty

Douglas criticized the guild socialist movement because "it has omitted entirely, in its proposals for the realisation of a sound ideal, to allow for the most important factor in modern civilisation – the unearned increment of association. . . ."[5] When an author identifies what he regards as the most important aspect of modern civilization, we need to pay attention to this supposed key to understanding, especially when he says that those closest to him – in Douglas' case, the guild socialists who subscribed to *The New Age* – have failed to recognize it. But Douglas did not properly identify the social arrangement by which capitalism structures the social division of labor.

Under free market capitalism, the consumer is sovereign. The producer must meet consumer demand or else go bankrupt. The consumer has the legal authority to say "no" to a producer. He can seek other producers to serve his desires.

Major Douglas did not believe this. He believed that the producer is sovereign under the present capitalist economy, not

5. *Ibid.*, p. 80.

the consumer. This is the belief of almost all critics of the free market. He said that millions of people owe their livelihood to the armaments industry. "That is to say, the producer controls the consumer."[6] But how does the producer control the consumer? There is surely a consumer of armaments: the State. The State can make these purchases because it taxes the real producers, that is, income-earning people. The State takes a portion of the fruits of their labor and spends it on weapons. This does not prove that the producer controls the consumer under capitalism. On the contrary, the consumer – in this case, the State – controls the producer: the armaments industry. Only in the sense that the armaments industry may have persuaded politicians to buy more armaments can we conclude that the producer controls the consumer.

This inversion of the free market's system of consumer sovereignty can be accomplished only by thwarting the free market through empowering the political process. Voters substitute the State for the free market. It redistributes wealth by compulsion. Sometimes this is legitimate. Societies do need national defense. But let us not blame capitalism for this political decision to buy armaments. Let us not say that the producer controls the consumer.

A False Diagnosis

Major Douglas offered a five-point diagnosis of society's economic problem. Then he offered a one-point prescription: fiat money issued by an elite group of credit masters.[7]

He made a series of assumptions. First, cooperation and real capital are the outstanding features of the machine age. This is correct, but he might better have called this the social division of labor.

---

6. *Ibid.*, p. 83.

7. See Chapter 10, below.

Second, "The link which enables numbers of individuals to co-operate is Credit based on Capital. . . ."[8] This is a correct description, but it is not economic analysis. Bank credit-debt is an aspect of capitalism, but is not inherent in the system. We can have the division of labor without bank debt. The only debt that is inherent in any economy is the debt of the laborer to the employer whenever the employer has paid the laborer in advance, or the debt of the employer to the worker whenever the worker has worked without pay in the expectation of payment. This need have nothing to do with bank debt.

Third, The material link is money. Money "derives its value solely from the belief, the 'credit,' that it is an effective agent for the realization of the proposition contained in (2)."[9] This is incorrect. *Money is merely the most marketable commodity*. Its value stems from men's confidence that other men will take it in exchange for goods and services. Credit is a legal obligation, a debt, an IOU: the debtor has signed an obligation to repay money (or perhaps a commodity or service) in the future. Free market money is not a legal claim to wealth, not an IOU; it is merely a commodity (or legal claim to a commodity) that men expect will be valuable in the future, so it is valuable today. A person may have a legal claim (receipt) to a commodity stored in a vault, but if the commodity falls to zero value, the receipt becomes worthless. It cannot then serve as money. This is what Douglas did not understand. "Coal is real wealth as distinguished from money, which is a claim on wealth."[10] Coal is indeed real wealth, but fiat money is not a claim on wealth.

Fourth, The mobilization of money rests with the banks. This is true in an economy that allows *fractional reserve banking*, where bankers are allowed to issue receipts for gold or silver without actually possessing sufficient quantities of gold or silver

8. *Ibid.*, p. 88.

9. *Ibid.*, p. 89.

10. *Warning Democracy* (2nd ed.; London: Stanley Nott, 1934), p. 204.

to redeem the claims. This is a fraudulent practice and inflationary, but it is not inherent in banking. It is possible to have banking without fractional reserves.

Fifth, the existence of bank money supposedly places power in the hands of bankers. He should have said *monopolistic, State-licensed central bankers*. Local commercial bankers have very little authority over the economy. They respond to market opportunities: taking in deposits and making loans.

Sixth, his solution: "The public, as individuals, can only acquire control of the policy of the economic and industrial system by acquiring control of credit-issue and price-making. The organ of credit-issue is the bank, and the meaning of price-making is credit-withdrawal."[11] Notice his words: *the public, as individuals*.

How can the public, *as individuals*, acquire such control? This cannot be done politically by nationalizing the banks, since politics is always representational. There must be another way if individuals are to regain control. There is a way for voters to achieve this goal, but Douglas believed this would not be sufficient: *voters must outlaw fractional reserve banking*. Banks promise to pay depositors cash on demand. Then they lend the money on the assumption that not all depositors will demand cash on the same day. This constitutes fraud: promising to pay on demand what cannot be delivered on demand because it has been transferred to someone else. The civil government should prosecute banks or anyone else who issues an open-ended, pay-on-demand legal claim to gold or silver or any other commodity if that person does not possess the commodity specified in the contract, meaning the warehouse receipt.[12]

---

11. *Ibid.*, p. 90.

12. Gary North, *Honest Money: The Biblical Blueprint for Money and Banking* (Ft. Worth, Texas: Dominion Press; Nashville: Thomas Nelson Sons, 1986). This is not an argument against commodity futures speculation. A commodity futures contract is not open-ended; it does not promise to deliver goods on demand. It promises to deliver goods at a specified time in the future, and, at such time, commodity con-

This law, if enforced, would place into the hands of individuals the decision over what money to use and what bank to use. Individual sovereignty is what Major Douglas said he wanted, but because he offered a false diagnosis of the economy, he offered a false prescription. He offered a magic pill. This pill is the ability of the State to transfer wealth from one individual to another. Douglas believed the State could and should do this without imposing taxes through the creation of an elite group of credit masters. He abandoned his stated goal: to return power over capital to individuals.

It is not enough to outlaw fractional reserve banking, he said. He recognized the existence of the practice and criticized it.[13] The problem is, what should replace this system?

Replacing One Group of Controllers With Another

Douglas called for point five of the *Communist Manifesto's* ten points to destroy capitalism and establish socialism: "Centralisation of credit in the hands of the State, by means of a national bank with State capital and an exclusive monopoly." The entrepreneur should be forced to come to a State-managed bank to get loans, Douglas said.

> If, however, the entrepreneur, while subject to all the desirable features of free competition between establishments, involved by effective cost-keeping, is obliged, in order to compete at all, to come to some publicly controlled credit-bank at short intervals for the means to make up the difference between a price regulated (not fixed) by a fractional multiplier applied to all costs of production of articles sold to the individuals composing the public (as explained in Chapter X., "Economic Democracy"), then, and it seems probable only then, do we acquire a valid, flexible, active control, not only of the initiation, but of the devel-

tracts are enforceable by law.

13. *Warning Democracy*, pp. 98-99, 130-31.

> opment and modification of production, by the public acting in their interest as individuals.[14]

The formula for setting prices is not clear, is it? He refers only to Chapter X of *Economic Democracy* (1920). On page 130 of *Credit-Power and Democracy*, he did offer a "ratio of real credit-production to credit-consumption." Here is the ratio:

Capital (appreciation) issue per annum +
credit-issues (cost of goods produced) per annum
divided by
depreciation + cost of goods consumed per annum

He said that the unit governing this ratio is arbitrary. It is not associated with gold. "The only possible standard which can be applied with accuracy to the measurement of economic values is that of ratio, a standard which does not require that we postulate anything at all about the unit used to establish the ratio, except that it is the same unit."[15]

Problems With the Formula

Think of the problems here. First, where do the central bankers get the money in order to make a loan? Not from depositors. There is no discussion in Social Credit of voluntary deposits into the State bank. To allow private lenders (bankers) to control the supply of credit would transfer sovereignty over credit to consumers. This is what Social Credit opposes. Thus, in Social Credit, the presence of lenders – people willing to do without present consumption – is not to become the basis of borrowing. Instead, a government bank creates credit: fiat money.

Second, is this ratio historical or predictive? Does the ratio express only the capital that *has been consumed* over the last 12

---

14. *Credit-Power and Democracy*, pp. 92-93.
15. *Ibid.*, pp. 130-31.

months? Or does it express the quantity of capital that the experts believe *should be consumed* over the coming year? Major Douglas never said, although it makes a huge difference.

Third, how do the experts gain the statistics needed? How does anyone measure depreciation in general? Depreciation for what items? In which industry? A computer depreciates by at least 50 percent every 18 months – the time it takes for the computer industry to double the computing power of microcomputer chips. A new convention center located in a growing city depreciates far less rapidly.

Fourth, what about capital accumulation? A growing economy requires more capital per worker. How do the credit experts decide how much new credit is necessary for what rate of growth? How do they keep these new issues of fiat money from becoming inflationary? If they issue new credit only when old debts are repaid, there will be no accumulation of capital.

Fifth, what if borrowers decide to go to banks outside their country? Does this mean that the world will need an international central bank and an international currency unit, a system run by a one-State world government's team of Social Credit experts? I think it does, although conservative Social Credit defenders will insist that it just couldn't mean that. If it doesn't mean that, then how can the experts in one country control the supply of credit scientifically? Any Social Credit defender who denies that Major Douglas' system requires a one-State world government banking system needs to show exactly how a nation-by-nation Social Credit system would work scientifically. (Warning: don't take seriously anyone's denial which is not accompanied with detailed, logical *proof* that Social Credit does not require a one-State world government in order to retain its scientific character.)

He offered another formula in *Social Credit* (3rd edition): p. 192. It suffers from the same criticisms.

Major Douglas' Confusion: Money and Credit

The problem for Social Credit is that Douglas confused the issue of credit with the issue of money. This was also Keynes' error and the error of most other central planners. Credit in a free market economy – one without fractional reserve banking – is identical with savings. When one person decides to forego the present consumption of goods and services by lending money (gold, silver, or whatever serves as money) to someone else for a period of time, the recipient of credit spends it, either for consumption or the purchase of capital: tools, including information. *One man's willingness to defer consumption is the basis of the other man's access to credit.* Individuals therefore decide how to allocate capital. Borrowers compete against borrowers (offering better terms); lenders compete against lenders (offering better terms). "To save or not to save?" That is the question. So is "To borrow or not to borrow?"

There is no need to transfer to the State the power to hire experts to decide who gets access to scarce capital. There is no need to create a nation of dependent businessmen who are completely at the mercy of a monopolistic State bank that controls the issue of credit. Such a monopoly is mandatory in Social Credit economics: for the experts to fill in the formula with accurate data, they would need to control the creation of credit. They cannot accurately guess what other businesses are doing with capital. As we shall see in the next chapter, Social Credit means State monopoly credit. In a free market economy, social credit means credit issued by savers who voluntarily lend money to borrowers. Bargaining individuals – savers and borrowers – set the terms of exchange: present goods (lent) vs. future goods (paid back). The creditor voluntarily becomes an economic partner with the debtor.[16] Individuals are sovereign over the creation and distribution of credit, not the State.

---

16. Ludwig von Mises, *Human Action* (New Haven, Connecticut: Yale University Press, 1949), p. 536.

Centralizing Power

What is clear is that Social Credit does not reduce State power; it increases it. It does not return sovereignty to consumers by preventing the fraud of fractional reserve banking; it removes sovereignty from consumers and transfers it to a group of central planners in the banks.

Warning: don't "throw the rascals (bankers) out" until you have replaced them with someone reliable, namely, individuals who are in control of their own decisions. Don't exchange one set of power-seekers for another.

Douglas called for an economic system in which "the public" is sovereign. But here is the problem: he defined the public politically, not economically. He offered a political solution: the public – *political* – control over credit. He did not call for free market control of credit, with the State serving only as a policeman to prevent fraud, such as fractional reserve banking. In the name of individualism, he called for statism:

> But by controlling *both* credit-issue and price-making the public acquires control of policy with all its attributes – the effective appointment and removal of personnel, amongst others. *The essential nature of a satisfactory modern co-operative State may be broadly expressed as consisting of a functionally aristocratic hierarchy of producers accredited by, and serving, a democracy of consumers.*[17]

"Accredited by"? This means *licensed by the State*. A democracy of consumers needs no State manipulation of credit and banks. It requires only the legal right to make bids to buy and sell. If a man wants to loan someone else some money, this is allowed. If someone wants to store an ounce of gold in a warehouse for a fee and issue a receipt for this single ounce of gold (and no more), this is allowed. If a person wants to put his money in a bank and have the banker lend it out at interest, this is allowed.

17. *Credit-Power and Democracy*, p. 94.

My point is that a *democracy of consumers* can be attained by only one way: where the "vote" is not political. The vote is economic – the private, personal decision to buy or sell, lend or borrow, deposit or withdraw.

A False Definition of Money: Tickets

The number-one analytical error in Major Douglas' criticism of capitalism was his definition of money. Because he did not understand what money is – the most marketable commodity – his solution was the creation of fiat money by the State.

He viewed money as a system of tickets for goods and services. "The money system can accurately be described as a ticket system. . . ."[18] In *Social Credit*, he described the operations of a railway ticket system. A railway ticket, he said, is a "limited form of money."[19]

A Legal Claim or the Most Marketable Commodity?

This is a complete misunderstanding of money. Money is a not a claim on goods and services in the way that a ticket is a claim on a particular good or service. Money is the most marketable commodity. In contrast, a ticket is a legal claim on a specific quantity of goods or services: "one seat per ticket" or "one car wash per ticket." The person who holds that ticket is *legally entitled* to whatever is promised on the ticket. A person holding a ticket faces no counter-bid from someone holding another ticket. He cannot lose his seat in the auditorium just because someone else has five tickets while he has only one. There is no system of competitive bidding, with the highest number of tickets offered entitling that bidder to one seat. On the contrary, a bidding process is what allocates the tickets: a bidding process involving money.

---

18. *Warning Democracy*, p. 50.
19. *Social Credit*, p. 62.

There is no good or service promised on a dollar bill or on any other modern currency unit. No longer does the possession of currency entitle the bearer to a specific quantity and fineness of gold or silver. No longer is cash a warehouse receipt for metal. But even when it was a warehouse receipt, it was not a claim on goods in general; it was a claim only to a particular quantity and fineness of a specific metal. The value of paper money was very closely associated with the value of the metal, but nothing was said on the currency about the quantity of other goods or services that money might (or might not) buy. The purchasing power of money at a particular time and place was established by competitive bidding among those who held money vs. the competitive bidding among sellers of goods and services ("buyers of money"): buyers vs. buyers, sellers vs. sellers. Remember my economic policy parrot: "High bid wins!" In a free market economy, no government official can say in advance what that high bid must be.[20]

Douglas did not understand any of this. Therefore, he made a key mistake, the error which above all his other errors doomed his system of economic analysis: *he denied the relevance of the monetary value of tickets*. He thereby denied the relevance of the free market's auction process, which creates specific money value for a particular scarce item. He denied the relevance of the auction process as the best means of allocating scarce resources. He wrote: "The fact that a railway ticket has money-value attached to it is subsidiary and irrelevant to its main function, which is to distribute transportation."[21] He got things exactly backwards: there can be no rational distribution of transportation without the money-value of tickets. A ticket without money value is a ticket to something nobody wants, i.e., a non-economic resource.

20. I am of course exempting public utility prices.

21. *Social Credit*, p. 62.

I Want In!

Consider a large auditorium. It has 5,000 seats. On a particular evening, a promoter has scheduled the appearance of the nation's most popular entertainment group. There will be one performance only in this city. A ticket entitles the bearer to occupy a particular seat during the performance. The ticket is a convenient device for allocating seats in advance. Instead of hiring people to take money from would-be members of the audience, one by one, in front of each seat, the manager of the auditorium sells tickets in advance. The tickets function as warehouse receipts, except that in this case, people want to sit in the "warehouse."

What is a ticket worth? As with every other resource, a ticket is worth whatever some buyer will pay for it. Prior to the performance, it may be worth a person's income for a week. Immediately after the performance, a ticket is worth whatever a collector of memorabilia is willing to pay for it.

The problem of allocating seats is not solved merely by printing up tickets. It is solved by selling them. Again, remember my *economic policy parrot*: "High bid wins!" The seller of seats – actually, he rents the seats – offers tickets for sale that legally entitle the holders to specific seats during the performance. The auction for seats now goes to work. If the tickets are priced too low, there will be people waiting outside to buy a ticket when the performance begins. If the promoter has priced the seats too high, the auditorium will have empty seats.[22]

22. The economic function of ticket "scalpers" is to transfer some of the risk from the promoter to the scalper. When he sells a ticket to a scalper, the salesman at the gate becomes a wholesaler. Those buyers who are willing to stand in line and buy blocks of tickets in advance can then enter the market and sell these tickets to latecomers or others who are willing to bid for them. If demand is heavy, scalpers make money. If it is lower than expected, scalpers lose money. The promoter is more likely to sell out all the seats when scalpers buy blocks of tickets. Also, the scalpers get all the bad publicity as price gougers if the promoter has priced the tickets too low.

The allocation of seats is not made by the tickets. The allocation is made by the auction process for tickets. Contrary to Douglas, it is the tickets' money-value (as Douglas put it) which performs the task of allocating scarce seats for the performance.

A ticket is a legal claim to a specific item. The economic value of that item is not established by the ticket; it is established by supply and demand. Douglas saw each unit of money as a ticket. This is incorrect: money is not a ticket; rather, it is the most marketable commodity. A ticket entitles its holder to whatever the ticket promises. It is a legal claim. Its value is determined by the value of the thing legally represented by the ticket. In contrast, fiat money entitles its holder to nothing. Economically speaking, it is not a claim to anything. Its value is indeterminate until the seller of some good accepts the buyer's money bid. A unit of money is a means of bidding at the auction, not a legal claim on anything offered for sale.[23]

I Want Out!

Consider that same auditorium. Instead of the nation's most popular entertainer or group, someone – not very skilled entrepreneurially – decides to schedule a debate on the economics of Social Credit. How much will each of the 5,000 tickets be worth? Not very much. In fact, to fill all 5,000 seats on the night of the debate, the sponsoring organization would probably have to pay people to attend. The fact is, most people would have to be compensated financially to keep them in their seats during a debate on Social Credit. They want out.

What is the difference between the value of the tickets in the first example and their value in the second? The seats are physically the same. The tickets may be the same color. But nobody wants to pay for them in the second example. What is the economic difference? Answer: the general desirability of

23. A warehouse receipt (IOU) can function as money only because the item against which the receipt is a legal claim is money.

sitting in the seats during a performance. In neither example does the ticket have any economic function except as a legal claim on a particular seat. The ticket is not a form of money in the second example. Hardly anyone wants to attend. In the first example, a ticket could become a means of barter, but only until the performance begins. It is not money unless it is the most marketable commodity.

Not Enough Tickets?

The economic problem is scarcity. When the nation's most popular entertainer comes to town, there are not enough seats available at zero price to meet all the demand. Let me say it one more time: *there are not enough seats to meet demand at zero price*. Competitive bidding establishes the price of each ticket. The problem is not an insufficient number of tickets; the problem is an insufficient number of seats available at zero price.

Major Douglas did not understand this. There are an insufficient number of tickets, he said.[24] There is not enough money. He insisted that "total prices produced over a given period of time are greatly in excess of total money distributed over the same period of time."[25] In short, the total number of goods and services offered cannot not be purchased by the total number of monetary units – "tickets" – created by the financial system.

Extinguishing "Tickets"

Here is the source of Douglas' conceptual error, the error that undermines Social Credit's economic analysis. He said that the credit issued by banks to producers in order to manufacture whatever it is they produce is extinguished when these debts are paid off. Thus, there are not enough "tickets" for

24. *Warning Democracy*, pp. 15-16.

25. *Ibid.*, p. 19.

consumers to purchase the consumer goods that have been produced. He believed that in order for the market to clear itself, the number of currency units in circulation has to match the value of economic output in the economy. But there is no way for a ticket to entitle anyone to "value." A ticket entitles a person to a specific item: a measurable unit of something that a civil court can enforce the ticket-issuer to deliver.

Douglas missed the point: the credit issued by banks – or any other agency – never was a ticket in the first place. It was never a legal claim to anything except, possibly, gold or silver. The money that was issued to a producer to buy capital goods, raw materials, and labor was not a legal claim to any of these items. The money was merely the most marketable commodity, which enabled its holder to enter the market and bid for goods and services. It is precisely because *money is not a legal claim on anyone else's goods* that the holders of money must bid against each other in order to buy anything.

If the ticket is a legal claim – say, to gold or silver – then the auction will be the other way around: sellers of goods and services will bid their less marketable goods to buy warehouse receipts for the most marketable good: money. The price will be established by supply and demand: high bid wins.

A unit of currency is not the same as a ticket. Consider tickets. When the scheduled performance is over, the ticket to that performance is indeed "extinguished." It has no further allocational function. The item promised by the ticket – a particular seat on a particular night at a particular time – is no longer "in the warehouse." It has been "consumed."

Consider modern fiat money. No commodity is promised for a particular currency unit. No specific item is "in the warehouse" waiting for you to claim it. Currency today is not a legal claim to anything. There is no conflict between holders of money that can be settled simply by looking at a number on the monetary unit and matching it to a particular item in inventory. Money is not analogous to some kind of laundry ticket. You do not hand over your ticket and get back your favorite pair of brown socks. There is no usher who looks at the number on your currency unit and says, "Yes, sir, this is your seat. The gentlemen presently sitting in the seat will have to leave."

Paying Off a Bank Loan

If a particular bank account is extinguished by the repayment of a loan, then there will be a reduction in the money supply, *if, and **only** if, the banking system is based on fractional reserves*. The only loan in a modern economy that has this contracting effect when it is paid off is a loan to the government by the nation's central bank. If the central bank sells the Treasury's IOU to a private investor, the total money supply shrinks, just as it expanded when the central bank bought the Treasury's IOU. On the other hand, if a private loan is paid off by a bank's debtor, that bank immediately makes another loan, either to an individual, or to a business organization, or to the Treasury. Therefore, the total money loaned out does not change. The bank makes its money by lending, and all deposits that are legally permitted by the central bank to go out as loans will go out, moment by moment. Once governments insure bank deposits, and once they allow banks to buy government IOU debt instruments, there is no question that every time a loan is paid off by handing a check or cash to the bank loan officer, either by a consumer or a business, *the bank will loan out the money that the former debtor has just used to pay off his loan*. This will happen before the bank closes that afternoon. So long as the government does not send bankers to jail for making bad loans, there is no reason for bankers not to keep their banks "loaned up and loaned out." Because governments never prosecute anyone who has bought the government's bonds, the bankers will at least buy government bonds rather than hoard cash. Then the government spends this money into circulation. The money supply does not shrink.

One more time: when a nation's central bank sells a credit-debt asset that had been in its possession, or when the government pays off this debt (ha, ha, ha – just kidding), the money supply is reduced *if the central bank does not immediately buy another government IOU in order to offset the shrinkage*. But this central bank decision to shrink the money supply makes the remaining units of money more valuable. Their purchasing power rises. Why? Because prices tend to fall. There is now less money in the hands of bidders to bid up the prices of goods and services. Sellers of goods and services will face less demand *at yesterday's prices*. Some of them will have to lower their prices.

Major Douglas did not understand how fractional reserve banking works. He did not understand that the only loans that contract a nation's money supply when they are paid off are loans by the central bank to the government. Because he failed to understand how the Bank of England and other central banks control the money supply from the top, he did not understand commercial banking. The local bank is under reserve requirement constraints established by the central bank. It is not what the local bank does with its depositors' money that affects the total money supply; rather, it is what the government-licensed central bank does with respect to holding government debt certificates and other reserve assets.[26]

Conclusion

Major Douglas came in the name of individualism. His policy recommendation, however, was collectivist. He rejected the legitimacy of private banking. He opposed the payment of interest, never suspecting that interest is a universal phenomenon that is not limited to money-lending. He proposed the creation of State-managed banks that would be run by experts who are beyond the control of consumers and producers. These

---

26. Murray N. Rothbard, *What Has Government Done to Our Money?* (Auburn, Alabama: Ludwig von Mises Institute, [1963] 1990), pp. 72-79.

expert planners would use a formula to regulate credit and set prices. He never explained how this formula would work. He never showed why an increase in the supply of credit (money) would not raise the monetary value of the nation's assets, therefore justifying another increase in the money supply, thereby raising the money value of the nation's assets, and so on until mass inflation finally destroys the economy.

This false prescription for economic democracy was the result of a false diagnosis: identifying credit as the basis of money in a capitalist economy. Douglas believed that credit must be controlled by bureaucratic experts who do not seek to make profits for themselves. These disinterested experts, he assured us, will be able to create just the right amount of credit to create unprecedented wealth. We consumers are to trust them with all our hearts and all our capital.

His policy error rested in an analytical error: money as a ticket. Money is not a ticket. A ticket is a legal claim to a specific good or service: "one ticket, one item." Money is not a legal claim. It is simply the most marketable commodity. Prices are announced in terms of money because money is the most marketable commodity. Prices are set by competitive bidding: consumers vs. consumers, producers vs. producers. High bid wins.

Douglas was wrong: when a private loan is repaid to a local bank, there is no reduction in the nation's money supply. The bank loans the money out almost immediately in order to receive interest. The central bank can increase or shrink the money supply in a fractional reserve system. Douglas never recognized that the size of the money supply is regulated solely by the central bank, not the commercial banking system as such, and surely not the commercial banking system in an economy that does not allow fractional reserve banking.[27]

27. North, *Honest Money*.

Summary

1. Major Douglas complained that the few control the many in today's capitalism.
2. The view that "the conspiracy" controls "the people" apart from their consent is not biblical.
3. It is dangerous to "throw the rascals out" before widespread morality and responsibility has prepared the way.
4. Social Credit insists that individuals can attain great wealth with very little labor.
5. The Bible teaches that men must labor six days a week.
6. Douglas correctly identified the division of labor as the key to wealth.
7. He did not identify the basis of capitalism's social division of labor: consumer sovereignty.
8. He offered a five-point diagnosis and a one-point prescription.
9. He argued that credit is the heart of modern capitalism.
10. Bankers control credit.
11. The State should control credit, he concluded.
12. This confuses individual control (consumer sovereignty) with political control (State sovereignty).
13. The problem with modern credit is fractional reserve banking and central banking, not credit as such.
14. Who will control the credit controllers?
15. Social Credit requires a one-state world government banking system to create capital scientifically.
16. Douglas defined money as tickets.
17. Tickets are legal claims to specific items.
18. Money is the most marketable commodity.
19. The value of money is indeterminate until actual transactions take place.
20. Money is not a ticket.
21. A ticket is a legal claim on a specific item or service.
22. Money is not a legal claim.
23. Money allocates scarce resources; tickets do not.

24. The money supply does not shrink when someone pays off a loan, unless. . . .
25. The borrower is the government, and the lender was the nation's central bank.
26. The central bank, not an individual bank, controls the supply of money.
27. If the central bank adds to its holdings of debt, the money supply rises.
28. If the central bank sells assets, the money supply declines.
29. When the money supply declines, sellers are pressured to lower prices.

9

DIVIDENDS UNDER CAPITALISM

Woe unto them that call evil good, and good evil; that put darkness for light, and light for darkness; that put bitter for sweet, and sweet for bitter! (Isaiah 5:20).

Major Douglas was a reformer. He insisted that "Capitalism in its present form has always been fundamentally bad."[1] Not kind of bad, or sort of bad, or bad in some areas, but *fundamentally* bad. But why? By 1920, capitalism had made people far richer than they had been in 1820 or 1720. Why is it fundamentally bad?

At the heart of capitalism, he argued, is a single problem, a single evil to be eliminated: the bank credit system. This system of credit supposedly does not provide sufficient money for workers to buy all the goods produced by the economy. Thus, capitalism suffers from chronic underconsumption. It is this credit-based restraint on the system that supposedly keeps capitalism from becoming productive beyond men's dreams.

We have seen in Chapter 8 that Major Douglas made a fundamental error: equating money with tickets, and then concluding that when a bank loan is paid off, this shrinks the

1. *Credit-Power and Democracy* (London: Cecil Palmer, 1920), p. 40.

number of "tickets," so that the sellers cannot make a profit. We saw that money is not a ticket system, that paying off a private loan to a local commercial bank does not shrink the money supply, and that the central bank controls the money supply under a system of fractional reserve banking. Consequently, in his desire to solve a non-existent problem – the shrinking supply of "tickets" – Douglas offered a solution: the creation of a State monopoly over all credit run by an elite group of credit masters.[2] He explicitly called capitalism bad and implicitly called the State good.

Major Douglas' error then spread out: from bad economic analysis to bad economic history.

Major Douglas vs. Economic History

When did capitalism take its present, supposedly perverse form? It must have happened late in the development of capitalism. Early capitalism, he said, had operated "to the ultimate advantage of everyone." He wrote that "at the beginning of the Machine Age, the capitalistic system had the effect of concentrating effort on the expansion of real capital to an extent which no other conceivable arrangement could have brought about in so short a time, to the ultimate advantage of everyone. Not only so, but the real competition which preceded the Trust Era kept production of ultimate products up, prices and profits down. . . ."[3] Then what went wrong? "The evolution from the individual entrepreneur and private banker into the limited liability company. . . ."[4]

There is a problem with this historical evaluation. The Bank of England was created in 1694. It is a privately owned, government-licensed monopoly. It is based on fractional reserve banking: the creation of fiat money out of nothing through the

2. See Chapter 10, below.

3. *Credit-Power and Democracy*, p. 42

4. *Ibid.*, p. 42.

credit system. The Bank loans money to the British government, money that it creates out of nothing using the government's IOUs as collateral. The government wants cheap loans, and the bank wants interest income from money it creates almost for free. Thus, for three centuries, a "sweetheart deal" has been in operation: the Bank of England creates fiat money, buys government IOU's, and collects interest. This increases the total money supply.

The government then spends this newly created money. The fractional reserve banking system multiplies this new money. The result has been a steady increase in the money supply, escalating rapidly after England went off the gold standard: from 1914 to 1925, and from 1931 to the present.[5] This story has been repeated throughout the world, since the world's money system in the twentieth century has been tied either to the British pound sterling or the U.S. dollar.[6]

The Bank of England preceded the Machine Age by about two generations. It preceded the late nineteenth century by over two centuries. Thus, the mere presence of the Bank of England and the English credit system apparently did nothing to make capitalism fundamentally evil. Then what ruined capitalism? Douglas blamed the limited liability corporation, which was primarily a late-nineteenth-century phenomenon, and "Joint-Stock Branch Banking Systems."[7]

Was he correct? Were these two institutional developments the cause of modern capitalism's crises? If so, how?

---

5. Chart II-4, "The British Price Level, 1661-1974," W. W. Rostow, *The World Economy: History & Prospect* (Austin and London: University of Texas Press, 1978), p. 82.

6. The Genoa agreement of 1922 (gold-exchange standard) and the Bretton Woods agreement of 1944 ended when President Nixon closed the U.S. "gold window" on August 15, 1971, thereby floating the dollar. Down went the dollar. See Alfred E. Eckes, Jr., *A Search for Solvency: Bretton Woods and the International Monetary System, 1941-1971* (Austin & London: University of Texas Press, 1975).

7. *Credit-Power and Democracy*, p. 43.

Limited Liability

We need to ask: What is wrong with limited liability corporations? They are legal entities that restrict the liability of investors to the amount of capital invested in the company. This allows investors to pool their capital, hire skilled managers, and create an entity that may outlive them. It opens up investment opportunities to people who in earlier generations would have been afraid of the liability involved in a partnership: if your partner goes bankrupt for any reason, his creditor can sue you to collect the debt. What is wrong with the legal protection offered by a corporation?[8]

Judicially, a limited liability corporation is like a church. Church members are not personally responsible for debts contracted by the church's hierarchy. The congregation can lose its collateral (probably its building) if the church cannot meet its debt payments, but the lender cannot attach the wages of church members. No one questions this system. Yet all that a limited liability company does is to extend this ecclesiastical principle of personal immunity to a business. Why is this corrupting to capitalism? Douglas never bothered to address this question. Neither do other critics of the limited-liability corporation.

Douglas never showed how the existence of corporations created the crisis in finance capital: the supposed Real Capital/Finance Capital gap. The supposed shortage of finance capital had nothing to do with the laws governing limited liability corporations. Then Douglas proposed a solution to modern capitalism's supposed problem, a solution that had nothing to do analytically with what he blamed for the failure of capitalism, namely, the limited liability corporation. This solution he called the National Dividend.

He proposed that the government create a credit system that

8. Robert Hessen, *In Defense of the Corporation* (Stanford, California: Hoover Institution Press, 1979).

would issue fiat money based on the monetary value of the nation's assets. This would replace the present system of corporate dividends to investors. In other words, Douglas adopted the same word, *dividend,* to describe two radically different systems: one compulsory and the other voluntary; one government-mandated and the other a matter of private decision-making. One system is based on a person's decision to turn his money over to a corporation in the hope of future income and capital gains, while the other is based on the government's issuing of fiat money in terms of a statistic: the estimated money value of all the assets inside the nation's borders.

Machines and Productivity

Major Douglas argued that "the increased utilisation of mechanical power and machinery . . . tends to contract the area of the distribution of wages."[9] Why should this be true? Some people are released from a particular type of service by the substitution of a machine, but humans are remarkably versatile. They are not highly specific capital goods. In short, men are not machines. The fact that a man loses one job to a machine does not mean that he cannot get another job, such as building more machines or repairing machines or selling the products of machines. If machines replaced men in general rather than specific men working on specific tasks, hardly anyone would be employed today. Machines in Douglas' view are like slaves prior to the mid-nineteenth century: low-paid servants.

But don't machines replace men? Yes: specific men in specific jobs. But machines also make men more productive. For example, a bulldozer can be used to build a road, and the road opens up new markets. If we argue that bulldozers lead to unemployment, shouldn't we conclude that the government ought to make the use of bulldozers illegal in order to further the hiring of lots of men using shovels? Taking this even far-

9. *Credit-Power and Democracy,* p. 43.

ther, shouldn't the government make shovels illegal, so that construction firms will have to hire even more men who use only stainless steel teaspoons? Would society be richer if such a law were enacted and rigorously enforced?

The argument that machines create unemployment are always variations of the teaspoon argument. Such arguments assume that most of those men who are freed up by labor-saving machines never get another job, never find other areas in which to serve their fellow men in the production system. These arguments do not view capital-intensive economic improvements as a means of producing greater wealth for all, or almost all, members of society.

Douglas argued the opposite: machines should be encouraged because they will produce unemployment. He wanted to take men out of the work place. He wanted the government to send "dividends" to them to make their early retirement possible. But this argument rested on the assumption that capitalism is capable of huge and rapid increases in productivity merely through the substitution of Social Credit (fiat money issued by the government). He never provided a single statistic to prove this assertion; he merely stated it repeatedly, using different figures every time, as we have seen.[10]

Both views are false: "abolish machines" and "abolish labor." The substitution of machines has reduced the need for men to labor in order to obtain a traditional income, but this added productivity opens up new possibilities for increased productivity and therefore increased income. Men stay in the work force in order to buy the ever-increasing output of capitalism.

The Lure of Dividends

The early Machine Age, which Douglas regarded as a good thing, was financed by a tiny number of people who bought equipment that employed laborers. The population of industri-

10. See above, pp. 109-10, 136. See below, p. 173.

alized companies expanded rapidly in the nineteenth century. These people got jobs in factories. The machines that investors provided to workers made life better for them; they increased labor productivity and therefore labor income.[11] Why would the opportunity to pool capital in a limited liability corporation reduce the number of wage-earners? Always before, an increase in the amount of capital had increased the productivity of labor and made possible an expanding labor market. How was this connection destroyed by the coming of limited liability companies and local banks? Douglas never said.

The return on invested capital has fluctuated over the years between six percent and twenty percent. For example, the yield to industrial capital in Germany, 1850 to 1910, stayed in the narrow range of 6.5% and 7%.[12] The reason for these fluctuations is often statistical; until the twentieth century, statistics on invested capital have been unavailable for most countries. This return is normally an interest payment. Rare is a company that earns above ten percent on capital invested, and even more rare is a firm that continues to do so year after year. Also, companies rarely pay out in dividends all of the profits earned. It is not uncommon for half of the profits to be retained for capital investment. How could this tiny percentage – a percentage that did not increase under limited liability – have affected the wage system? Employee compensation in the United States has remained in the narrow range of 65% to 73% of national income since 1930.[13] This is not fundamentally different from other industrial nations. Dividends play a very small role in the overall demand for consumer goods, but they play a crucial role in persuading investors to forfeit present consumption.

---

11. R. M. Hartwell, "The Standard of Living Controversy: A Summary," in Hartwell (ed.), *The Industrial Revolution* (New York: Barnes & Noble, 1970), ch. 8.

12. Solomos Solomou, *Phases of Economic Growth, 1850-1973* (Cambridge University Press, 1990), p. 109.

13. Herbert Stein and Murray Foss, *An Illustrated Guide to the American Economy* (Washington, D.C.: AEI Press, 1992), p. 47.

Douglas vaguely understood this. He said that "probably 94 per cent. of the purchasing power which constitutes the distribution system of this country, is wages and salaries, and, on the whole, this percentage of the total tends to increase, and dividends collectively tend to decrease. . . ."[14] But if this is true, then Social Credit is irrelevant. If 94% of national income is going to wage earners, and this percentage is rising, *there is hardly any break in the flow of funds to consumers*. With this one admission, Douglas introduced what he regarded as statistical evidence of the ultimate success of finance capitalism. His reform would not be needed. He never seemed to recognize just how damaging this admission was.

If this growing percentage of national income accrues to wages, what will be the source of Social Credit's proposed National Dividend? Wage-earners are steadily absorbing the bulk of production. Consumers are buying up their own production! But *excess production* – production not being gobbled up by wage-earners – must accompany the mailing of government checks if society is to avoid mass inflation. We know that dividends under capitalism are related closely to the return on capital. Yet dividends represent a small percentage of national income, as Douglas freely (and fatally) admitted. Social Credit cannot overcome this limitation on dividends except by reducing wages as a percentage of national income. This is exactly what Major Douglas promised – the replacement of wages by the National Dividend – but he never indicated how this vast increase in the post-reform productivity of capital will be accomplished by the State credit masters. He merely announced that this will surely occur once society adopts Social Credit:

> The scientific organisation of industry and the introduction of increased quantities of solar energy into the productive system means, and can only mean, the displacement of human labour

14. *Warning Democracy* (2nd ed.; London: Stanley Nott, 1934), p. 86.

> from the economic process. Even now there is very little doubt that the present standard of living can be maintained by the working efforts of 10 per cent. of the population if the productive system were not so largely directed towards money-making rather than goods-making. . . .[15]

Here is the reality: there are no dividends for investors until after the firm has paid wages, rent, raw materials, interest payments (usually three to ten percent), insurance, capital replacement, capital improvement, advertising expenses, and taxes. *Dividends are a small percentage of national income because the bulk of most people's income comes from wages*. This has not changed despite the advent of modern machinery. Dependence on wages is an aspect of creation: man was placed on this earth to extend his dominion as God's agent, and when he sinned, his labor was cursed (Genesis 3:17-19).

Perhaps the best definition of "rich" is this one: a person is rich if his lifestyle would not change even though he lost his job today and never again gained employment. Douglas wanted all people to become rich in this sense. He believed that a restructuring of the allocation over credit would achieve this goal. Do this, he promised, and governments can cut taxes permanently. This was why he called for a National Dividend program. This would create wealth for all.

What Are Dividends?

Dividends are that portion of a firm's income that is paid to investors who have provided capital to the firm. This return normally fluctuates from about three percent to ten percent, paralleling the rate of interest.

A firm can borrow money to buy capital goods. It can seek investors who will provide funds to buy capital goods. In the case of interest payments, those providing the money do not

15. *Ibid.*, p. 87.

participate in the profits of the firm. Whether the firm makes a profit or not, the lenders must be paid. Not so the owners of common shares. They receive payments at the discretion of the firm's management. While management will try to find enough money to pay investors in order to keep share prices high, the managers are not legally compelled to pay dividends to common stocks.

Share owners may be willing to receive a reduced rate of return from dividends in order to participate in greater capital gains, meaning an increase in the value of ownership shares. In effect, they re-invest their dividends. A lender does not participate in a company's capital gains. He also does not participate in a company's capital losses unless it goes totally bankrupt. The shareholder has different financial expectations from those of the lender. He expects capital gains: profits from owning the shares of an unexpectedly more profitable company.

Except in public utility corporations, where a rate of return is guaranteed by government regulatory agencies, the rate of return from dividends is normally below the rate of return from interest. The reason for this is simple: investors expect to receive capital gains, i.e., increases in the market value of the shares. Lenders demand and receive a higher rate of return, since they do participate in capital gains, i.e., profits.

Reducing the Need to Work

Douglas wanted to substitute a National Dividend because he believed it would be large enough to relieve people from any need to work for a living. The modern economic system, Douglas said, "has widened the area of the distribution of purchasing-power through the agency of *dividends*, while, at the same time, the actual necessity for 'direct' wage-earning labour has been diminished by the increased utilisation of mechanical power and machinery, which tends to contract the area of the distribution of wages."[16] This was incorrect. It still is.

Dividends in today's economy, Douglas said, go to a "large body of shareholders. . . ."[17] This was incorrect. If his estimate was correct, namely, that 94% of national income went to wages, then there clearly was no "large body of shareholders" in his day. Prior to the late twentieth century, the number of shareholders in corporations was a tiny fraction of any nation's population. Only with the rise of tax-deferred pension funds and mutual funds has this situation changed.[18]

Profits

What is the source of profits? This has baffled many economists. Profits are a residual that is left over after all expenses have been paid. Where do they come from? From the difference (spread) between what the producer has paid out for all operating expenses and what he has taken in from buyers. But how can there be a spread between costs and income in a system that pays everyone the value of his output?

The answer is: *entrepreneurship*. An entrepreneur is an economic forecaster who buys resources in order to sell them for more later. He believes that some resource factors are priced too cheaply compared to what they would be worth if every producer could correctly forecast the *future* state of consumer demand. That is, the entrepreneur buys up raw materials, labor, and all other factors of production that will be used to produce a product or service for *future* consumers. He guesses that consumers in the future will be willing to pay more for the product than what rival producers presently estimate.

The only way he can make a profit is if his competitors, meaning other producers, have not spotted the opportunity. As

16. *Credit-Power and Democracy*, p. 43.

17. *Ibid.*, p. 43.

18. Peter F. Drucker, *The Unseen Revolution: How Pension Fund Socialism Came to America* (New York: Harper & Row, 1976).

soon as they spot it, they will enter the markets for production factors and *bid up the prices*. (Remember my parrot: "High bid wins.") Also, because there will be more producers, they will increase the supply of the product or service. This will lower the selling the price of each unit unless there is an even larger (unforecasted) increase in demand. The presence of profits for company A alerts companies B through Z that there are factors of production in today's market that are priced too low compared to their future value in the form of consumer goods. The price spread between today's factor prices and tomorrow's product prices will soon be reduced to the discount rate, i.e., the rate of interest. That is to say, profits will disappear.[19]

Profits are not automatic. This means that capital gains are not automatic. If a firm's profits get higher than the rate of interest on loans, other firms will be alerted to the opportunity. Thus, it is rare for any company to be able to produce profits – income higher than what it could get simply by lending the money – year after year.

Profits come only from correct forecasting and efficient organizing. *Profits are a residual*. Profit is whatever is left over after all the previous exchanges have been made. Profit is always threatened by loss: less than what the entrepreneur started out with when he began to produce the product. There can be no guarantee of profits or dividends. Losses always threaten them.

All of this was known when Major Douglas began publishing. Economist Frank H. Knight's classic book, *Risk, Uncertainty and Profit*, appeared in 1921. It provided a detailed examination of the origin of profits. But Major Douglas never quoted from Knight or from any of the economists who followed his lead. Neither have his followers. This places them at a tremendous intellectual disadvantage. They do not understand profits.

---

19. Ludwig von Mises, *Human Action: A Treatise on Economics* (New Haven: Yale University Press, 1949), ch. 19.

Douglas said that "the root motive of human nature and the mainspring of human advancement is profit."[20] But he meant this only in the sense of working for our own individual advantage. He never provided an economic definition of profit with respect to planning in the present for an uncertain future.

Douglas Confused Dividends With Wages

Douglas insisted that "the *dividend* is the logical successor to the wage, carrying with it privileges which the wage never had and never can have. . . ."[21] This analysis is incorrect. A wage comes from the temporary sale of labor services, just as rent comes from the temporary sale of land's services. Something *known* is voluntarily exchanged. Not so with dividends. The investor turns over his money to a seller of shares to buy a share of ownership. He may or may not receive a future payment from the company. There is no assurance that he will receive any dividends. *A dividend is not guaranteed by any firm to holders of its common stock.* He cannot sue the management simply because they refuse to pay dividends to shareholders.

What does Douglas say a dividend is? A dividend is "a payment, absolute and unconditional, of something due."[22] This is what distinguishes a wage from a dividend, he insisted. "The first is servitude, however disguised, the second is the primary step to economic emancipation."[23] Once again, he had things exactly backwards. First, a wage is based on a contractual arrangement between the seller of labor services and a buyer of these services. Wages are money due to the wage-earner for services received by the employer. Wages owed are *legal claims* by wage-earners against money in the possession of employers. In contrast, a dividend is not received on the basis of a contrac-

20. Warning Democracy, p. 125.
21. *Credit-Power and Democracy*, p. 43.
22. *Ibid.*, p. 44.
23. *Ibid.*, p. 44.

tual agreement. Second, a wage is not a form of servitude. *A wage is legal payment for agreed-upon services rendered.* The free market economist teaches this. So does the Bible.

The Parable of the Righteous Employer

In the parable of the just employer, Jesus defended the principle of voluntary contracts for labor. A farmer hired men in the morning to work at an agreed-upon wage. He hired other laborers later in the day. He paid them all the same daily (not hourly) wage, which he and they had agreed upon. At the end of the day, he paid them exactly what they were due. *This payment was a legal entitlement on their part.* But those workers who had worked longer complained. They wanted more than what they had agreed to in the morning.

> But when the first came, they supposed that they should have received more; and they likewise received every man a penny. And when they had received it, they murmured against the goodman of the house, Saying, These last have wrought but one hour, and thou hast made them equal unto us, which have borne the burden and heat of the day. But he answered one of them, and said, Friend, I do thee no wrong: didst not thou agree with me for a penny? Take that thine is, and go thy way: I will give unto this last, even as unto thee. Is it not lawful for me to do what I will with mine own? Is thine eye evil, because I am good? (Matthew 20:10-15).

The employer's answer was to the point: "Didst not thou agree with me for a penny? Take that thine is, and go thy way." The employer was a free man. He was under no moral or legal obligation to pay them more. Nevertheless, their pay was theirs. It belonged by law to them. This was not servitude.

Douglas Confused Dividends With Interest

Having completely misrepresented wages as a form of servitude, Douglas then misidentified the source of dividends. He confused dividends with interest.

Interest is what borrowers pay to "hire" money or goods for a period of time. Because present goods are more valuable to us than those same future goods are, a borrower has to pay the lender something extra when the lending period has expired for the privilege of using the money in the meantime. Every lender discounts in his own mind the present value of future goods in comparison to the present value of those same goods available today. To offset the lender's inescapable mental discount, the borrower has to agree to pay an extra quantity of *future goods* to gain access to the lender's supply of *present goods*, i.e., the goods that his loan money would otherwise have made available to him.

Let me offer this example. Rolls-Royce automobiles do not change style very often. They still look like a 1953 car. I shall therefore use the example of a Rolls-Royce: no change in taste by consumers or change in style by the producer. (I could also use the example of London's black cabs, which look like 1938 automobiles, but who among us would want to own one?)

Let us say that you just won a Rolls-Royce. You subscribed to a magazine and this was the grand prize. All taxes have been paid on it. You are now given a choice. Would you like the Rolls-Royce delivered right now or in five years? I know your answer: right now. Why? Because a Rolls-Royce is worth more to you right now than the same Rolls-Royce delivered five years from now is worth to you right now. Present goods are more valuable to us than identical future goods, other things remaining the same. Because of this, the person who wants you to put off delivery for five years will have to offer you something extra for the privilege. *This is your interest payment*. It is a payment for *forfeited use over time*.

All this was known by economists as early as 1884, when the Austrian economist Eugen von Böhm-Bawerk wrote *The History and Critique of Interest Theories*. In Chapter 12, "The Exploitation

Theory," he used this insight to destroy the economics of Karl Marx and Communism. But, like the Marxists, Major Douglas and his followers have never understood this argument, or else they have refused to admit its truth. Both Karl Marx and Major Douglas argued that workers are being exploited because some people invest money to buy machinery and provide employment for other people. Both men relied on "the exploitation theory." It is easy to see how Hewlett Johnson, the Red Dean of Canterbury, went from Social Credit to Marxism, never abandoning Social Credit.

Payments to Banks?

As we shall see, Douglas incorrectly argued that dividends are payments to banks. On this error he built his version of Marxism's exploitation theory. He argued that capital – money loaned by individuals to borrowers in the credit markets – belongs not to individuals but to the community. Question: If you loan me some money, do I then have a right to protest my obligation to repay this loan because the money you loaned me actually belongs to the whole community, and I am part of that community? This would seem to be an implication of Douglas' view of the legal basis of the National Dividend.

Furthermore, your control over your own money is somehow the cause of my near-starvation, or, as Douglas also called it, my servitude. He wrote:

> Because the credit of the community – which, if distributed, would have resulted in universal dividends – has been largely centralised in the hands of the Banks and industrial combines, all of them struggling for power, that part of the community which still gets its purchasing-power through the medium of wages and salaries has been faced with starvation, unless it "earned" them, machinery or no machinery.[24]

---

24. *Credit-Power and Democracy*, p. 45.

Worse, the trusts and banks then suppress output. They get rich only when others get poor. This, too, is Marx's argument: the supposed impoverization of the proletariat, the declining condition of the working class. Marx wrote that "the general tendency of capitalistic production is not to raise, but to sink the average standard of wages, or to push the *value of labour* more or less to its *minimum limit*."[25] Douglas wrote: "Similarly, the Trusts and Banks, obliged, as a condition of existence under the system, to reabsorb the majority of the credit distributed as wages, through the agency of prices, restricted the supply of ultimate commodities, not only by their own forms of sabotage, but by directing production more and more to capital goods and goods for export."[26] The banks sabotage the system that feeds them. If we believe this, we must believe that capitalism is indeed a paradoxical system. Or could it be that Major Douglas could not keep his arguments straight?

Underconsumption or Underproduction?

I feel compelled to ask: Is Douglas' theory a theory of undercomsumption or underproduction? In this place, he wrote that capitalism restricts "the supply of ultimate commodities," by which he seems to have meant consumer goods: *underproduction*. Elsewhere, he argued repeatedly that Finance Capital reduces the availability of funds for consumers to buy the existing consumer goods: *underconsumption*. Well, which is it? Capitalism is apparently the worst of all possible production systems. It reduces consumption by not making consumer goods available, but also by not creating enough "tickets" for consumers to buy goods that it does produce. Capitalists invest in capital goods in order to increase production of future consumer goods, yet the system somehow suppresses the sales of these

25. Karl Marx, *Value, Price and Profit* (1865), in Marx and Engels, *Collected Works*, Vol. 20 (New York: International Publishers, 1985), p. 148.

26. *Credit-Power and Democracy*, p. 45.

goods by creating too few tickets (money): underconsumption. Meanwhile, capitalism does not actually produce all the consumer goods possible, leaving us to condemn it for underproduction.

If you are a banker, and you have loaned me money, do you want me to make a lot of money or to become impoverished? Which people do bankers prefer to make loans to: poor people who may not be able to repay the loans or successful people who will repay and then borrow again? The answer is obvious: bankers usually loan money to successful people who are expected to do well, not to people who are getting poorer year by year. Sadly, this motivation of bankers was not discussed by Major Douglas, as far as his books indicate.

Is capitalism really this paradoxical? Or was Major Douglas totally confused? I vote for the latter possibility.

Conclusion

Major Douglas confused wages with dividends, and on this basis predicted that dividends would steadily replace wages as the source of income: "[T]he dividend is the logical successor to the wage, carrying with it privileges which the wage never can have. . . ."[27] The dividend was his version of the welfare dole.

He also confused dividends with interest, blaming the supposed concentration of power in banking and the trusts with their control over credit. He did not understand that interest is the payment for time, wages are the payment for labor, rent is the payment for land, and profits are a residual that will remain if an entrepreneur has correctly forecast future consumer demand and has organized production on an effective, low-waste basis. Profits are not automatic; dividends are not automatic; and both are low most of the time. Profits are rarely above a ten percent return on invested capital most of the time.

Douglas used Marx-like arguments regarding the exploita-

27. *Credit-Power and Democracy*, p. 43.

tion of labor by capital. Like Marx, he refused to acknowledge that in a competitive economy, men are paid what they contribute to the production process. Douglas appealed to his A+B Theorem to show how capitalists drained off the productivity of workers. Marx appealed to his doctrine of surplus value. Both theories suffered from the same error: not understanding that competition rewards men according to their productivity. Both Marx and Douglas wrote that the proletariat – the workers – would be progressively impoverished under capitalism.

Douglas called labor under capitalism a form of servitude. Marx said the same thing. The Bible says that labor is service to God. It is cursed because of man's sin, but it can be restored through faith.

Douglas said that capital belongs to the community. So did Marx. The Bible teaches that God grants property to individuals. They serve as God's stewards in history. Private property is honored by the eighth commandment: "Thou shalt not steal" (Exodus 20:15). The Bible does not say, "Thou shalt not steal except by majority vote." It does not say, "Thou shalt not steal except by proletarian revolution."

When the vast majority of mankind saves half their income, generation after generation, for a few centuries, we will be able to speak of a society in which most people live on the money derived from dividends, meaning interest. There will still be jobs, however: people must direct investments, design capital equipment, and employ these tools to meet consumer demand. Was Douglas a utopian in calling for such a world? You decide. The idea that most people will be capable of living well without earning a wage is no more utopian than the idea that most people will invest half their income for many generations – and no less utopian.

Summary

1. Major Douglas said that today's capitalism is "fundamentally bad."

2. The banker and the limited liability corporation made capitalism bad.
3. He said that dividends in private hands are the fundamental evil of modern capitalism.
4. He did not discuss the low level of dividends, century after century: under ten percent.
5. Dividends come from profits.
6. Profits are not automatic.
7. Profits are a residual after all operational expenses have been paid.
8. Profits come from accurate forecasting and efficient production.
9. Profits alert other producers to the existence of factors of production that have been priced too low.
10. Competing producers then bid up the price of these previously underpriced resources.
11. Profits are not automatic because losses are also possible.
12. Douglas argued that dividends are replacing wages.
13. He argued that unlike wages, a dividend is a guaranteed payment.
14. Jesus said a wage is a guaranteed payment.
15. Douglas confused dividends with interest payments.
16. Interest is a payment for time: the use of an asset over time.
17. Douglas said that dividends are payments to banks.
18. The fact is, interest is the payment to banks.
19. Douglas said credit (capital) belongs to the community.
20. Credit is misused by private individuals, Douglas said.
21. Marx said the same thing.
22. Banks and trusts suppress the wealth of workers, Douglas said.
23. Marx said the same thing.
24. Bankers want borrowers to be economically successful.

10

SOCIAL CREDIT MEANS STATE MONOPOLY CREDIT

> Nationalisation without decentralised control of policy will quite effectively instal [*sic*] the trust magnate of the next generation in the chair of the bureaucrat, with the added advantage to him that he will have no shareholders' meeting.
>
> C. H. Douglas, (1921)[1]

I regard this citation as the most accurate policy assessment Major Douglas ever wrote. He made this much clear: without the decentralization of economic policy-making, Social Credit is just one more political dead end, one more call to "throw the rascals out (and put in ours)!"

With this suggestion in his first book, Douglas presented himself and his disciples with Social Credit's most important challenge: to devise the blueprint for a State-administered alternative to private capital markets, one which would not lead to centralized control over national capital in the hands of just this type of bureaucratic tyrant. As I hope to show in this chapter, Douglas never provided so much as a hint of how Social

1. *Economic Democracy* (2nd ed.; London: Cecil Palmer, 1921), pp. 27-28.

Credit's proposed reforms could install a decentralized political authority over credit. All he ever discussed were such topics as the statistical estimate of the nation's capital, the National Dividend (fiat money) program based on this estimate, and the national Just Price allocation of business capital from the national government's credit masters. He never answered his own challenge.

We can see his dilemma in a book published over a decade later, in which he insisted that "the essential point to recognise in regard to finance is the question of the *beneficial ownership* of public credit, whether public credit be administered under a de-centralised or private system of administration or by a public authority."[2] Notice the contrast between the phrases *decentralized or private system* and *public authority*. There is no discussion here of a *decentralized* **public** *authority*. Yet it was this which he said is vital to preserve the economy from bureaucratization. To keep his proposed reform from becoming a centralized tyranny, he needed to explain exactly how the national credit masters would apply the monetary statistic of the inventory of national assets on a decentralized basis. He never did explain this. *A national State monopoly over credit necessarily means centralized political control over production.* The credit masters at the top "hold the hammer." They not only hold it; their monopolistic control over credit decides who manufactures any additional hammers.

Society and State in Social and Political Thought

Under Social Credit, the central government must control the distribution of business capital, as we shall see. This recommendation is the technical heart of Social Credit's proposed reform. This is why it is called *Social* Credit. Major Douglas' system is governed by a formula even more fundamental than his A + B theorem.[3] The heart of Social Credit's political anal-

2. *Warning Democracy* (2nd ed.; London: Stanley Nott, 1934), p. 104.

3. See Appendix A, below.

ysis is this equation: *society* = *State*. This is why Social Credit economics is not conservative.

There are few propositions more hostile to conservatism than the "society = State" formula. From the days of Edmund Burke, England's social philosopher and member of Parliament in the late eighteenth century, until today, conservatives have maintained that society is much more than the State. Society is a vast association which includes families, churches, voluntary associations of all kinds, businesses, etc. And from the days of the French Revolution, which Burke so eloquently opposed, radicals and socialists have insisted that society is the State, that the State must exercise ever-increasing control over all these social organizations.

There are very few conservative professors of sociology in today's world, but the most famous of them, Robert Nisbet (under whom I studied), made his position plain: "In the first place, State and society must be sharply distinguished."[4] *It is the essence of totalitarianism that the State gains control over the institutions we call social.* Any move at this late date in history toward the expansion of State power in order further to empower the State at the expense of society is a move away from freedom. Any attempt to make State bureaucrats the monopolistic economic agents of individuals in the quest for a better, more productive economy is one more step toward the triumph of the State over individuals and the social groups they belong to. Yet there are people who call themselves conservatives today who promote the creation of just such a State monopoly: supporters of Social Credit. Even more astounding, they promote this in the name of the consumer.

Consumer sovereignty is undermined by almost every transfer of power over the economy to State bureaucrats. Taking money away from citizens and placing it in the hands of politi-

---

4. Robert A. Nisbet, *The Quest for Community* (New York: Oxford University Press, 1954), p. 99.

cians and unelected bureaucrats thwarts consumer sovereignty. Consumer sovereignty rests on a single legal principle: *the lawful authority of the consumer over the allocation of his money and other assets*. Yet the technical heart of Social Credit's proposed reform is the forcible transfer of the authority over capital allocation from consumers to the State. A. R. Orage set forth the justification for this massive transfer of authority in his section of *Credit-Power and Democracy*, and Douglas allowed this to be published in the name of Social Credit: the State is the lawful custodian of the nation's wealth, for it is the true representative of the community. He wrote:

> Economically regarded, a nation is an association of people engaged in the production of Real Credit, and in this sense the State, as the custodian of the Real Credit of the community, may be said to represent the interests of Producer and Consumer equally, since both are equally necessary to the creation of Real Credit. Since, however, Producers and Consumers between them make up the whole community, we may conclude that Real Credit is social or communal in origin; that it belongs neither to the producer nor to the consumer, but to their *common* element, the community, of which they each form a part.[5]

Let the reader be reminded: the idea that the community (society) owns the wealth of the nation, and the State alone represents all members equally, is the heart, mind, and soul of every socialistic theory of economic reform. (See Chapter 5, above.)

Bureaucracy

By law, the State is always a bureaucracy. Its employees are salaried. They do not own the State; they work for the State. They cannot legally share as owners in the economic successes of the State. That is, it is difficult for a bureaucrat to benefit

---

5. A. R. Orage, "Commentary," *Credit-Power and Democracy* (2nd ed.; London: Cecil Palmer, 1920), pp. 157-58.

directly from his role in producing any positive sanctions from the State. He receives only his salary, his appropriate "perks," and a sense of power (maybe). So much for positive sanctions from the State. What about negative sanctions: State-engineered failures? Every bureaucrat seeks to minimize his risk for having participated in the economic failures of the State. This means that risk-avoiding bureaucrats, not profit-seeking investors, will control the society's supply of credit. People who cannot legally be fired if they invest the State's money unwisely will decide which projects are financed with State capital, and which are never begun for lack of capital. This will inevitably lead to the total bureaucratization of the economy.

Major Douglas did his best to counter this conclusion. He insisted that his proposal in no way would stifle creativity. The problem is, his argument in this regard was inconsistent with the details of his proposed reconstruction of economic policy. Toward the end of his section of *Credit-Power and Democracy*, Douglas insisted: "There is no suggestion intended in the foregoing pages that any restriction whatever should be placed in the way of anyone who wishes to make a new machine or devise a new process, or that he should be hindered in so doing – very much to the contrary."[6]

This sounds very reassuring. But Douglas faced the problem that every social reformer faces: to see to it that the reform he proposes has judicial laws and sanctions attached to it that assure voters that his stated policy goals are likely to be attained by the actual social order that will be produced by his recommended reform. It is not sufficient to proclaim one's good intentions, as Douglas himself insisted: "Unselfish aspirations, good intentions, beautiful phrases – none of these by themselves will affect the issue by so much as one hair's breadth."[7] The many roads to social hell on earth have always been paved

6. *Ibid.*, p. 142.

7. *Ibid.*, p. 85.

with good intentions. The question is: What built-in legal safeguards does the proposed reform possess that will insure that the reformer's good intentions will become social realities?

Consumers' Control Over Credit

Major Douglas stated, but could hardly prove, that his system would produce the consumers' control over credit. I ask: Which consumers? How? Under free market capitalism, the supply of credit is determined by competition. Lenders compete against lenders to supply funds, while borrowers compete against borrowers by offering future rewards to lenders. The result of this bargaining process is the rate of interest. The lenders must assess the likelihood that the borrowers will repay the loans. These loans may be consumer loans or business (producer) loans. If they are producer loans, then the future consumers of the goods produced will determine which producers will be able to receive additional loans. *Consumers decide who fails and who succeeds in business.* This is what the free market economist means when he says that consumers control credit. They control the potential borrowers' eligibility for credit.

This is not what Major Douglas meant. He meant that *voters* will authorize *politicians* who will appoint *bureaucrats* who will determine who gets business loans. The bureaucrats will decide which manufacturer is producing desirable goods, and which is producing unneeded luxuries. The bureaucrats' tastes and forecasts will determine who gets the money to produce goods and services, not the economic forecasts of bankers whose banks' survival is on the line. An elite of unelected bureaucrats will make these investment decisions.

Elitism

Douglas was an elitist, and said so repeatedly. In the 1934 edition of his book, *Warning Democracy*, he wrote about the great evil of "the continuous extension of the voting franchise, and a very Machiavellian policy it is, resulting as it does in the intelligent voter being completely disfranchised."[8] In other words, too many citizens are allowed to vote. In *Social Credit*, he wrote that under his proposed reform of society, the voters will be allowed to vote on general economic policy, but they must not be allowed to dictate to the elite credit masters exactly how the nation's capital shall be allocated – a merely procedural matter. "To submit questions of fiscal procedure, of foreign affairs, and other cognate matters to the judgment of an electorate is merely to submit matters which are essentially technical to a community which is essentially non-technical."[9]

So, when Douglas spoke of consumers' control over credit, he meant the elite credit masters' control over credit in the name of consumers. Under Social Credit, the representation of consumers will be political and ultimately bureaucratic. Bankers will not represent the interests of depositors. An unelected elite group of central planners will represent consumers and producers equally. We know where this system of bureaucratic representation always leads, on both sides of the now-defunct Iron Curtain: the elitists who disburse the money will pursue their own economic interests and, if they should get caught, will then claim that they were only representing "the People."

Procedure and Responsibility

Douglas wrote as if the allocation of a nation's capital were a procedural matter only, as if the money elite's crucial decisions were as economically neutral and simple as drawing up plans to build a bridge. Yet we know how politically corrupt something as narrowly constrained as building a bridge can be: who gets paid how much for the land, who gets awarded the contracts, etc. Nevertheless, Douglas recommended the creation of a political elite that would finance thousands of projects every

8. *Warning Democracy* (2nd ed.; London: Stanley Nott, 1934), p. 8.
9. *Social Credit* (3rd ed.; London: Eyre & Spottiswoode, 1933), p. 125.

year, and turn down tens of thousands of other projects. Did I say tens of thousands? Why not hundreds of thousands – or as many as the creative minds of men might devise each year?

Douglas never answered this key fundamental question, *the most fundamental economic problem facing any State planning bureaucracy*: How can any State bureaucracy know what the most socially beneficial projects are? This is the question that free market economist Ludwig von Mises asked in 1920 in his classic essay, "Economic Calculation in the Socialist Commonwealth."[10] In the absence of a free market, Mises argued, especially a market for capital goods, no one can rationally calculate the economic value of anything. When Communism openly collapsed in 1989, it became clear even to Mises' critics that no one has ever been able to answer Mises' question. The defenders of Social Credit have never even tried to answer it. They act as though it had never been asked.

Good Intentions Are Not Enough

Douglas provided a list of good intentions. But there is no doubt what he was proposing: an economy controlled at the top by bureaucrats. These bureaucrats must somehow monitor every aspect of production in order to make sure that the public is getting its money's worth. He offered no suggestion as to exactly how production would be monitored from the top. He proposed no system of rewards and punishments over bureaucrats that would insure that they act in the public's interest. He did not even offer a working definition of the public interest, as we shall see shortly. But he did insist that these public-spirited bureaucrats will do their job faithfully.

> The materialisation of the proposals for consumer-control of credit, outlined in the foregoing pages, would make it far easier

10. Reprinted by the Ludwig von Mises Institute, Auburn University, Auburn, Alabama, USA.

> than it is now, to experiment with any idea, however apparently wild it might appear at first sight. What they would prevent is the manufacture for sale, at the expense of the public, of armaments, machinery, factories, "luxuries," shoddy articles, etc., without the public as individuals having any opportunity to express an opinion as to whether such articles are or are not a fit object on which to expend the capacity of the community to deliver goods and services – *i.e.*, its credit.[11]

Douglas' promise is a statement of good intentions. It is hardly proof of the real-world correspondence between his recommended reform and its outcome. How, precisely, would *the public as individuals* have an opportunity to *express an opinion* regarding which businesses will receive credit, that is, social credit, meaning *the community's credit*? Will the experts have to seek the approval of the public in some sort of national or international referendum every time some businessman comes to the bank for a loan? Of course not. Douglas labeled majoritarian rule as "the ultimate Terror."[12]

High Demand for Below-Cost Loans

Will the public appoint committees to oversee the experts who make the loans? He did not say. If such an added layer were appointed, this would only add another layer of bureaucratic inefficiency to the Social Credit program. Some group would still have to decide who gets the limited (scarce) supply of credit. We cannot reasonably hope to solve the fundamental problem – guaranteeing honesty and efficiency from the credit masters of a State monopoly banking system – by adding layers of representation. The problem remains: *someone has to decide who gets the credit*. Douglas admitted as much:

---

11. *Credit-Power and Democracy*, p. 142.
12. *Ibid.*, p. 7.

> In other words, and more concretely, persons who wished to avail themselves of the facilities which enable them to so use the public credit as to sell "below cost" would only be able to do so after obtaining the necessary decision that their product is in the public interest. No definition of the public interest is either necessary or desirable – it is quite sufficient that public agreement is obtained in the matter without depriving minorities of the opportunity of proving the majority wrong.[13]

As cricket fans say, this proposal creates a sticky wicket. First, a potential borrower must prove to the State's bankers – let's face it, Social Credit's credit masters are still bankers, for they are money-lenders – that his project is in the public interest. Second, "public interest" is deliberately left undefined in Douglas' proposed reform. This transfers total sovereignty to the State's bankers in their decision to lend or not to lend. Third, to keep us from drawing this obvious conclusion, Douglas assured us that "public agreement is obtained," but he did not reveal the judicial or bureaucratic mechanism by which this agreement could be obtained. Fourth, he was concerned with the problem of "depriving minorities of the opportunity of proving the majority wrong." But being concerned with the problem is not the same as coming up with a workable organizational solution to the problem. Good intentions are not sufficient.

If someone came to you with this same proposal, but he called it Communism, would you accept it? Probably not. Yet this system is exactly what Karl Marx proposed in the *Communist Manifesto* (1848): a State-run banking system. If someone proposed this plan in the name of Fascism, would you accept it? Probably not. Yet the German Nazis and the Italian Fascists created State monopoly over banking: credit controls.

---

13. *Ibid.*, pp. 142-43.

Our acceptance or rejection of a reform proposal should not be based on what it is called. Our decision should be made on what the specifics of the proposal are.

"Effective Demand"

Major Douglas insisted that "The scarcity of money and the consequent restriction of effective demand is unquestionably the most important, and in fact, the vital point on which the future of the present financial system turns. . . ."[14] This phrase, "effective demand," became important in the writings of another economist, one far more influential than Major Douglas, as we shall see: John Maynard Keynes.

Douglas also insisted that "an enormously increased use of credit facilities is the only radical solution of the present difficulties. . . ."[15] He called for consumer credit to match producer credit. This credit should be issued "below cost." (Below cost? This is a familiar socialist slogan, not a conservative one.) He assured his readers that "it is just as feasible to issue this credit to the consumer by selling 'below cost' as it is to issue it to the producer by anticipating payment. In both cases it is public credit which is used. . . ."[16]

Someone or some process has to balance supply and demand. In a free market society, this balancing is done through flexible pricing. But Douglas did not believe that the voluntary decisions of buyers and sellers, lenders and debtors, can perform this balancing function. He did not believe that freely fluctuating prices are the best way to balance supply with demand. Balancing must be done through the issue of credit, he insisted. This means that merely producing goods and services is not sufficient. There must be *effective demand*, a phrase which Keynes was later to adopt. Douglas wrote: "Now, one of the

14. *Warning Democracy*, p. 100.

15. *Credit-Power and Democracy*, p. 143.

16. *Ibid.*, p. 143.

components of the capacity of a society to *deliver* goods and services *is the existence of an effective demand* for those goods and services."[17] He had used this same phrase in his first book, *Economic Democracy*.[18] Therefore, he concluded, "*The business of a modern and effective financial system is to issue credit to the consumer, up to the limit of the productive capacity of the producer, so that either the consumers' real demand is satiated, or the producers' capacity is exhausted, whichever happens first.*"[19]

Four practical questions need specific answers. The first question is: What is this limit on productive capacity? The second question is: How can any bureaucracy estimate this accurately? The third question is: When is consumers' real demand satiated? The fourth question is: How can any bureaucracy discover this point of satiation? *Bureaucrats are not omniscient.* Douglas never answered any of them. No one ever has.

John Maynard Keynes

Let us turn to Keynes, the most prominent economist of this century, the promoter of the idea of the so-called "mixed economy": part capitalist, part socialist. He, too, centered his economic theory around the concept of effective demand. He clearly recognized that this focus was also Major Douglas' focus. Keynes wrote: "The great puzzle of Effective Demand with which Malthus had wrestled vanished from economic literature. . . . It could only live on furtively, below the surface, in the underworlds of Karl Marx, Silvio Gesell or Major Douglas."[20] (It is worth noting that Gesell was recommended by Douglas as a reliable economist.)[21] When John Maynard Keynes praises

---

17. *Ibid.*, p. 106.

18. *Economic Democracy* (2nd ed.; London: Cecil Palmer, 1921), p. 67.

19. *Credit-Power and Democracy*, p. 106.

20. John Maynard Keynes, *The General Theory of Employment, Interest, and Money* (New York: Macmillan, 1936), p. 32.

21. *The Monopoly of Credit* (London: Chapman & Hall, 1931), p. 4, footnote.

your ideas, and when he links them with the ideas of Karl Marx, you have a problem if you are presenting yourself as a conservative, let alone a Christian.[22] This is the dilemma of Social Credit.

The Sovereignty of the Credit Masters

In a world of scarcity, there is always more demand than supply at zero price. This means that consumer demand can never be satiated. Consumer demand at zero price is analogous to an internal combustion engine with no governor and a driver who will race faster and faster until the engine blows up or the car crashes. Presumably, Major Douglas did not intend to blow up the economy. He surely did not intend to crash it. Therefore, Social Credit's elite credit masters have a responsibility to estimate maximum productivity, i.e., Real Capital. How they can do this, Major Douglas never said. The experts who issue social credit must also somehow decide which consumer demand should be filled with the available production.

There is a word for a State-planned system of production and distribution: *socialism*. But Major Douglas knew that this word would alienate respectable voters. Thus, he refused to use the word. Major Douglas was a prudent man.

The number-one feature of his proposed reform was the substitution of social credit for private credit. This meant the replacement of private bankers with State bureaucrats. It meant, in short, *State* credit. In his economic analysis, credit is the heart of modern capitalism. It is what keeps the economy moving. Thus, the transfer of control over credit from private bankers to public officials would place in the hands of State-appointed bureaucrats the power to direct the system of production and also distribution: producer debt and consumer debt (if any).

---

22. Ian Hodge, *Baptized Inflation: A Critique of "Christian" Keynesianism* (Tyler, Texas: Institute for Christian Economics, 1985).

Major Douglas wanted to resolve the seeming alternatives of freedom and authority. "And so we arrive at the same position as that reached in the consideration of various Socialistic proposals – we are confronted by the fundamental alternatives of freedom and authority. But it should be possible, if the previous pages have conveyed the intention of their writer, to see that these are not necessarily alternatives at all – they are policies each fundamentally 'right' on its own plane of action."[23] Freedom and authority, he insisted, need not be rivals at all. They are both "right." He puts "right" in quotation marks, presumably because he began the book with a disclaimer in its Preface that he would avoid any consideration of morality: "That is moral which works best."

Even if these credit masters were elected rather than appointed, what fundamental difference would this make? The consumers as consumers and lenders still would have no say in the allocation of credit except as voters. Production would shift to meet the preferences of politicians who spend *other people's money* rather than the preferences of consumers who spend and save their own money. I ask: What is conservative about such a State-administered, centrally directed economy? What is Christian about it?

Major Douglas always maintained that he opposed socialism. He opposed "Nationalising."[24] He therefore opposed Communism: the ownership of the tools of production by the State. But by refusing to recommend free market credit and free market money, he adopted the National Socialists' and Fascists' version of economic control: almost total control over credit and prices by the State, but with legal title to property remaining officially in private hands. This is still State planning. Douglas said he opposed those forms of socialism that deprived the individual of "economic independence," either through conscription or

23. *Credit-Power and Democracy*, p. 144.

24. *Ibid.*, p. 146.

nationalization. *But if the experts can use political power to nationalize the allocation of credit, thereby "conscripting" credit, what is the economic difference?* The difference is merely rhetorical.

Men can resist the evil side of socialism, Douglas insisted. How? By his magic pill, the creation of a State monopoly bank which will issue below-cost, zero-interest loans to favored producers who are registered with the State: his Just Price scheme.[25] He ended his portion of *Credit-Power and Democracy* with these stirring words: "Into the temple of this faith the money-changers have entered; and only when they have been cast out shall we have peace."[26] The problem is, slogans are not a reliable institutional defense against State monopoly power. Karl Marx also wanted a State monopoly bank in the transition stage to his recommended Communist society. Why? Because he understood that *they who control the allocation of capital thereby control the economy*. If this control is forced on producers and lenders by the State, then the State has become the true owner. The tools of production are in the hands of the State. This is the essence of socialism.

Decapitalization Through Mass Inflation

During the French Revolution, the government confiscated the monasteries and landed estates of those who had fled the country. This decapitalized Christians and conservatives. The government then issued paper money with these lands serving as collateral. The problem was, as these lands appreciated in value because of this monetary inflation, their collateral value rose. This allowed the government to issue even more money. Year by year, the government destroyed the French economy by means of monetary inflation.[27] But the politicians through-

25. See Chapter 4, above.

26. *Ibid.*, p. 146.

27. Andrew Dickson White, *Fiat Money in France* (Irvington, New York: Foundation for Economic Education, [1912] 1959).

out the revolutionary era proclaimed their devotion to the public interest, and castigated producers as greedy enemies of the People. The government went from castigation to decapitation, all in the name of the People. This was the ultimate decapitalization of France.

Social Credit proposes that the national government conduct an inventory of all capital in the nation, including "human capital," meaning the value of everyone's potential output.[28] The problem is, this inventory has to be made in terms of money prices. There is no other way for such an inventory to be taken. It is not sufficient to count machines, land, and people. Who knows what any given piece of land or equipment is worth? Is an acre of swamp land or desert equal in value to an acre of land in the path of a major city's development? Is a worn-out machine equal in value to a new model? So, the estimators must place a money value on this gigantic inventory of assets, both physical and intellectual (patents and copyrights, for example).

Once the estimators place a monetary value on this inventory, they must continually track its value. Some capital wears out. New inventions are introduced. Some are valuable; most aren't. The estimators must make adjustments for changes in price of everything in the economy. This means that the monetary system is fundamental in this enormous, never-ending task. Without money and prices denominated in money, there would be no way to estimate the value of the national wealth, meaning national capital.

Every time Social Credit's credit masters made a loan, and every time the dividend masters sent out monthly checks, they would do so not simply on the basis of tax revenues collected – Douglas hated taxes – but on the basis of the estimated monetary value of the nation's capital, meaning Real Capital. But because the government would not officially own this capital, it

28. *Social Credit*, pp. 205-6.

would not collect money from rents. It would not participate in any profits. There would be only an estimation of the national capital's total money value. A true dividend could exist only when there were actual profits and rents collected, but since a Social Credit government would not own the nation's assets, but would merely control the money (credit) supply, it would not participate in any profits or rents. The State would merely print up checks and mail them to all citizens (except the rich).

Fiat Money

The Social Credit system is one among many fiat money schemes.[29] It adds extra features, such as the national inventory, the National Dividend (money sent to citizens), and the "Just Price" (money issued to producers), but it is ultimately a fiat money scheme. Every such scheme promises to keep the increase in the money supply tied statistically to the increase in production.[30] The well-acknowledged practical problem with all such schemes is the same: *how to keep the increase in money from producing rising prices*. There has to be a judicial or economic limit in the system that keeps the central bank, government, or other money managers from creating too much money. Without a gold standard or other commodity standard, where individuals can exchange money for a fixed supply of the commodity, what institutional restraint exists?

There is another practical problem, but it is rarely acknowledged, even by economists: how to keep an injection of fiat money from causing distortions in *relative prices*. That is, how to keep new money from causing price distortions at those points in the economy where this new money arrives first, such as in the accounts of the businesses that get government credit. It is

29. See Appendix C, below.

30. Gary North, "Gertrude Coogan and the Myth of Social Credit," in Gary North, *An Introduction to Christian Economics* (Nutley, New Jersey: Craig Press, 1973), ch. 11.

not just that injections of fiat money tend to raise prices in general (or keep prices in general from falling); it is that these injections of new money raise some prices sooner than others. Those people who get their hands on the new money first have a competitive advantage over those who get access later, after prices have risen, after resources have been bought by those who got access earlier. This is the issue raised by Professor Mises in 1912,[31] by Professor Knight in 1921,[32] and by Professor Hayek from 1931 through the 1970's.[33] (Hayek died in 1992, still writing: an amazingly long and productive career.)

Speaking of monetary inflation, Knight wrote in 1921: "When inflation occurs, therefore, purchasing power is not created, but merely transferred from the previous owners of circulating medium to the persons into whose hands the new currency is placed for its first expenditure. The enormous role played in history by inflationism and the persistence of the heresy rest upon the fact that the effects of the expenditure of the new money are more conspicuous than the diminished effects of that which already existed."[34] *Monetary inflation does not create wealth; it merely* ***redistributes*** *it.* We can easily identify the winners; we tend to ignore the losers, at least during the early stages of an economic boom – a boom created by false signals, namely, lower interest rates produced by the injection of new fiat money. At the end of the process, most people lose.

Monetary inflation is not economically neutral. Its price effects are not simultaneous. It creates winners and losers over time. We see winners in the early stages of the boom; we see a

---

31. Ludwig von Mises, *The Theory of Money and Credit* (New Haven, Connecticut: Yale University Press, [1912] 1953), pp. 139-43.

32. Frank H. Knight, *Risk, Uncertainty and Profit* (New York: Harper Torchbooks, [1921] 1965), p. 166n.

33. F. A. Hayek, *Prices and Production* (London: Routledge & Kegan Paul, 1931); Hayek, *Monetary Theory and the Trade Cycle* (New York: Augustus M. Kelley, [1933] 1966); Hayek, *A Tiger by the Tail*, edited by Sudha R. Shenoy (London: Institute of Economic Affairs, 1972).

34. Knight, *Risk*, p. 166n.

growing number losers in the final stages, as price inflation destroys the value of savings; and we see the almost universal crisis in the deflationary depression that inevitably follows the period of the fiat-money-generated boom. But very few people understand economics well enough to blame the depression on the prior monetary inflation and its distortion of relative prices, as well as its subsidy to businesses that began projects that proved unprofitable when the monetary inflation slowed, ended, and turned into deflation, when depositors make cash withdrawals from banks and hoard the cash.

Who Decides What the Market Can Produce?

We return to the question of the limits on the creation of fiat money by the State's monetary authorities. Douglas wrote: "*The only sane limit to the issue of credit for use as purchasing-power is the limit imposed by ability to deliver the goods for which it forms an effective demand, providing that the community agrees to their manufacture.*"[35] But who is to decide this limit on the ability of the economy "to deliver the goods"? He never said.

Furthermore, who is to determine if "the community agrees to their manufacture"? The credit masters act in the name of the community, but how can they know what the community – meaning every individual – needs or wants? As he wrote: "Centralised *financial* credit is a technical possibility, but centralised *real* credit assumes that the desires and aspirations of humanity can be standardised, and ought to be standardised, and ought to be standardised. . . . [N]o man, or body of men, however elected, can represent the detailed desires of any other man, or body of men."[36] If Real Credit cannot be defined scientifically – Douglas offered several incompatible definitions[37] – then on

---

35. *Credit-Power and Democracy*, p. 101.
36. *Ibid.*, p. 57.
37. See above, pp. 96-98, 136.

what basis can the credit masters decide how much fiat credit to issue? The answer is obvious: there is no scientific basis.

Major Douglas offered no formula to guide the credit masters, no mechanism for the public to control the credit masters, no legal limits to the creation of credit, meaning money. Social Credit is therefore an open-ended invitation to the creation of money by the State in an attempt by politicians to attain their political goals without increasing taxes. This is the traditional political motivation for every mass inflationist regime in history. There have been many of them.[38]

Follow the Money

In his first book, Major Douglas wrote emphatically that "*the State should lend, not borrow, and that in this respect, as in others, the Capitalist usurps the function of the State.*"[39] He never changed his mind about this usurping of a State function by private lenders. Everything he ever wrote on economic reform rested on this fundamental presupposition. This was the heart of his judicial criticism of capitalism, not his technical A + B Theorem. He made his position clear: "There is no doubt whatever that the first step towards dealing with the problem is the recognition of the fact that what is commonly called credit by the banker is administered by him primarily for the purpose of private profit, whereas it is most definitely communal property."[40] Here it is again: *your bank account belongs to society.*

I have stated that in seeking answers to questions of operational authority, we should begin with a plan: *follow the money.* Let us do so now. Question: Where does the State obtain assets (money) to lend? Ah, there's the rub! It possesses no wealth of its own. The State has to take assets from individuals in order

---

38. Forrest H. Capie (ed.), *Major Inflations in History* (Brookfield, Vermont: Elgar, 1991).

39. *Economic Democracy*, p. 125.

40. *Ibid.*, p. 121.

to become the nation's banker. It then transfers these confiscated assets to an elite group of money masters. They then become the source of all future productivity. Douglas believed that this elite could produce wealth so great that the rest of mankind would have to labor only a few hours per week to enjoy ever-increasing wealth.

What distinguishes Social Credit from conventional socialism is that Douglas did not call for an open confiscation of capital by the State. Titles of ownership remained with private owners. Then how does the State under Social Credit remove assets from one group and transfer them to another? Through the monopoly of money creation and credit allocation.

The State's credit masters reward favored producers at the expense of their competitors. The credit masters decide what kinds of goods will be produced and in what quantities. In order to secure capital to launch new projects or sustain old ones, producers must come to the credit masters with plans. They must "sell" the credit masters on the viability of these plans. (If you think corruption is not lurking in the shadows behind this arrangement, you are terminally naïve.) As surely as private bankers have the power to allocate capital, so will Social Credit's credit masters. The difference is, private bankers act as economic agents of depositors, who retain the authority to remove their deposits. No similar economic threat hangs over the heads of the bureaucratic State credit masters. They face political threats, not economic ones.

This is true of every system of socialism: *the sanctions facing the bureaucrats are political rather than economic*. This is what Major Douglas specifically proposed as the ultimate justification of Social Credit: the removal of economic sanctions and the substitution of political sanctions.[41] This is the moral heart of Social Credit. This is why at bottom Social Credit is socialistic. In Germany in 1935, a similar system was called National Socialism.

---

41. See Chapter 11, below.

Douglas vs. Democratic Capitalism

Major Douglas always attacked private bankers. He never pursued the answer to the obvious question: Where do they get the money they lend? Once again, *let us follow the money*. Under capitalism, individual owners of assets (you and I) deposit money in a bank, thereby hiring the banker to make decisions regarding where to lend our money. In short, we hire a specialist in lending. What is so terrible about this? We also go to mechanics, physicians, and other specialists. Or perhaps we invest in a business and become part owners. Perhaps we loan money directly to a business. The point is, *as the owners of capital, you and I retain sovereignty over how our wealth is to be distributed*. We retain authority, for we retain responsibility. We can delegate this responsibility to a businessman or a banker, but ultimately, the decision is ours. It is our loss if we delegate unwisely. Again, what is wrong with this? What is wrong with personal responsibility? What is wrong with capitalism's principle of consumers' sovereignty?

Everything, said Major Douglas. He despised capitalism. Capitalism is much too democratic. It delivers too much authority over wealth to individuals. It leaves the consumers with too large a hammer over private producers, both as buyers of consumer goods and investors. Douglas wanted an elite minority of central planners – the credit masters – to decide what should be produced, by whom, at what prices, and at what profit to producers: the Just Price system. As he wrote so clearly, he wanted the State to be the only lender of capital. This means that the State must become the primary *owner* of capital.

Douglas did allow existing home owners to retain ownership, just so long as they do not move out of their homes.[42] He wanted the State's credit masters to place extensive restrictions around all forms of privately owned productive wealth. Douglas

42. "No transfer of real estate directly between either persons or business undertakings will be recognised." *Social Credit*, p. 206.

made this so clear in his writings that it is astounding that many of his followers today promote his ideas in the name of both conservatism and Christianity.

Then again, there is some doubt that they actually promote his ideas. There is at least some evidence that they have whitewashed Major Douglas by suppressing information about what he actually wrote. I ask you if you are a follower: Have you read these citations from Major Douglas' books in the materials published by his followers? If not, think twice about your commitment to Social Credit.

Conclusion

Social credit means State credit. State credit means State control over what gets produced. State control means State ownership. State ownership is socialism. Let us not be deceived about this. Major Douglas, in the name of conservatism, was a promoter of socialism. This is why Hewlett Johnson, the Red Dean of Canterbury, began his march into Communism by way of Major Douglas. This is why the poet Ezra Pound, who became a radio propagandist for Mussolini during World War II, began and ended as a disciple of Major Douglas.

Summary

1. Social credit means State-controlled credit.
2. Conservatism teaches that society is much broader than the State.
3. Radicals and socialists equate State and society.
4. Consumer sovereignty means control over spending and saving by consumers.
5. State credit thwarts consumer sovereignty.
6. Bureaucrats do not own the money they spend.
7. They seek to avoid risk in allocating capital.
8. If bureaucrats control credit, they will bureaucratize the entire economy.

9. Major Douglas insisted that the bureaucrats would allocate the State's capital wisely.
10. He had good intentions.
11. His theory offered no specific ways to insure that his good intentions would result in a productive economy.
12. He never said how the State's money masters would be controlled.
13. He did not offer any economic guidelines to these money masters.
14. He said that credit should be supplied below cost.
15. He did not say how the public interest can and will be maintained by these money masters.
16. Karl Marx recommended the same sort of central bank.
17. Major Douglas insisted that the free market does not provide effective demand.
18. John Maynard Keynes insisted that the free market does not provide effective demand.
19. State credit produces State control over the economy.
20. We normally call such State-controlled economies socialist economies.
21. Douglas provided no formula for governing the creation of credit.
22. Social Credit therefore opens the door to mass inflation.

11

SANCTIONS: FROM ECONOMICS TO POLITICS

It seems indisputable that no modern economic system can be based on any theory of rewards and punishments.

C. H. Douglas (1931)[1]

Behind any mechanism, you always have to have a sanction. It is the sanction which is the important thing. If you have the sanction, the mechanism can always be devised.

C. H. Douglas (1937)[2]

Well, which is it? Are sanctions – blessing and cursing, carrot and stick – irrelevant to economic theory and economic systems, or are they crucial? For economics, he said they are irrelevant. For politics, which was the focus of his 1937 essay, Major Douglas said sanctions are inescapable. Yet earlier he had rejected the long-term legitimacy of economic sanctions. He distinguished between political sanctions and economic sanctions. This is a very important distinction, one which I believe lies at

---

1. *The Monopoly of Credit* (London: Chapman & Hall, 1931), p. 86.
2. *The Policy of a Philosophy* (Liverpool: K.R.P. Publications, 1937), p. 7.

the heart of his system of political economy. He wanted to shift control over capital from the free market (which supposedly overcomes sanctions) to the State (inescapable sanctions).

He proposed a system of political economy, no doubt about that. Yet in his first book, *Economic Democracy*, he claimed that all intellectual systems are limited. We should not take any system too seriously. "Systems were made for men, and not men for systems, and the interest of man which is self-development, is above all systems, whether theological, political, or economic."[3] He was paraphrasing Jesus' words regarding the sabbath: "The sabbath was made for man, and not man for the sabbath (Mark 2:27). This was a very odd statement for an author who was proposing a system of economic reform and who later became the titular head of a reform movement. As he wrote in 1937, "You could not have a country which was pursuing a consistent policy unless somewhere at the back of it there was a consistent philosophy."[4]

As we have seen, he rejected ethics as the foundation of his critique of capitalism. "In what is undoubtedly an attack on certain features of the so-called Capitalistic system, in this book, no attempt or desire to judge that system on any grounds but those of workability is made or implied. The business of an economic system is to deliver the right goods to the right users, and the private financing of public production is doomed because it is failing signally in delivering the goods."[5] He claimed to base his critique only on practical matters.

I contend that Major Douglas had a theology as well as a proposed economic system. What was this theology? Above all, it was his rejection of the New Testament's teaching on heaven and hell: the Bible's doctrine of final sanctions.

---

3. *Economic Democracy* (2nd ed.; London: Cecil Palmer, 1921), pp. 6-7.

4. *Policy of a Philosophy*, p. 9.

5. *Credit-Power and Democracy* (London: Cecil Palmer, 1920), p. vii.

Darwinian Evolution

Douglas was committed to the doctrine of Darwinian evolution. In the language of evolutionism, he called his readers "back to first principles – to an attempt to define the purposes, conscious or unconscious, which govern humanity in its ceaseless struggle with environment." This process he called "the drive of evolution."[6] He referred favorably to evolutionist Benjamin Kidd's *Science of Power*, which defended the survival of the fittest.[7] While there are some questions about the term "fittest," Douglas said, "it is not of course necessary to question the soundness of Darwin's theory."[8]

He observed that "It is even probable that all life on this planet is compelled by the nature of things thus to change on to a different plane on pain of extinction."[9] All of life evolving to "a different plane"? This sounds more like New Age mysticism than science. It is not difficult to see why A. R. Orage, a Theosophist and Eastern mystic, adopted Social Credit so readily. Eastern mysticism is evolutionistic.

A Rejection of the Bible

As we have seen in Chapter 10, Douglas expected Social Credit to remove steadily the role of labor as a source of a person's income.[10] He made this the touchstone of his economic reform:

> 1. That the cash credits of the population of any country shall at any moment be collectively equal to the collective cash prices for consumable goods for sale in that country, and such cash credits shall be cancelled on the purchase of goods for consumption.

6. *Economic Democracy*, p. 4.
7. *Ibid.*, p. 10.
8. *Ibid.*, p. 10.
9. *Warning Democracy* (2nd ed.; London: Stanley Nott, 1934), p. 73.
10. *Ibid.*, pp. 34-35.

> 2. That the credits required to finance production shall be supplied, not from savings, but be new credits relating to new production.
>
> 3. That the distribution of cash credits to individuals shall be progressively less dependent upon employment. That is to say, that the dividend shall progressively displace the wage and salary.[11]

Here is the long-term economic goal of Social Credit: "The dividend shall progressively displace the wage and salary." He believed that there should be no connection between labor and income, between working and eating. He knew exactly who his opponent was in this recommendation: the Apostle Paul.

> You will see, I think, without difficulty that the solution of this situation is easy if you will only divest it of any preconceived ideas of social morality, and turn your back on such ideas as "if a man will not work neither shall he eat," a sentiment which in my opinion was merely a statement of fact in the conditions under which it was written and not intended to be a canon of ethics.[12]

What did Paul say? "For even when we were with you, this we commanded you, that if any would not work, neither should he eat. For we hear that there are some which walk among you disorderly, working not at all, but are busybodies. Now them that are such we command and exhort by our Lord Jesus Christ, that with quietness they work, and eat their own bread. But ye, brethren, be not weary in well doing. And if any man obey not our word by this epistle, note that man, and have no company with him, that he may be ashamed" (II Thessalonians 3:10-14). *This sounds exactly like a canon of ethics*. But it was ethics,

---

11. *Ibid.*, p. 42.
12. *Ibid.*, p. 36.

above all biblical ethics, that Douglas opposed. It was a system of sanctions like the one found in Leviticus 26 and Deuteronomy 28 that outraged him. He wrote:

> Closely interwoven with the classical and moral theory of society, is the theory of rewards and punishments. So familiar is this idea, through education and experience, to most people, that it is only with some difficulty that they are brought to realise that it is an artificial theory and not inherent in the nature of things; that the statement "be good and you will be happy" does not rely for any truth it may possess on any fixed relation between the abstract qualities of goodness and happiness, but upon the fixed relation of cause and effect between certain actions to which the title "goodness" may arbitrarily be applied, and their reactions which we term "happiness." This may appear to be word splitting, but when we realise that the whole of the industrial, legal, and social system of the world rests for its sanctions on this theory of rewards and punishments, it is difficult to deny the importance of an exact comprehension of it.[13]

The Issue Was Moral Law

He wrote a lengthy passage against the Salvation Army, one of the most successful anti-poverty, self-help organizations in history. Douglas despised it. He especially despised a statement by the head of the Salvation Army that was critical of the dole, meaning the welfare system. Douglas went into a tirade against the Salvation Army as a manifestation of Puritanism, which he regarded as a negative influence. He ended with an appeal to the Great Reformer (Jesus) who supposedly was opposed to "formalism," meaning Puritanism.

> There are certain factors operative in human psychology which it is possible to recognise as helpful or the reverse. During a visit to New York I saw considerable numbers of fervent men

13. *Social Credit* (3rd ed.; London: Eyre & Spottiswoode, 1933), pp. 10-11.

> and women carrying sandwich-boards and collecting-boxes through the financial quarters in and around Wall Street, bearing on them the legend, "The Salvation Army is Father Knickerbocker's best friend." It is perhaps hardly necessary to explain that Father Knickerbocker is generally taken to represent the respectability of solid, or perhaps preferably, liquid capital. That is to say, it may be taken as a scientific statement of fact that one of the most dangerous opponents of a better, cleaner world, is the sentimental spirit which is entirely concerned with the beauties of a prospective Heaven, whether that Heaven is theological or moral. The head of the institution to which I have just referred, has recently elaborated the preceding statement by an intemperate attack on the "dole," basing his objection to it on the "demoralisation" of the recipient and not, of course, on the financial jugglery which accompanies it – an attitude entirely similar to that of the Puritan in his abolition of bear-baiting; not because it was cruel to the bear, but because it gave pleasure to the populace. The practical outcome of this Puritanism is always negative. In short, there is a type of sentiment which, under existing conditions, is able to attain great respectability, but which can, with very little difficulty, be identified with the formalism against which the Great Reformer of nineteen hundred years ago launched his most bitter invective; and wherever that is found, the prospect of effective assistance is not encouraging.[14]

Yet it was Jesus who warned: "And fear not them which kill the body, but are not able to kill the soul: but rather fear him which is able to destroy both soul and body in hell" (Matt. 10:28). This is formalism with a vengeance: God's vengeance.

The Decline of Economic Sanctions

Douglas attacked modern taxation. He regarded the modern State as a robber. This, despite the fact that the technical heart of his proposal for reform was the permanent transfer of con-

14. *Ibid.*, pp. 200-1.

trol over capital to the State: the pool of capital from which all future dividends would be paid on an equal per capita basis. With respect to modern taxation, he predicted that modern economic theory was about to go through a transformation: the disappearance of any theory of rewards and punishments.

> In passing it may be noted how the power of taxation has grown into a form of oppression beside which the modest efforts of the robber barons of the Middle Ages must appear crude. While the system is fundamentally based upon a theory of rewards and punishments, modern financial methods, in conjunction with the taxation system, would appear to suggest that the acquisition of the reward is proper ground for the imposition of punishment in the form of taxation which will distribute the reward amongst those who have not worked for it. I have very little doubt that in this we are witnessing not merely the decay of the financial system, but of the whole theory of rewards and punishments as applied to economics.[15]

That final sentence is crucial. From Adam Smith to the present, economists who have defended the free market system have focused on the power of the consumer to reward some producers by buying from them, and to punish other producers by not buying from them. A theory of sanctions is central to all economic theory, just as it is central to all social theory.[16] It is worth noting that Douglas did not say that rewards and punishments would disappear only if his proposed reform were enacted. He said that sanctions were disappearing from all forms of economic theory. What evidence he had for this statement remained his secret. I am aware of no economist who has not suggested a system of rewards and punishments. Scarcity in a fallen world itself is a sanction. To escape its cursed effects, men require a system of economic sanctions: positive and negative.

---

15. *The Monopoly of Credit*, p. 72.
16. See Gary North, *Sanctions and Social Theory*, forthcoming.

Douglas vs. Negative Economic Sanctions

Major Douglas offered a theory of economic productivity unique in modern history. He argued that the fear of poverty is the cause of poverty. That is to say, he argued that people who are not fearful are more efficient. I suppose we might ask: All of the time? In every case? He thought so: all of the time, in every case. (Notice his phrase, "tend automatically.")

> I have no hesitation whatever in saying that the most important work, the hardest work, and the most work per man in the world is done by men who have no fear whatever of poverty and no human likelihood of ever being poor. Conversely, these sections of society which are constantly faced with the fear of poverty tend automatically to become incapable of anything but the lowest grade of work, and ultimately do even this work less efficiently than better-paid and socially better-placed individuals. Whatever function it may have fulfilled in the past, it is my personal opinion that fear of any kind is the most destructive and generally undesirable motive which can be imported into any human action, and that no greater service can be made to mankind that its elimination.[17]

He wanted to eliminate the fear of economic failure. But if there is no fear of economic failure on the part of producers, how can consumers impose their will on producers? Only politically. The credit masters will impose fear and trembling on producers, not consumers. The credit masters will impose this fear politically. All registered companies – the only ones with access to the government's below-cost credit – will be guaranteed an average rate of profit for five years. "Undertakings unable to show a profit after five years' operation to be struck off the register."[18] That is, these firms will be cast out into the outer darkness of competition without government subsidies.

---

17. *Warning Democracy*, p. 29.
18. *Social Credit*, p. 209.

Yet even in this case, there will still be economic sanctions. The political threat is economic: the removal of government subsidies to the company. The trigger is also economic: the failure of a company to make a profit after five years. Douglas could not show that in the early stages of Social Credit economic sanctions would be removed. They would still be used to direct production. This was comparable to the *Communist Manifesto*'s ten points of socialism: they only provided a means into the millennium of full communism. The date of the post-revolution society's transition to full communism was left indeterminate by Marx. The same is true for Social Credit.

The Coming Millennium

Douglas predicted a new millennium of wealth under Social Credit. As with most millennia, its arrival is conditional on our obeying the Prophet. Yet this transition will be easy to achieve, he said. All it will take is the abolition of private banking. Just transfer the banking function to an elite group of government credit masters, and a new age of prosperity becomes not only possible but probable – "easy," he said. First comes the expropriation of the expropriators, the exploitation of the exploiters, the bankers.

> It seems difficult to doubt that the efforts of those in control of financial policy are primarily, if not entirely, concerned with making the world safe for bankers, rather than making the world safe. By one of those curious ironies which seem to be present in great crisis, it happens, as one might say by a sidewind, that the world cannot be made safe without removing the banker, painlessly or otherwise, from the commanding position which he now occupies.[19]

But once the banker is separated from his money – meaning,

19. *Monopoly of Credit*, pp. 83-84.

once you and I will no longer have the legal right to deposit our money in a bank – then will come the millennium!

> If we are to emerge from this period into the millennium which is easily possible, although by no means certain, the re-organisation necessary must be based on a philosophy which, whatever other elements it may contain, will certainly not enthrone the productive and industrial systems in the preponderantly important position which they have occupied for the past 100 years.[20]

Who Brings Sanctions Against the Credit Masters?

In a free market, the saver has the legal right to determine where his savings will go. Not so under Social Credit. The free market gives the saver the right to withdraw his savings from the bank, or sell his shares of ownership, or sell his real estate. Not so under Social Credit.

Douglas understood that there must be a hierarchy in society: rulers and ruled. He also understood that for rulers to control the ruled, there must be appropriate sanctions. What he failed to understand is that under capitalism, the consumers are the rulers, while the producers are the ruled. He did not understand the dual sanctions of profit and loss. Most socialists regard the producers as the masters. Douglas differed from them only in regarding the bankers as the masters.

There must be hierarchies in every society. There must also be sanctions. But, he insisted, economic sanctions – rewards and punishments – are fading from the modern economy, except for the final sanction: the smash-up. With respect to the coming economic breakdown – his version of final judgment – Douglas said, in effect, the quicker the better. "Whatever may be the case in other matters, compromise in arithmetic seems singularly out of place, and it is much better that the present defective system should be allowed to discredit its upholders, and so

---

20. *Ibid.*, pp. 84-85.

render genuine reconstruction possible, than that an alternative, of which the effects are not sufficiently beneficial as to place it at once in an impregnable position, should be substituted for it."[21]

Then what kind of hierarchy should there be? Douglas answered: a political hierarchy. The public will set policy; the elite credit masters will execute this policy. Thus will the economy move from economic sanctions, which Douglas despised, to political sanctions, which he affirmed.

> We do not acquire, by these suggested methods, control by the public, as such, of the processes of production – the "how" it shall be done. That is not the business of the public, as such, but of experts. But by controlling *both* credit-issue and price-making the public acquires control of policy with all its attributes – the effective appointment and removal of personnel, amongst others. *The essential nature of a satisfactory modern co-operative State may be broadly expressed as consisting of a functionally aristocratic hierarchy of producers accredited by, and serving, a democracy of consumers.* The business of producers is to produce; to take orders, not to give them; and the business of the public, as consumers, is not only to give orders, but to see that they are obeyed as to results, and to remove unsuitable or wilfully recalcitrant persons from the aristocracy of production to the democracy of consumption.[22]

Hierarchy is an inescapable concept.[23] Sanctions are inescapable concepts.[24] The questions are: Which hierarchy? Which sanctions? In the case of Social Credit, how will this "aristocratic hierarchy" of producers be controlled by the "democracy of consumers"? How will the latter be able to bring sanctions against the former? Through politics. Thus it must

---

21. *Monopoly of Credit*, p. 88.

22. *Credit-Power and Democracy*, pp. 94-95.

23. Ray R. Sutton, *That You May Prosper: Dominion By Covenant* (2nd ed.; Tyler, Texas: Institute for Christian Economics, 1992), ch. 2.

24. *Ibid.*, ch. 4.

always be: when reformers remove from consumers the sanction of profit and loss, the State steps into the vacuum.

Douglas had a doctrine of final sanctions. Prophets generally do. He warned that the day of judgment is coming! The final conflict fast approaches. "No peace will ever settle on the distracted earth until this matter has been fought to a finish, and it rests with the intelligence of those who are from time to time in a position to guide popular movements, whether a mere remnant of civilisation will achieve the Golden Age awaiting the settlement, or whether a decisive verdict is close at hand."[25]

What was the motivation of Major Douglas? His hatred of the banking system. But there was something else: *his hatred of biblical morality, especially the Old Testament law*. Now we are beginning to get close to the heart of the matter. It was all too easy for Douglas to move from these two hatreds to a more familiar hate: the Jews.

Anti-Semitism

Major Douglas was an anti-semite who wanted to remove what he regarded as Jewish control over England, which, he insisted, Jews maintained through their control of banking. Let us begin with his rejection of any connection between morality and prosperity. He called such an outlook "semitic."

> A conception which is closely connected with the theory of rewards and punishments, is that of "Value." In effect, value may be defined, to fit the orthodox conception of it, as that quality which gives to anything maximum exchangeability under present conditions. Rewards and Punishments, Justice, i.e. the assessments of desserts, and "Value," i.e. the basis on which desserts are assessed, may be said to be the corner stones of the Semitic structure of society.[26]

---

25. *Credit-Power and Democracy*, p. 95.

26. *Social Credit*, p. 44.

Douglas hated private banking. He believed in an international bankers' conspiracy: ". . . I have come to the conclusion that we are witnessing a gigantic attempt, directed from sources which have no geographical nationality, to dispossess a defective democracy, and to substitute a dictatorship of Finance for it."[27] He implied that the major bankers are almost always Jews: "Rothschilds, Sterns, Schiffs, and others."[28] He called them "sons of Levi." These sons of Levi have adopted a policy of "divide and conquer," which consists in "attacking one section of the public after another." This policy can be thwarted only by a true statesman.

> So long as this condition of affairs remains...so long indeed as the financial system remains unmodified...statesmanship would thus appear to consist in attacking one section of the public after another, and steadily reducing the power of resistance of each while consolidating the position of the financial hierarchy. There can be no remedy for this state of affairs, so fatal to morale, until a statesman is in power who is prepared to face squarely the issue that either finance will rule the world and the statesmen will become a species of bank clerk; or, on the other hand, a halt will be called to the aggression of the financier, sanctioned and assisted by the law, upon each section of society in turn, and he will be reminded of the warning given many hundreds of years ago: "Ye take too much upon yourselves, ye sons of Levi." (ellipses in original)[29]

This raises what Douglas called "the Jewish question." Here is what he had to say about this matter:

> No consideration of this subject would be complete without recognizing the bearing upon it of what is known as the Jewish Question; a question rendered doubly difficult by the conspiracy

27. *Warning Democracy*, p. 62.
28. *Ibid.*, p. 120.
29. *Ibid.*, pp. 154-55.

> of silence which surrounds it. At the moment it can only be pointed out that the theory of rewards and punishments is Mosaic in origin; that finance and law derive their main inspiration from the same source, and that countries such as pre-war Germany and post-war Russia, which exhibit the logical consequences of unchecked collectivism, have done so under the direct influence of Jewish leaders. Of the Jews themselves, it may be said that they exhibit the race-consciousness idea to an extent unapproached elsewhere, and it is fair to say that their success in many walks of life is primarily due to their adaptation to an environment which has been moulded in conformity with their own ideal.[30]

He even went so far as to rely on the notoriously anti-semitic "Protocols of the Learned Elders of Zion" in his attempt to persuade his readers of the centrality of finance and the evils thereof. The Protocols were in fact a forgery produced by the Czar's secret police in the late 1890's.[31] He dismissed as irrelevant the criticism that the document was a fake: "The authenticity of this document is a matter of little importance. . . ." He called it "a remarkable document . . . a Machiavellian scheme for the enslavement of the world. . . ."

> It was explained in that treatise that the financial system was the agency most suitable for such a purpose; the inculcation of a false democracy was recommended; vindictive penalties for infringements of laws were advised; . . .[32]

And so on. Then came a reference to racial character: ". . . the Anglo-Saxon character probably remains the greatest bulwark against tyranny that exists in the world to-day."[33] The proper

30. *Social Credit*, p. 29.

31. Norman Cohn, *Warrant for Genocide* (New York: Harper & Row, 1967), p. 103.

32. *Social Credit*, p. 146.

33. *Ibid.*, p. 147.

strategy of these non-Anglo-Saxons would be to "concentrate on such methods as would paralyse the Anglo-Saxon."[34]

Douglas understood that ideas are important in a civilization. As a result, he offered this explanation of socialist ideas in his day: the Jews invented them and now promote them.

> . . . we have a good many more Jews in important positions in this country than we deserve. And not only in this country, but in every country, certain ideas which are the gravest possible menace to humanity – ideas which can be traced through the propaganda of Collectivism to the idea of the Supreme, impersonal State, to which every individual must bow – seem to derive a good deal of their most active, intelligent support from Jewish sources, while at the same time a grim struggle is proceeding in the great international financial groups, many of which are purely Jewish, for the acquisition of key positions from which to control the World-State when formed.[35]

Unlike many anti-semites, Douglas seems not to have devised his system as a way to "get even" with Jews as such. He seems honestly to have come to his anti-semitic conclusions by way of his hostility to private banking and his hostility to Mosaic law. But this does not change the fact that he blamed Jewish bankers for the ills of the nation and the world.

Conclusion

Major Douglas hated the existence of moral cause and effect in economic matters. He hated economic sanctions, and he predicted their demise, whether under capitalism or Social Credit. He also hated thrift, since it was in the hands of private individuals rather than the State's credit masters.

I think this hostility to the free market and his acceptance of

34. *Ibid.*, p. 148.

35. *Control and Distribution of Production* (2nd ed.; London: Stanley Nott, 1934), pp. 106-7.

the State was part of his overall hostility to the Bible and his acceptance of Darwinism. He regarded Social Credit as an evolutionary step toward an earthly millennium. This millennium would be brought in, not by religious revival, not by moral reform, but by a simple transfer of the control over credit from private bankers to the State. A new elite of capital managers would be reliable. They would bring in a world without fear, a world without negative economic sanctions.

Then what negative sanctions will the public be able to bring against failed credit masters? The voters – or their representatives – will "remove unsuitable or wilfully recalcitrant persons from the aristocracy of production to the democracy of consumption." In short, we are back to politics, i.e., back to an economy run by an elite bureaucracy.

What else could we expect from a Darwinian socialist? This is where all Darwinian socialist systems end: with politics and political sanctions.[36] They promise economic abundance, but they deliver only political battles and bureaucracies that blame others for their failure.

Summary

1. Douglas denied the permanency of economic sanctions.
2. He affirmed the inevitability of political sanctions.
3. He rejected ethics as the basis of his critique of capitalism.
4. Nevertheless, he had a theology and a system of ethics.
5. His theology was Darwinism.
6. He rejected the idea that under Social Credit, a man's labor will remain important in the income he receives.
7. He rejected the biblical idea that there is close correspondence between righteousness and prosperity.
8. He predicted the decline in importance of economic sanc-

36. Gary North, *The Dominion Covenant: Genesis* (2nd ed.; Tyler, Texas: Institute for Christian Economics, 1987), Appendix A: "From Cosmic Purposelessness to Humanistic Sovereignty."

tions.

9. Douglas opposed the idea that the fear of poverty spurs men on to greater productivity.
10. He called such an idea "Puritan."
11. He predicted a coming millennium of wealth, a new golden age.
12. He moved negative sanctions from consumers to voters.
13. He replaced economics with politics.
14. He predicted a kind of final judgment: the breakdown of capitalism.
15. This day of judgment will surely come.
16. His hatred of banking was linked to his hatred of biblical law.
17. This two-fold hatred produced an open anti-semitism.

CONCLUSION

> Unselfish aspirations, good intentions, beautiful phrases – none of these by themselves will affect the issue by so much as one hair's breadth.
>
> C. H. Douglas (1920)[1]

> . . . a bad system is still a bad system no matter what changes are made in personnel.
>
> C. H. Douglas (1921)[2]

I agree entirely with Major Douglas on these two points. First, good intentions are not sufficient to save a bad system from producing bad results. Second, the issue is not the moral character or the efficiency of the personnel running the system. The issue is the moral character of the system. By this I mean both its moral character and its efficiency. The reason why I reject Social Credit is because Major Douglas' good intentions could not overcome the really bad system he recommended as a substitute for free market capitalism.

The overall moral issue of political economy in its broadest sense is the economy's conformity to God's law. Most economists do not believe this. Neither do most political reformers. The secondary issue of political economy is the system's built-in

1. *Credit-Power and Democracy* (London: Cecil Palmer, 1920), p. 85.
2. *Economic Democracy* (2nd ed.; London: Cecil Palmer, 1921), p. 40.

limitations on power. Are there built-in safeguards in the economy that will restrain the accumulation of power in the hands of an elite?

The Premise of Inflationism

Social Credit is one more scheme in a long list of fiat money inflation schemes which stretch back to the Israelites of Isaiah's day: "Thy silver has become dross" (Isaiah 1:22a). Each of these schemes is promoted by defenders as unique, but all of them indulge in the same group of errors: "The State is capable of fine-tuning the economy with fiat money. The State can balance supply and demand. Without the State as the balancing agent, the free market inevitably falls into chronic unemployment." From John Law's inflationary scheme of the 1720's in France to the modern Keynesian's prescriptions, the argument is the same: "Without the State to direct fiat money into its most productive avenues, capitalism will fail. Free market capitalism provides insufficient money to assure effective consumer demand." So we are told.

Each of these schemes argues that there is some way for bureaucrats to assess the productive capacity of men, the economic desires of men, and the motivations of men to produce. In other words, State planners can somehow estimate accurately both the potential supply of a society's producers and the demand of consumers, and then create a system of appropriate sanctions to bring supply and demand into balance. No one argues that this can be done moment by moment, yet to match the free market's system of supply and demand – freely fluctuating prices – it *must* be done moment by moment.

The free market provides an institutional and legal arrangement that offers moment-by-moment opportunities to buy and sell, to "truck and barter," as Adam Smith put it. The free market provides economic order. Those who claim that the free market has failed in some fundamental way to deliver the goods to consumers who are willing and able to buy must show how their recommended reform will improve on what the market already accomplishes. The inflationists claim that a scientifically organized injection of fiat money will accomplish this.

The problem is, there is no formula that provides the money manipulators with a reliable, "scientific" guide. There is no formula to get inside the minds of men, to reveal their innate capacities and their range of desires. There is no way to collect national price data that will reveal the true state of the "real" economy – Douglas' Real Credit, for example – but will not be affected by the subsequent issuing of fiat money. There is no way for politicians or bureaucrats to estimate scientifically the degree to which the new money is inflationary. There is no way for the money manipulators to be sure who wins and who loses from each injection of fiat money, each at a specific point and time in the economy. The economic effects depend entirely on people's present conditions and their expectations about the economic future. No one knows what these conditions and expectations are today or will be tomorrow.

Social Credit Is Not Unique

Social Credit is not a unique reform proposal. It is one among many: Proudhonism, "free silver," greenbackism (in the late nineteenth-century United States), Lawsonomy, Gesellism, Keynesianism, and many others. They all promote the same economic premise: "The voluntary exchanges of free men under a system of predictable civil law are not sufficient to bring forth the immense natural abundance of nature and society."

Major Douglas argued that inherent in every economy is this built-in tendency for centralization of authority over production and distribution. The only question for society to settle is this one: Which elite group should exercise this power, private, profit-seeking bankers or State-appointed scientific credit masters?

A free market economist rejects this assessment. The consumers have final earthly sovereignty over distribution, and therefore consumers possess final earthly sovereignty over production. *Producers act as the economic agents of consumers under capitalism.* Producers have no choice in the matter. If consumers fail to buy the products of a particular producer or a particular industry – for example, the proverbial buggy whip industry – then producers will sustain losses. Producers do not set final prices; they set on provisional asking prices. They ask consumers to buy their products at these prices. Consumers have the legal authority to say no. Therefore, consumers ratify or reject the prices set by producers. Consumers are sovereign.

Why the Money Supply Expands or Contracts

The free market's process of the production and distribution of money is the inherent weak link of capitalism, Douglas and all other underconsumptionists have maintained. Douglas taught the following. First, banks create credit and supply producers with this credit. Second, when these loans are repaid, this shrinks the money supply. Third, consumers do not have sufficient money to buy the total output of consumer goods. Fourth, there is an inherent downward tendency of both prices and profits under capitalism. What is needed, Douglas taught, is some means to increase the nation's money supply until the consumers make their purchases. As Louis Spadaro pointed out in 1955, this is a variant of an old error in economics, the "real bills" doctrine. Economists have repeatedly called for an "elastic currency" that grows or shrinks with the "real" economy.

Businesses do need money when they begin production. Let us consider what happens if there is no central bank. Commercial banks create new money through the fractional reserve process. Consider the system if it operates in terms of a ten percent reserve requirement. A depositor deposits a hundred monetary units in cash. The bank puts ten units aside as a reserve, and then lends out 90 units. The borrower spends these 90 units to buy something. The recipient takes the 90 units and deposits them in his bank. His bank sets aside nine units and lends out 81 units. On and on the process goes until the banking *system* has created 900 units in fiat money based on the original hundred units deposited.

If all these loans are paid off and no new loans are made, the money supply shrinks back to the original 100 units in cash. This is Douglas' version of the underconsumption thesis. The problem is, the money supply does not shrink back to the original deposit under fractional reserve banking unless all of the banks' depositors demand payment in cash and then refuse to redeposit this cash in another bank. Unless this bank run happens, when one loan is repaid, another loan will be made. Banks make money lending money, after all.

Under a central bank, the system is somewhat different. The counterfeiting process never begins with cash. It begins with an issue of fiat credit. When a nation's central bank buys government bonds, it creates money and gives it to the government's Treasury. The Treasury then spends this newly created money. The money goes into circulation. If the nation's central bank later sells these government debt certificates into the market, and does not purchase new assets to offset the sale, then the original expansion of fiat money that took place when the central bank created it to buy the debt is now reversed. The nation's money supply contracts. Commercial banks make fewer new loans. They have no choice; the assets in the central bank's portfolio is no longer there to support the creation of new money, meaning new commercial bank loans. This contraction of the money supply is not initiated by business lenders who pay off their loans. It is initiated by the central bank that sold some of the government's IOU's that had formerly been in its portfolio.

The Crucial Constraint: Money or Scarcity?

It was basic to Douglas' system that a break in the flow of money to consumers is the restraining factor in capitalism, not technical factors of production. Capitalism "does not provide enough purchasing power to buy the goods which are produced."[3] Again, "the amount of money available as purchasing power is insufficient to buy the goods available for sale at the prices at which they were made."[4]

To use an analogy which he did not offer, the economy is like a gigantic engine of production that does not have enough lubrication to run it at full speed. The missing lubricant, he believed, is money at the disposal of consumers. Producers can obtain credit from banks, but consumers cannot. (It is strange that never in his books did Douglas discuss consumer credit in relation to his theory of capitalism's inevitable tendency to underconsumption.) His reform proposed dual injections of new money: the Just Price (production) and the National Dividend (consumption).

"Ticket, Please!"

He argued that a unit of money is the same as a ticket. There is a shortage of tickets at the end of the structure of production. Consumers cannot buy all the goods and services that have been produced by capitalism. Prices fall or inventories remain unsold. Most producers then suffer losses. They reduce present production. They cut back. This restrains the inherent productivity of modern technology.

What was wrong with this analysis? His failure to understand that paper money is not a ticket that enables the holder to buy someone else's production. It is rather a receipt for goods in storage. In a free market monetary system, paper money is a legal claim on the person who issued the receipt. The holder of the receipt has a "ticket" to a fixed quantity of a specified commodity. Thus, as a potential buyer of goods, he does indeed hold a legal claim, but not on the *seller's* goods; his legal claim is on the *receipt issuer's* goods – usually gold or silver. The po-

3. *Warning Democracy* (2nd ed.; London: Stanley Nott, 1934), p. 41.
4. *Ibid.*, p. 88.

tential goods buyer's "ticket" is redeemable on demand. This is what gives paper money its value in the eyes of sellers of goods and services. How much value? That is for competitive bargaining to determine. The "ticket" will not be worth more than the value of asset for which it is a legal claim.

Douglas and other underconsumptionists– Gertrude Coogan comes to mind[5] – regarded money as an *economic claim* of the buyer of goods and services (a seller of money) on the seller of goods and services (a buyer of money). On the contrary, paper money the free market is a *legal claim* on the issuer of money. He issued paper money or a check that is redeemable in gold or silver or whatever. The potential buyer holds a legal claim to a specific quantity of a commodity. When he buys something, he transfers the ownership of this legal claim to the seller of goods or services. The reason why the "ticket" functions as money is because the ticket is redeemable on demand for the commodity promised on the warehouse receipt-ticket.

In a pure fiat money standard economy, paper money is at least legal for paying taxes to the nation that issued it. Thus, it has value at least as a method of tax payment. Fiat money is not a legal claim on anything unless the issuing government has declared cash as legal tender for all debts within that government's jurisdiction. In this case, an offer to sell at a price in "dollars" is a declared by civil law to be a promise of the seller to accept the government's fiat money from the buyer: cash. Politicians adopt legal tender laws in order to force sellers to accept the government's fiat money.

Scarcity

The number of goods and services offered for sale is not constrained by the money supply. Rather, it is constrained by scarcity. Buyers use money to make their competitive bids

5. Gertrude Coogan, *Money Creators* (Hawthorne, California: Omni, [1935] 1963).

against each other. Sellers use money to calculate profits or losses. But changes in the size of the money supply are relevant only when these changes have not been predicted by the participants. This is the advantage of monetary systems based on precious metals: it is easier to predict the size of the money supply. Mining is expensive. The amount of new metals coming into the economy through mining is always very small compared to the quantity of those metals already in the reserves of individuals, businesses, governments, and banks. Thus, a metallic money standard makes the growth of the money supply far more predictable. It is a lot more expensive to mine gold than to print pieces of paper with officials' pictures on them.

The Rate of Interest

Interest is not a product of any specific monetary system. It is not the product of any specific system of borrowing and lending. Interest is an inherent aspect of human action. The present value of present goods is greater than the present value of those same goods in the future. That is to say, everyone applies a *discount* to future goods. This is why a new Rolls-Royce is worth more to me today than exactly the same Rolls-Royce delivered a year from now is worth to me today. (I am assuming here that there is no new Rolls-Royce model offered for sale in the interim, and also that very rich people's tastes in automobiles do not change.) If anyone offers me a gift of a new Rolls-Royce, delivered either today or a year from now, I will have it delivered today.

This is why there is a rate of interest. It is not because bankers are greedy. It is not because of a shortage of money. It is because every acting person applies a *discount* to the value of future goods as compared with the value of identical present goods.

This means that the government cannot *permanently* lower the rate of interest by creating money. Because people can be deceived, the government or the banking system can lower short-term rates *temporarily* because those who use money do not recognize that the newly created money does not in fact represent additional new supplies of gold or silver or other valuable commodity. When the fractional reserve banking system creates new money by lending fiat money either to producers or to consumers (rarely considered by Douglas), this money has not been made available by depositors. No depositor has voluntarily delayed consuming some scarce economic resource today in order to deposit money in the bank so that the bank can lend money to someone else for a period of time. Therefore, the banking system's injection of fiat credit money is inflationary. This is the fault of the government: it allows fractional reserve banking. It wants cheap loans for its own purposes, so it legalizes private counterfeiting: fractional reserve banking.

Any artificial lowering of interest rates by means of an the issue of fiat money, either by the government or the banking system, will be followed by a rise in rates during the resulting inflationary boom period and the credit crunch (preliminary to a recession) that follows.[6] Fiat money creates the boom, but the result is either a recession when the increase of money ceases, or mass inflation and an inflationary collapse if the government, with or without a central bank acting as its agent, continues to spend new fiat money into circulation.

Estimating the Value of the Nation's Capital

The credit masters will control the money supply under social credit. As we saw in his blueprint for Scotland, the credit masters will first take an inventory of all the goods and services in the economy, including the estimated value of everyone's work in the future. This inventory will be expressed in monetary terms. Then they will assign an arbitrary percentage to this total value of national capital. Based on this percentage, the

---

6. Ludwig von Mises, *Human Action: A Treatise on Economics* (New Haven, Connecticut: Yale University Press, 1949), ch. 20.

credit masters will issue fiat money every month to all citizens except wealthy ones. This is the **National Dividend.**

The credit masters will also provide all business loans. These loans will go only to government-registered companies. These loans will be interest-free. Meanwhile, private banks will have to charge at least 25 percent. This will pressure private companies to register with the government to get access to the cheap, interest-free government credit, i.e., *social* credit. Most businesses will register with the government. They will be given the money they need to begin production and complete it. Prices and wages will be regulated by the credit masters. So will profits. This is the **Just Price.**

What will the National Dividend and the Just Price do to market prices? They will raise them. If the government sets price control ceilings, this will create shortages. It will lead to black markets for the price-controlled goods.[7]

Furthermore, as the money value of consumer goods rises, so will the money value of capital goods. This will increase the national capital base. This will require further issues of National Dividend fiat money, which will raise prices again, which will increase the monetary value of the nation's capital, and so forth. An inflationary spiral is inevitable unless the credit masters decide not to take any more inventories of the nation's capital. But then how will technological progress be capable of adding to the value of capital and therefore also increase size of the National Dividend? Douglas never even raised this question. Neither have the other credit reform inflationists.

The system was offered as scientific. It is not scientific; it is merely inflationist. An illusion of science is conveyed by the very incoherence of Major Douglas' language. Most people do not expect to be able to understand scientists.

---

7. *Prices and Price Controls* (Irvington, New York: Foundation for Economic Education, 1992).

Incoherence

I have argued that you should not commit yourself to any political reformer whose reform cannot be put into simple, straightforward language. Any political reform that is not clear would be dangerous if implemented. Those doing the implementing could then claim almost anything in the name of the reform. You must demand clarity from every economic reformer. *Do not trust his reform if he cannot express himself clearly.* With this in mind, consider Major Douglas' description of his theory:

> The fundamental idea which it is necessary to grasp is that you cannot get existing and future credit-power into the hands of the community, unless the distribution of purchasing-power, both in respect of capital increases, as well as in respect of ultimate products, is only taken back from the community in the proportion that consumption bears, not only to these products, but to capital production as well, using capital in just as wide a sense as the credit-issuer uses it.
>
> The result of this is that as a condition of such a state of affairs, prices of ultimate commodities would have to be fixed, not with regard to what they would fetch, but with regard to the above ratio, which would result in a price which would be a fraction of cost; the difference being made up to the entrepreneur by an issue based on the actual capital still remaining as a result of effort represented by total "cost."[8]

You do not understand this, do you? This is not because you are stupid. Do not blame yourself. Major Douglas was confused.

One of the reasons why Social Credit has attracted such religiously and philosophically diverse supporters (but not economists) is that the confusion of his presentation allows people to imagine that somehow or other, "Douglas believed what I believe." Some advocate of Social Credit may say that it is truly conservative. Others say Sócial credit is "truly, deep

---

8. *Credit-Power and Democracy*, pp. 46-47.

down inside" socialist, Fascist, capitalist, or Christian. Social Credit has attracted conservatives (T. S. Eliot), socialists (G. D. H. Cole), Fascists (Ezra Pound), capitalists, and evangelical Christians (the Social Credit League of Alberta in the late 1930's)[9]. Even Hewlett Johnson, the apologist for Josef Stalin, never lost his admiration for Social Credit. All have been equally enthusiastic; all have claimed Social Credit as the economic system most conformable to their beliefs. This should serve as a warning that something is seriously wrong with Social Credit.

The Appeal of Millennial Rhetoric

I think Professor Macpherson has accurately identified the appeal of Social Credit: its break with the Establishment world and its promise of a utopian, millennial world to come after the Great Reform. The details of Social Credit have not interested most of his followers. What has mattered has been Major Douglas' hostility to the present economic order and his assurance of his technical reform's ability to deliver a prosperous world without poverty. It is the promise of the return of the Golden Age, the restoration of Eden, where men shall live in comfort in history apart from the sweat of their brows. It is the millennialist element in Douglas' writings, as well as his identification of a Hidden Hand – an international bankers' conspiracy (mostly Jewish) – that has gained him the utter devotion of his followers. This is why evangelical Christian farmers in Canada during the worst of the Great Depression could embrace the rhetoric (though not the actual program) of a reform scheme promoted by a man who proclaimed pragmatism as his foundation and Darwinism as his worldview. Macpherson is on target:

> Social credit's remarkable similarities with evangelical religious doctrine, which so many Albertans found the most satisfy-

9. C. B. Macpherson, *Democracy in Alberta: Social Credit and the Party System* (2nd ed.; Toronto: University of Toronto Press, 1962), chaps. 4, 6.

> ing, recommended it still further. Combining in itself a root-and-branch denunciation of the world as it was with a magical promise of a new secular life for all who were suffering, social credit had a peculiar affinity to the fundamentalist and prophetic religious gospel of which Aberhart was a vigorous preacher. An evangelist whose mind ran powerfully to prophetic interpretation of the Bible could take the fullest advantage of the social credit doctrine, unhampered by those analytical misgivings which prevented its whole-hearted reception by the more rationalist U.F.A.[10] leaders. There were, indeed, things in Douglas's doctrine that Aberhart could scarcely have comprehended and could certainly not have agreed with. Aberhart's puritanism was too strong to allow him to accept Douglas's denigration of work and praise of abundance not earned in the sweat of the brow; it is doubtful if Aberhart ever grasped Douglas's denunciatory concept of the "work fetish." But he found no difficulty in merging the positive side of the Douglas doctrine with his own prophetic gospel.[11]

In this regard, Aberhart has not been alone. Major Douglas' modern fundamentalist disciples have followed Aberhart's lead: recruit supporters with the rhetoric of social salvation and the promise of thwarting a hidden conspiracy, but defer indefinitely the task of spelling out in detail exactly how society can get from here to there.

Conclusion

Major Douglas was a self-proclaimed pragmatist, a Darwinian, and a man who opposed the biblical idea of economic sanctions in history. He rejected as "semitic" any suggestion that there is a cause-and-effect relationship between "Puritanism" – the morality of the Old Testament – and economic pros-

10. United Farmers of Alberta.
11. Macpherson, *Democracy in Alberta*, p. 145.

perity. On this philosophical foundation, he constructed Social Credit.

His reform program rested on a fallacious economic analysis. He argued that there is a break in the flow of funds under modern capitalism, though not under capitalism prior to the era of the joint-stock, limited liability corporation (late nineteenth century). This break comes in either of two ways. *First,* bank credit – fiat or fiduciary money – which had been extended to producers is extinguished when the loans are repaid, that is, before consumers gain access to the money. Thus, consumers have insufficient purchasing power to buy all of the output of capitalist firms. *Second*, payments by factories to their employees (people) and their suppliers ("organizations") also suffer a breakdown: the suppliers do not spend all of the money they receive. Why, we are not told. This is Douglas' A + B Theorem.[12] These two arguments are completely separate analytically. They have nothing to do with each other. Also, both are incorrect. There is no permanent break in the flow of funds under capitalism.

The alleged break in the flow of funds is said to doom capitalism to shrinking productivity. This raises hope regarding Social Credit's promised reform. By creating fiat money, the State's credit masters can restore the flow of funds in two ways: (1) interest-free credit to State-registered producers to buy materials below cost; (2) automatic monthly dividends to consumers. This creation of fiat money will close finance capitalism's gap between the money spent by producers to bring goods to the market and the lack of purchasing power in the hands of consumers.

The analytical problem with Douglas' analysis is simple to state: *money never leaves the hands of potential consumers*. Money is always in someone's possession. There is no break in the flow of funds except in those rare occasions when people physically

12. See Appendix A, below.

lose cash. Flexible pricing is capitalism's way to clear the market of goods and services. Except when fractional reserve banking and government issues of fiat money lead to a boom which then collapses into recession, the free market supplies all the money necessary for consumers to buy whatever is offered. This or that producer may suffer losses, while others make profits, but there is no break in the flow of funds. There can be temporary breaks in trade when governments enact restraints on trade – tariffs, quotas, price controls – but then people will then spend their money on something else, although not the things which they would have purchased apart from interference by the politicians.

Major Douglas offered a solution to a non-existent problem: the supposed break in the flow of funds. The solution Major Douglas offered was fiat money. This is the perennial solution offered by economic cranks of all persuasions, from the economics departments of the world's most prestigious universities to the smeared-ink newsletters of the most hate-filled anti-Semite. We have seen it all before. It is the monetary reform program of the morally debased: "Thy silver is become dross" (Isaiah 1:22a). God promises to reform any society that has gone through a fiat money reform:

> Therefore saith the Lord, the LORD of hosts, the mighty One of Israel, Ah, I will ease me of mine adversaries, and avenge me of mine enemies: And I will turn my hand upon thee, and purely purge away thy dross, and take away all thy tin: And I will restore thy judges as at the first, and thy counsellors as at the beginning: afterward thou shalt be called, The city of righteousness, the faithful city. Zion shall be redeemed with judgment, and her converts with righteousness. And the destruction of the transgressors and of the sinners shall be together, and they that forsake the LORD shall be consumed (Isaiah 1:24-28).

A word to the wise is sufficient. But because not everyone is wise, I wrote a whole book.

APPENDIX A

MAJOR DOUGLAS' A + B THEOREM

From this disparity between purchasing power and goods available arises almost every material economic ill from which the world suffers to-day, including in that category the imminent risk of devastating wars.

C. H. Douglas (1934)[1]

From whence come wars and fightings among you? come they not hence, even of your lusts that war in your members? (James 4:1).

The cause of man's predicament is sin. What is sin? It is knowing what to do morally but then failing to do it. "Therefore to him that knoweth to do good, and doeth it not, to him it is sin" (James 4:17). So, we can speak of a single cause of our problems, but it is a very broad cause. It is not some technical omission. Tinkering with the economy will not save it or mankind. Neither will a single "revolutionary" transformation. But some men still want to tinker, while others call for revolution. What is needed is regeneration.

---

1. *Warning Democracy* (2nd ed.; London: Stanley Nott, 1934), p. 103.

It is typical of cults and fringe groups that they identify one error as *the* cause of all our problems. This one mistake, or this one evil, is seen as central to all of man's crises. If we could just change our minds or change our ways in this one area, the cult member assures us, everything good and wonderful could be achieved. The greatest evils in life could be overcome. This is what I call *the magic pill solution*. Like the magic pill that allows fat people to eat everything they want and still lose weight in all the right places, so is the mentality of the single-cause cultist.

Race is one of these commonly identified single problems. The single solution is said to be laws against race mixing. In economics, the Henry Georgist movement identifies inappropriate taxation as the single problem. The recommended solution is the single tax: a tax on land values that will replace all other forms of taxation. Far more common in fringe-like economic groups, however, is the belief that the money problem, usually coupled with the banking problem, is the number-one cause of all economic backwardness and poverty.[2] If society would simply adopt the group's recommended solution – its magic pill of fiat money – then there would be wealth for all.

Major Douglas was a cultist as I have defined it here. He identified a single flaw in capitalism, as we have seen: "From this disparity between purchasing power and goods available arises almost every material economic ill from which the world suffers to-day, including in that category the imminent risk of devastating wars."[3] His single solution was the creation of government credit masters who would control a nation's credit by granting State-subsidized loans to producers.

Single Cause, Single Formula

Major Douglas offered a single-cause theory of man's ills – the classic mark of a utopian social reformer. To match his

2. See Appendix C, below.

3. *Warning Democracy*, p. 103.

single-cause theory, he offered a single formula. This formula was not a formula to guide the State's credit masters. Rather, it was a formula which he believed had, once and for all, revealed the central flaw of finance capitalism. It was supposedly the very encapsulation of his critique of finance capitalism. It has been called the A + B Theorem.[4] He believed that it revealed, in stark, scientific neutrality, the central technical flaw of capitalism. He used it to augment his verbal critique.

What was this verbal critique? He argued that capitalism suffers from a fundamental flaw: the inability of the private banking system's *finance credit* to keep pace with what he called *Real Credit.* When producers repay business loans, he said, they thereby extinguish finance credit, meaning money, thus depriving consumers of the purchasing power necessary for them to buy the full output of industry. Thus, workers under capitalism cannot afford to buy back all of their production. There is not enough money – "tickets," as he referred to money – remaining in the economy at the end of the production process to enable producers to sell all of the output of the system of production. *This supposed break in the flow of funds must lead to losses for most producers.* Producers will eventually reduce output unless this break in the flow of funds is overcome by the issue of fiat money. This is an underconsumptionist criticism of capitalism.

The curious fact is this: Douglas' A + B Theorem did not analytically link his verbal critique of capitalism's supposed break in the flow of funds with the supposed problem supposedly identified by the Theorem: a break in payments to the "organizations" that supply factories with raw materials. As we shall see, this was a completely separate argument: the identification of another break in the flow of funds. Douglas was incorrect on both counts. There is no break in the flow of funds under capitalism. But the A + B Theorem hypothesized a

4. *The Douglas Manual,* edited by Philip Mairet (London: Stanley Nott, 1934), pp. 68-74.

different kind of break from the one he hypothesized in his critique of bank credit. The A + B Theorem has nothing to do analytically with the credit system.

A Series of Mistakes

We have seen in earlier chapters that Major Douglas' analytical error began with his misunderstanding of money and credit. There is no break in the flow of funds under capitalism. His assertion that there is such a break rested on at least four fundamental misunderstandings of capitalism.

First, money is not a system of tickets; money is the most marketable commodity. Tickets are legal claims to specific goods: "one ticket, one item." Money, on the other hand, is the means of competitive bidding for goods: "high bid wins."

Second, money (credit) is not issued to a prospective producer by a bank so that a specific worker can in the future buy back exactly the good or service which he has produced. Credit is issued so that the producer can hire land (*rent*), labor (*wages*), and capital goods (land plus labor) over time (*interest*) in order to produce consumer goods. The bank lends money to enable the producer to bring a final product to market.

The bank is equally willing to issue consumer credit to buyers. If anything, the bank is more willing to do this. In the late 1980's, consumers in the United States were paying interest rates on bank credit card debt that were twice as high as the rates which businesses were being charged. But Douglas never discussed consumer debt, for obvious reasons. *The presence of consumer credit in finance capitalism makes his critique of capitalism look silly, at least in the eyes of those who have not adopted a cult-like attitude toward Social Credit.*

The producer, if he is to make a profit, must buy these factors of production less expensively than he can sell them in their final composition as consumer goods. He makes his profit (if any) by buying these factor inputs for less than they are really worth, given the actual conditions of future consumer demand. He guesses correctly; his competitors do not. He puts his money where his guess is. If he makes a profit, he does so at the expense of other producers who did not see the opportunity – cheap factor inputs – and did not bid up their prices. As information on his profits spreads to his competitors, his profits steadily disappear as his competitors begin to imitate him. Profit is therefore a residual. The quest for profit is what drives producers, but nothing in free market capitalism guarantees profits.

Third, money is not extinguished when a producer repays a business loan. This is the case whether the banking system is a fractional reserve system or not. The money used to repay the loan is immediately loaned out again unless the depositor simultaneously withdraws his money. If the depositor withdraws his cash, he either spends it, hoards it (rare), or deposits it in another bank. Repaying a business loan does not extinguish money in a fractional reserve banking system that is governed by a central bank. Repayment need not extinguish money in a fractional reserve system that is not governed by a central bank.

Fourth, capitalist producers can still make profits when they lower selling prices. Indeed, this is the essence of capitalism, as Henry Ford learned: innovative manufacturers are willing to risk paying more for economic inputs today than they can get back in revenues tomorrow if they can buy inputs even cheaper tomorrow because of volume purchases. Falling prices and rising output and wealth are basic to capitalism. The economic issue is not falling *money* prices; the issue is *purchasing power*: How much will money buy when the producer sells his goods?

I argue in this Appendix that these four major errors have nothing to do analytically with the A + B Theorem. The A + B Theorem offers a wholly new analytical error. This theorem does not complement the original error: the supposed break in the flow of funds due to the repayment of business loans. It adds a new error: a separate break in the flow of funds.

To understand what Major Douglas failed to understand, we must first be clear in our minds regarding what is true. We must analyze capitalism's system of rewards. Specifically, we need to understand why labor, as is true of every other factor of production, is paid very nearly the value of its output under competitive capitalism. If men were omniscient, the owner of every factor of production would receive exactly the value of his factor's output. Profits reveal underpaid factors of production.

Free Market Wages Approach the Value of Labor's Output

What if some employer is paying his work force below-market wages? Some of his workers will move to another place of employment if they discover that another producer is paying more, and this move will alert those workers who remain behind that their employer is not paying them the full value of their output. They will ask for more money. If they do not receive the raise, more of them will quit. The employer will lose to his competitors these crucial factors of production.

Any producer who discovers that his competitor is paying his workers too little can and will try to lure the best workers away from the competitor. This is not because employers are always people with charitable inclinations. It is because they discover that their competitor is buying a factor of production at a below-market price. Wise competitors move in and bid up the price of that factor of production. Remember the words of my economic policy parrot: "high bid wins." Given free movement of labor and open competition, workers will tend to be paid the full value of their output. The profit motive of both the workers and their employers will see to this. Producers compete against producers, while laborers compete against laborers.

The System as a Whole

I will assume that Major Douglas was referring to the factory system as a whole. His criticism was that the system of production in a capitalist economy does not allow the workers as a whole to buy the totality of the goods they have produced. That is, *workers are being exploited*. For once, he mentioned consumer credit. The credit system does make money available for the workers to buy the fruits of their labor, but they must go into debt. This creates a system of growing indebtedness. Douglas quoted the mysterious (and incoherent) H.M.M., who wrote:

> The goods we buy are produced on borrowed money; the money we buy them with goes to extinguish the debt; but it itself is derived from credits that have been borrowed from the banks, and consequently its value must reappear in selling prices somewhere, and be recovered again from the consumer if the banks are to be repaid their advances. It is clear, therefore, that one credit is only cancelled by the creation of another and larger credit.[5]

(Over two decades later, H.M.M. reciprocated the favor, citing Major Douglas as the man who "had analysed the problem into its basic elements, and devised a solution for it that fitted all the facts, and was watertight in every particular; . . .[6])

One thing needs to be mentioned in this context: *services*. In a growing economy, services steadily replace manufacturing as the primary source of wealth. Decades ago, management expert Peter Drucker called this new phenomenon "the knowledge economy." This phrase has become widely accepted. The wages paid to knowledge workers account for most of the expenditures in a modern economy. For example, the raw materials in a computer disk on which magnetic impulses are embedded cost less than a dollar. The disk may sell for two hundred times this because of the information contained in those magnetic impulses. So, even if Douglas' theoretical analysis were correct, as time goes on it would become increasingly irrelevant eco-

---

5. *Credit-Power and Democracy* (London: Cecil Palmer, 1920), p. 24.
6. H.M.M., *The Struggle for Money* (Glasgow: William Maclellan, 1957), p. 14.

nomically. The share of expenditures paid for raw materials normally is dropping in modern capitalist economies.[7] More and more, total wages will approach total business income.

The Flow of Purchasing Power

Major Douglas argued that there is a single flaw in capitalism that dooms the system. What his followers have failed to perceive is that Major Douglas adopted two versions of this single flaw: one in his verbal critique of the credit structure, and the other in the A + B Theorem, which analytically has nothing to do with credit.

According to the A + B Theorem, what is the origin of this supposed flaw? He said the flaw is the factory payment system. Note: not the bank credit system, but the factory payment system. Note: not limited liability corporations but factories. Two types of recipients are involved in the factory payment system, he argued, and therefore there are two types of payment: **Group A**: payments "made to individuals (wages, salaries, and dividends)." **Group B**: payments to "other organizations (raw materials, bank charges, and other external costs)."[8] We must pay close, careful attention to the words he used: *individuals* and *organizations*. These words are central to his analysis.

The key to his analysis is his consideration of the *flow of purchasing power.* (Let me remind the reader: whenever you find an economist or economic writer whose explanation does not make sense, it is probably not your fault. Either the economist is a poor communicator or else his theory is nonsense.) Here is what Douglas wrote, word for word (his italics):

> Now *the rate of flow of purchasing-power to individuals is represented by A, but since all payments go into prices, the rate of flow of prices*

---

7. E. Calvin Beisner, *Prospects for Growth: A Biblical View of Population, Resources, and the Future* (Westchester, Illinois: Crossway, 1990), ch. 7.

8. *Credit-Power and Democracy*, p. 21.

cannot be less than A + B. The product of any factory may be considered as something which the public ought to be able to buy, although in many cases it is an intermediate product of no use to individuals but only to a subsequent manufacture; but since A will not purchase A + B, a proportion of the product at least equivalent to B must be distributed by a form of purchasing-power which is not comprised in the descriptions grouped under A.[9]

This passage was reprinted in the 1934 compilation of the most important passages in Major Douglas' writings, *The Douglas Manual.*[10] Even though it is verbally and analytically incoherent, it must be taken seriously as a definitive statement of his position as far as the Social Credit movement is concerned.

Note at this point that Douglas made no reference here to the issue of credit by a bank or the supposed extinguishing of money with the repayment of the loan to the bank. He said that "A will not purchase A + B," but this equation has nothing to do with credit. It also has nothing to do with limited liability. It rests on a completely different line of reasoning.

A Supposed Break in the Flow of Funds

What was Major Douglas arguing? He was arguing that there is a break in the flow of payments. The factory's payments to **Group A** – payments made to *individuals* – is smaller than the total payments by the factory: A + B. Members of **Group B,** who receive payments made to *other organisations*, apparently (he never actually said this) do not go out and buy goods and services produced by the factory system as a whole. What they do with this money remains a mystery: the supreme mystery of Social Credit.

He said that we should consider "Labour as an intermediate product, the raw material of further production, which is, of

---

9. *Ibid.*, p. 22.

10. *Douglas Manual*, p. 68.

course, the orthodox capitalistic view. . . ."[11] Consider, he said, a "Labour corporation – for instance, a trade union – as being in a position to make up the costs and consequently the selling price of this commodity on orthodox principles."[12] (If you do not know what this sentence means, do not feel stupid; neither I nor his disciples know what it means either.) Fact: "orthodox principles" do not teach that a trade union makes up these costs, unless we are talking about orthodox Marxism, which attributes all productivity to human labor. Orthodox economics regards labor as only one factor of production. Land is the other.[13]

We come now to the heart of the A + B Theorem:

> In this case using small letters, group *b* would include all the costs of living – *i.e.*, the overhead charges of the men who are the "machines" for the production of Labour – and group *a* would be their direct remuneration, and the "factory cost" of the commodity would again be *a* + *b*. Let us call this "factory-cost-of-Labour" *c*. Now *c* cannot be greater than A in the preceding formula for material-production cost, and yet if human beings are to buy A + B with their earnings and dividends, A + B must be included in *c*. Again we see that this is only possible by the inclusion of an external factor – credit – which allows an ostensibly stable value *c* to mean different things at successive intervals of time.[14]

Here he finally mentioned credit. But the A + B Theorem has nothing analytically to do with credit. It has to do with payments made to "other organizations," including the repayment of bank loans but also including payments for "raw mater-

11. *Credit-Power and Democracy*, p. 22.

12. *Ibid.*, p. 23.

13. Capital is a product of land plus labor over time.

14. *Ibid.*, p. 23. Perhaps you may disagree with me, but this is not what I call clear writing. Let us do our best to give Major Douglas the benefit of the doubt. Let us assume that there is some sort of logic in this argument.

ials" and "other charges."[15] What does the supposed break in payments to owners of raw materials, plus "other external costs," have to do with a supposed lack of bank credit? Analytically, not a thing. Thus, the A + B Theorem has introduced a new element: a different break in the flow of payments, one not dependent on the "extinguishing" of money.

The A + B Theorem assumes that payments to B are significant. As the total of A (wages) + B (other charges) grows, the overall economic importance of A payments is reduced. That is, the percentage of payments to wage-earners falls in relation to payments to other factors. If this were not the case, then capitalism would soon solve its supposed problem: payments to wage-earners would constitute an ever-growing percentage of total factor payments. (This is exactly what capitalism does.) *The supposed break in the flow of funds would steadily disappear.* This development would remove the need for Social Credit. Thus, his implicit argument in the A + B Theorem was that payments other than wage payments would grow in importance, thereby augmenting the supposed break in the flow of funds.

The problem is, Douglas emphatically *denied* that there was any evidence of this development! He correctly argued that the proportion of national income going to wages was very high in his day and getting higher. He said that "probably 94 per cent. of the purchasing power which constitutes the distribution system of this country, is wages and salaries, and, on the whole, this percentage of the total tends to increase, and dividends collectively tend to decrease. . . ."[16] There is no way to reconcile these opposing assertions: a declining proportion of national income going to wages vs. an increasing proportion.

Douglas was arguing in *Credit-Power and Democracy* that the money paid by a factory to its *workers* plus its *suppliers* is insufficient to allow its *workers* to buy back their stream of production.

---

15. *Ibid.*, p. 21.
16. *Warning Democracy*, p. 86.

I shall not ridicule this argument by commenting that no worker in a Rolls-Royce automobile factory is likely ever to want or buy the visible product of his labor. This is because no worker produces an entire Rolls Royce. He may produce a bumper, or perhaps a headlight, but not the whole car. He has no use for a Rolls Royce bumper or headlight.

Then what did he mean? The error in Douglas' analysis was that he spoke of factory payments to two kinds of recipients – *workers* (A) and *suppliers* (B) – but he focused his attention (and the reader's attention) solely on the money (purchasing power) paid to the factory's workers. He ignored the money paid to the factory's suppliers. He wrote as if spending by the workers employed by the factory's suppliers was nonexistent, and therefore the purchases made by the capitalist *system's* entire work force would not clear the market of consumer goods. Suppliers of raw materials to factories somehow do not count in the A + B Theorem as being part of the capitalist *system*. This, Douglas said, is the central flaw of capitalism. This, he said, is why capitalism must eventually collapse without Social Credit.

The question is: Does any of this correspond to the real world?

What Major Douglas Forgot: Organizations Are Fictions

Major Douglas made a fundamental mistake in his analysis. He neglected to honor the most important task in economic analysis. *He neglected to "follow the money."*

Think about the logic of the A + B Theorem. Group A – *individuals* – receives part of the money. Group B – *organizations* – receives the remaining part. Those who receive the wages and dividends (Group A) do not get all of the money, he said, so they cannot buy back the whole of their production. Thus, he concluded, capitalism is plagued with *underconsumption*: waste. "The existence of a poverty problem face to face with an unemployment problem and side by side with a marvelously effective production system ought to direct our attention unfailingly to the fact that it is something that stands in between consumption and production which is the cause of our difficulties."[17]

Douglas rested his entire system and public career on this argument. We can spot the error in one phrase: "All payments made to other organisations (raw materials, bank charges, and other external costs)."[18] This was **Group B**. He forgot the obvious: payments are never made to *people-less* organizations. Payments are never made to *raw materials*. Payments are never made to *other costs*. On the contrary, payments are made to living, breathing human owners of these resources. *Payments are made to people*. He neglected to follow the money beyond Group B to those who sell goods and services to members of Group B.

People do something with the money they receive: deposit it in a bank, or invest it, or spend it on consumer goods and services (most of what they receive), or carry cash (not too much because of the cost of forfeited interest), or hide it (rare – no interest income). The point is, virtually all of this money goes from one group of people – **Group B** – to other people. Here is what underconsumptionist critics of capitalism never discuss: *every unit of money is owned by someone at all times, unless someone has inadvertently lost it*. (If this lost money is somehow economically significant, then sellers will lower selling prices in order to clear the market of excess goods and services.) Thus, there is no shortage of purchasing power. There is no inherent need in a capitalist economy for credit-debt. (Remember: credit and debt are different sides of the same borrowed coin.) *Bank credit-debt is convenient but not mandatory*. The A + B Theorem acknowledges this reality. It does not rest on the assumption of bank credit. The Theorem has nothing to do analytically with Douglas' other argument for the break in the flow of funds: the repayment of bank loans. They are two separate arguments.

17. *Ibid.*, p. 31.

18. *Credit-Power and Democracy*, p. 21.

Following the Money

Consider this example: a person owns some land. A factory manager pays him a monthly rent. The land-owner then buys something with this rent money. Or maybe he invests it. Maybe he buys more land. It does not matter what he does with the money he receives from the factory owner. *The money never leaves the total economy*. This is equally true of the person who sells raw materials to the factory.

The point is this: the factory manager buys factors of production. ("Factory" is linked etymologically to "factors.") He buys a factor called *labor services* and a factor called *land services*. He is not legally allowed to buy the worker, since slavery was abolished in the nineteenth century. He buys labor services. He also buys factors of production that produce certain services.

If we were to take Douglas' Theorem literally, we would conclude that factories could eliminate all factor payments by going out and buying up the mines that produce raw materials and the land on which factories sit. That way, they could reduce **Group B** payments to zero. But the factory that owns all these factors is nonetheless paying for their use, since by using up these assets, the company is forfeiting the money it could get by selling or renting these factors. Whether the factory rents these land services (raw materials) or buys the land and suffers asset depletion as they are used up, credit is not theoretically necessary to the transaction. With or without bank credit, someone gets paid, and if someone gets paid, the money gets spent. *There is no break in the flow of money payments*. Therefore, Social Credit's fundamental argument collapses.

What About the Rich?

It is possible to argue that the rich will save more and therefore will be able to lend. This is as it should be. The Bible says: "The LORD shall open unto thee his good treasure, the heaven to give the rain unto thy land in his season, and to bless all the work of thine hand: and thou shalt lend unto many nations, and thou shalt not borrow" (Deuteronomy 28:12).

What do the not-so-rich need? They need ways to invest their money as effectively as the rich do. This is what modern capitalism has provided: stock markets, bond markets, money markets. Thousands of mutual funds have been created since the late 1950's. This process has democratized capitalism.

The point is, when an employer pays a worker, the worker does something with the money. There is no break in the flow of funds.

He Tried to Answer This Objection

In *The Monopoly of Credit*, Douglas responded to this objection. "Now the first objection which is commonly raised to this statement, is that the payments in wages which are made to the public for intermediate products [capital goods – G.N.] which the public does not want to buy and could not use, when added together, make up the necessary sum to balance the B payments, so that the population can buy all the consumable products."[19] He then referred the reader to a diagram on the previous page which supposedly explained why this objection is false.

There was a problem with this defense: the diagram proved no such thing. The diagram was an attempt to trace the payments made to the owners of each factor of production at each stage of the production process. Douglas tried to prove that the money spent today on wages will not allow wage-earners to purchase all the consumer goods available today in the market. Why not? Because the money spent by consumers supposedly will not cover the manufacturers' costs of production. (Note: he ignored savings and interest in his diagram, a key mistake.) I reproduce his diagram on the next page.

19. *The Monopoly of Credit* (London: Chapman & Hall, 1931), p. 32.

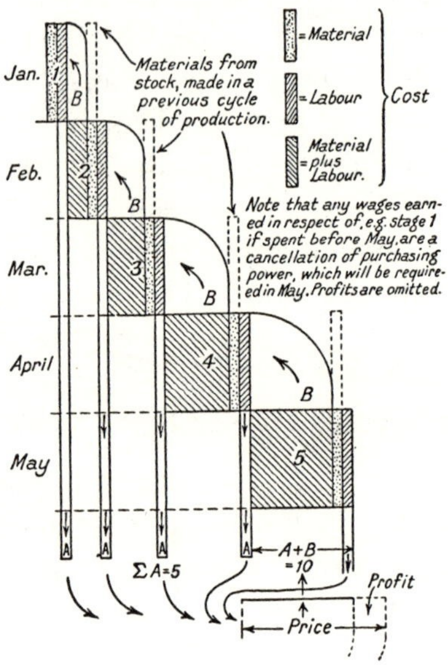

But the total money spent at each stage in the production process *will* cover all costs of production. He identified materials, labor, and material plus labor (capital). He ignored interest payments. He could safely ignore profit, for profit is a residual for correct forecasting; therefore, it may or may not appear in any given entrepreneur's accounts. The main issue is this: *Will the total payments by consumers match the payments to land (raw materials, space), labor, and interest?* The answer is clear: *yes.*

We need to add interest payments to our diagram of the structure of production. An accurate diagram will reveal that consumers pay more to sellers than producers have paid to owners of land and labor. The difference between what consumers pay to sellers and what producers paid for land and labor is *interest*: the payments made by producers to suppliers of capital during the period of production. Interest does not appear in Douglas' diagram. This was a crucial mistake on his part. (For the record: in 1931, the year of Douglas' diagram, F. A. Hayek provided a far more accurate series of diagrams of the structure of production in his book, *Prices and Production*. He showed that the structure of production is consistent: total payments to all factors of production at every stage of the production process equal total income from the sale of factors.)

In 1962, Murray Rothbard provided a diagram that showed that money paid by consumers to retailers at the final stage of production (delivery) exactly matches the total payments by manufacturers to owners of the factors production, land and labor, plus interest. Rothbard's diagram does not consider profits: an economic residual. For analytical purposes, this is a valid procedure in order to identify total payments to factors of production. (For this zero-profiit world to exist, the producers would have to forecast perfectly future supply and demand. Such perfect foreknowledge cannot happen in the real world.) While we can safely ignore profits for analytical purposes, we dare not ignore interest payments. (Rothbard uses ounces of gold as money in his diagram in order to avoid confusion over national currencies.)

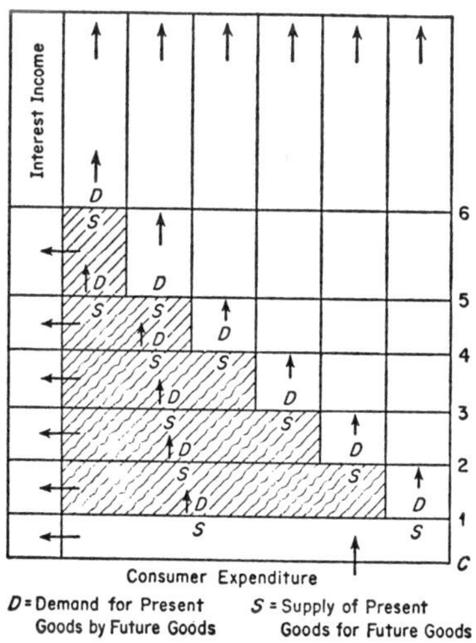

On the same page, Rothbard commented on the meaning of this diagram: "Now, instead of collecting interest income for services in one lump sum at the final stage, the capitalist or capitalists acquire interest income *at each stage*. If each stage takes one year, then the entire production process for the good takes six years. When the stages are all lumped together, or vertically integrated, then one capitalist (or set of capitalists) advances the owners of original factors their money six years ahead of time and then waits for this period to acquire his revenue."[20]

As you can see, total payments from consumers at the end of the production process exactly match the total payments for the factors of production – land and labor – plus interest. Or, as we might put it, A + B (payments *received* by producers and lenders) = A + B (payments *made* to producers by consumers). Thus, Major Douglas' analytical tool of criticism is wrong. To the extent that Social Credit economics relies on the A + B Theorem, Social Credit economics is wrong.

What About After the Reform?

For all the attention focused on the A + B Theorem by Douglas, his followers, and his critics, one fact should not be ignored: Douglas never once returned to this Theorem to show *mathematically* why or how this supposed flaw would cease to operate in the world of Social Credit. That is, his discussions of the A + B Theorem always are confined to his discussions of the inescapable dilemma of capitalism. *Never once in his books did Major Douglas show from his actual A + B formula how this supposedly fatal flaw of capitalist finance will be avoided in the world beyond his proposed reform.*

As we saw in Chapter 4, his proposed reform involved having the national government take a census of all the property in

20. Murray N. Rothbard, *Man, Economy, and State: A Treatise on Economic Principles* (Princeton, New Jersey: Van Nostrand, 1962), p. 314.

the nation. The national government then appoints an elite group of credit masters who will decide which privately owned businesses will receive credit. (Interestingly, he never discussed where consumer credit would come from. With all the private commercial banks shut down by the government, who would issue consumer loans? Perhaps Douglas believed that the National Dividend payments would replace consumer credit.)

Money paid today to "organizations," as he put it, would still have to be paid to the same kinds of organizations after his proposed reform: payments for raw materials and "other external costs." Money will be paid to businesses. There will still be bankers to repay: the government's credit masters. There will still be payments to the owners of capital: the national dividend. As today, *these payments will be made to individuals*; organizations are a legal fiction.

The Flow of Funds After "The Revolution"

Capitalism's problem, as he explained it, is not a shortage of money as such; rather, it is a problem of distribution: the breakdown in the flow of payments to individuals, i.e., consumers. So, the critic of Social Credit has a right to ask this question: Why won't the A + B Theorem also operate on the far side of Social Credit's reform? The critic is also entitled to ask this question: Why didn't Major Douglas ever discuss this problem in those passages where he brought up the A + B Theorem? In short, *why does the supposed dilemma of the A + B Theorem apply only to today's capitalism?*

If the answer is "bankers," then the defender of Social Credit must answer this question: Why won't Social Credit's money masters also have to be paid? What about raw materials owners, whether public or private? Defenders must also answer this question: Why is *interest paid by private banks to their depositors* any more of a break in the flow of payments than Social Credit's *automatic dividend payments to individuals*? Why is money received from interest payments today a break in the flow of funds, but

National Dividend payments under Social Credit not a break in the flow of funds? The answer is obvious: there is no difference. In neither case is there a break in the flow of payments.

Every economy must pay the owners of the factors of production: *land and labor*. Every economy has to cope with the existence of *interest*: today's discount of the value of future goods compared to the value of those same goods in the present. Why is a Social Credit economy immune to these inescapable restrictions on wealth? In short, *how can Social Credit escape the universal fact of scarcity and time?*

Conclusion

Major Douglas invented his A + B Theorem to explain why capitalism is so inefficient compared to what it could be under Social Credit – an assumption without proof. He argued that payments to *individuals* only count for part of the total distribution of money. Payments to *organizations* constitute the other part. But only individuals buy things; therefore, he concluded, the payments to organizations bleed off purchasing power from the economy. This, he argued, is why modern capitalism requires additional infusions of bank-created credit money: to make up for this lost purchasing power, by which he meant money. He forgot the obvious: *organizations are legal fictions; only individuals receive payments*. Thus, the entire money supply – "purchasing power" – is always in the possession of specific individuals. There can be no shortage of purchasing power as a result of payments by factory managers to sellers or renters of the factors of production: *real, live human beings*.

There is no single cause of the problems of the free market except the most general kind of cause: a refusal to allow men to compete without government interference. There is no inherent necessity for a capitalist economy to depend on fiat money created by commercial banks. Here is **capitalism's A + B theorem**: payments to Group A (suppliers of labor services) plus payments to Group B (suppliers of land services) are equal to the spending of Group A plus the spending of Group B. The money income *to* each group equals the money outflow *from* each group, assuming that people in Group B do not decide to light their cigars with the paper money or checks they receive from those producers who buy factors of production. Even if they did use all their money to light cigars, this reduction in the total money supply would lead to lower prices for the rest of us. Wage-receiving workers could then afford to buy additional goods and services. *There is still no break in the flow of money payments.* Besides, all of those rich cigar-smokers would eventually run out of cigars. When they at last stopped burning money and started buying more cigars, this would end the supposed break in the flow of money, even if there were one, which there isn't.

As I have shown, the A + B Theorem has nothing to do with Douglas' other explanation of the break in the flow of payments: his theory of private banking, producer loans, and the extinguishing of money upon debt repayment. The two analyses are conceptually different. Douglas made no attempt to fit them together into a coherent discussion of capitalism's supposed tendency to underconsumption. Nevertheless, he still proclaimed a single cause of capitalism's crisis: insufficient funds.

Without a single cause, there is no need for a magic pill. Without a psychological need for a magic pill, nobody will embrace Social Credit as the solution to society's ills. So, the defenders of Social Credit cling fanatically to Major Douglas' imaginary single cause. They need a market for the magic pill that Social Credit's proposed credit reform alone can provide.

The weavers who sold the emperor his invisible clothes knew it was all a hoax. They were in it for the money. In contrast, Social Credit's defenders honestly believe they are in the magic pill business. They honestly believe in the A + B Theorem. My suggestion to the reader: *don't buy any magic pills.* There are better ways to spend your hard-earned money and your dreams.

Douglas referred to "This somewhat elusive conception, the grasp of which is vital to an understanding of the modern economic problem. . . ."[21] Elusive indeed! Here is my strong suggestion: until you fully understand this highly elusive argument, and are able to explain it in your own words to anyone, as well as explain in your own words some of its economic implications, do not embrace Social Credit. Do not become an advocate of anything that does not make sense to you.

Finally, the A + B Theorem has to be wrong if it does not account for time. But any discussion of time must also discuss the rate of interest. Any explanation of the A + B Theorem which does not account for interest payments (time-preference) is not based on economics. Beware of any supposed revision of the original A + B Theorem which appeals to "time periods" unless it discusses the interest rate factor.

Summary

1. Fringe social critics identify single causes of society's evils; then they propose single solutions ("silver bullets" and "magic pills"). Major Douglas was such a fringe critic.
2. Free market economics teaches that wages in a competitive economy will approach the value of labor's output.
3. Producers compete against producers to bid up the price of labor (wages).
4. Major Douglas said there is a single cause of capitalism's ills: the factory payment system.
5. Factories pay two groups: wage earners and others.
6. He called the factory's wage-earning employees "individuals"; the other recipients of factory payments he called "organizations."

21. *Credit-Power and Democracy*, p. 22.

7. He implied that the money paid to "organizations" does not go to people who then buy consumer goods.
8. This gap in payments must be followed by extensions of credit in order to keep capitalism going, even though the A + B Theorem does not have anything to do with bank credit, analytically speaking.
9. Commercial bank credit grows proportionately to wages – the opposite of what he said was the case in *Warning Democracy*.
10. Douglas argued that the modern capitalist system does not allow workers to buy back the value of their output. That is, workers are exploited: debt servitude
11. The A + B Theorem does not limit payments to B to debt repayment; it includes payments for raw materials and other costs.
12. Douglas forgot to "follow the money": from Group B to those who sell goods and services to Group B.
13. He forgot that those who receive money spend it or save it.
14. When they spend it, it goes to other workers.
15. Most money is spent.
16. Not much of it is saved.
17. The Bible teaches that it is the blessing of God to become a lender.
18. Modern capitalism makes this possible: the democratization of investing.
19. Why doesn't the "problem" of the A + B Theorem also exist beyond the day of Social Credit reform?
20. How can any economic system avoid paying the owners of all factors of production?

APPENDIX B

MY CHALLENGE TO SOCIAL CREDIT LEADERS

> Those who have read *"The North-South Dialogue"*, which is the publication of correspondence between Australian Social Creditor Chas Pinwill, and Dr. Gary North, the North American who claims to be a Christian economist, and a critic of Social Credit, will recall how Dr. North cut short his correspondence with Chas Pinwill when it became clear that he was losing the debate.[1]

> He that passeth by, and meddleth with strife belonging not to him, is like one that taketh a dog by the ears (Proverbs 26:17).

To Social Credit Leaders in
England, Canada, Australia,
New Zealand, and South Africa

Gentlemen:

Whoever wrote the article in Australia's *New Times* which took up Mr. Pinwill's cause did not heed the warning in Prov-

1. "Dr. Gary North and Social Credit," *New Times* (Oct. 1992), p. 3.

erbs. His decision to publish that editorial served as a prod in my backside. Frankly, I had forgotten all about Mr. Pinwill and his little book. (Anyone who has read it will understand why.) That article or editorial or whatever it was persuaded me to begin a project that I had been talking about starting since 1965: write a book refuting the economics of Social Credit.

Gentlemen, I realize that most of you are unfamiliar with the rules of scholarly debate. You have had no experience with formal academic debate, since no economist since the beginning of World War II has written a book refuting Social Credit's economics.[2] Your generation has never seen a full-scale challenge to Major Douglas' system. Therefore, I realize that I ought to allow you considerable latitude – "cut you some slack," as we say in the U.S. But *New Times* really should not have taken advantage of my patience. The reference to my supposed inability to answer Mr. Pinwill is an example of a decided lack of wisdom. If I can answer Major Douglas, I can surely answer Mr. Pinwill. I have now answered Major Douglas. If you think I haven't, one of you is going to have to prove your case against me. In print, I mean, and preferably in a book, not in your little newsletters written for the already converted. More about this later.

Mr. Pinwill Broke the Rules

With regard to my private correspondence with Mr. Pinwill, you need to understand why I cut it short. When Mr. Pinwill sent me a manuscript in 1990 critical of my writings on monetary theory, I did respond privately. I hoped to save Mr. Pinwill the embarrassment of going into print with numerous errors. I had assumed, however, that Mr. Pinwill was aware of, and would abide by, international copyright law, which says that not more than ten percent of an author's private letter may

2. I do not regard Dr. Spadaro's 1955 critique as public: it was a Ph.D. dissertation. Almost no one reads them.

be reproduced verbatim without his permission. He did not abide by the law.

Instead, without my permission, he published my privately penned, line-by-line notes, which I had written in the margins of his manuscript. I did not put these comments in the form of a detailed scholarly response, ready for verbatim citation. Instead of revising his manuscript's text to counter my criticisms – which is why I replied to him in the first place – he published his 110-page book, *The North-South Dialogue*. It is a completely different manuscript from the one he originally sent me. Mr. Pinwill used my notes as a series of launching pads for another round of criticism. He quoted in bold type face my brief marginal notes, as if they constituted a detailed formal response.

I am not charging him with a moral failure. Mr. Pinwill is probably a very fine fellow. He just knows nothing about academic etiquette and international copyright law. This is the problem facing any movement which is run by amateurs. They don't know what they're doing.

I am no fool, gentlemen. I was not going to provide Mr. Pinwill with any new launching pads by sending him additional private letters. When I decide to reply publicly to an idea, especially to a critic of my writings, I do so in a very thorough manner, as several recipients of my responses are willing to verify (in private).[3] Had Mr. Pinwill's book been worth the effort, I would have responded in print in early 1991, when he sent me a copy. I ignored it because I intended eventually to complete a project which I had begun talking about in 1965, when I was 23 years old: the refutation of Major Douglas. But I kept putting off the project, year after year. I continued to do so even after I received Mr. Pinwill's book. Then came the unsigned article in the *New Times* (October 1992).

---

3. See, for example, my response to the faculty of Westminster Theological Seminary, *Westminster's Confession: The Abandonment of Van Til's Legacy* (Tyler, Texas: Institute for Christian Economics, 1991).

The article was FAXed to me by Mr. Ian Hodge on November 9. That FAX persuaded me to write this book. I completed the manuscript on December 31. I would have completed it earlier, but I was in the process of completing two other books.

Why Economists Have Long Ignored Social Credit

I have now written the first scholarly book published since the late 1930's that refutes the economics of Social Credit. The lack of such a book prior to mine was not due to the intellectual inability of many, many economists to respond to the details of Social Credit's proposed reforms. It was due to the fact that no economist thought it was worth his time to respond, and every publisher agreed with this assessment.

Social Credit as an economic doctrine has always been a peripheral affair, a part-time pastime of poets, mystics, and Christian fundamentalists who confuse Major Douglas' ideas with biblical wisdom. After the Social Credit government of Alberta failed to implement Social Credit's reforms (I hesitate to call Major Douglas' almost random suggestions a program) in the late 1930's, it became obvious to any secular economist that no book on Social Credit was needed, nor would there be much demand for one. The public forgot about Major Douglas after 1939, as the good major knew very well before he died. So, the professional economist asked himself, why spend time, effort, and publishing capital to beat an obviously dead horse? Social Credit economics is an exceedingly dead horse.

Were I not a Christian, I would have agreed with this assessment. Had a remnant of God-fearing Christians around the English-speaking world not been lured into the economic and political errors of the late Mr. Douglas and his promoters, this book would not have been worth my effort and ICE's money. Those defenders of Social Credit who have come in the name of Major Douglas alone are simply not worth anyone's time or energy to challenge. They are defenders of what is clearly a long-lost cause. They are intellectually incapable of writing books. All they publish are little pamphlets and an occasional newsletter. With nothing but pamphlets and newsletters, they cannot recruit those well-educated people and professionals who are vital for leadership in a serious economic reform movement. But several of you have come to the general public in the name of Jesus Christ. I regarded it as my God-given assignment to reply in His name. Because I could do it, I did do it. Let me review at this point exactly what I have done.

What I Have Done in This Book

I have set forth a challenge to the "laymen" in your tiny movement: those who occasionally may read but do not write unsigned articles in your low-circulation newsletters. First and foremost, I have challenged them to think through what Major Douglas actually wrote – not what leaders of the Social credit movement would like for him to have written, or what you say that he wrote, but what he really did write. This is why my book is so long: I have filled it with verbatim quotations from Major Douglas' books. I have proven from the public record that he really did write nonsense, over and over.

Second, I have shown from his writings that Major Douglas was not only *not* a Christian philosopher. He openly opposed the moral legitimacy of the biblical idea of economic rewards and punishments. It was this underlying motivation, deeply religious in origin, which was the heart of Major Douglas' writings, not his various technical criticisms of capitalism.

Third, I have shown, one by one, that Major Douglas' specific criticisms of the free market were either incorrect or were misdirected. As an example of one of his comparatively rare accurate but misdirected insights, he criticized fractional reserve banking. That is fine with me; this institutional arrangement deserves criticizing. The "Austrian School" economist Murray Rothbard has been saying so since at least 1963,[4] and I have

4. Murray N. Rothbard, *What Has Government Done to Our Money?* (Auburn,

been saying so in print since at least 1973[5] (as Mr. Pinwill is well aware). Major Douglas criticized fractional reserve banking mainly for its supposed tendency to reduce the money (credit) supply when a business repays a loan. No such tendency exists. The opposite tendency exists, due to the bankers' desire to make money. Under free banking, a profit-seeking bank will immediately loan out the money unless it is suffering from a bank run. In an economy in which the State has chartered a central bank, every bank will immediately lend out the money again, if only to buy government debt. So much for the technical criticism which Major Douglas offered. It was incorrect.

Douglas denied that his criticisms of capitalism were in any way moral criticisms.[6] But the main problem with fractional reserve banking is its immorality. The moral defect of fractional reserve banking is its fraudulent issuing of warehouse receipts for which there is no cash or money metals in reserve. Bad morality produces evil results. The economic problem with fractional reserve banking is its creation of an economy's boom-bust business cycle: the expansion of credits (fiduciary money), which produces a temporary lowering of short-term interest rates, followed by an economic boom, followed by a rise in interest rates, followed by a recession.[7]

Major Douglas' suggested solution to fractional reserve banking was equally as inflationary and probably far more inflationary. Central bankers at least want to make a personal profit for themselves, a profit denominated in money. They have an economic incentive to preserve the purchasing power of money. Major Douglas called for the creation of politically appointed monopolistic credit-masters who will have the legal

---

Alabama: Ludwig von Mises Institute, [1963] 1990).

5. Gary North, *An Introduction to Christian Economics* (Nutley, New Jersey: Craig Press, 1973).

6. Preface, *Credit-Power and Democracy*.

7. Ludwig von Mises, *Human Action: A Treatise on Economics* (New Haven, Connecticut: Yale University Press, 1949), ch. 20.

authority to issue money without limit. I say "without limit" because the statistical device they would use to limit the issue of credit – the national accounting of total available capital – is itself affected by the issuing of credit. The monetary value, though not necessarily the real value, of a Social Credit nation's capital will rise every time a new round of government-created fiat money is issued, thus requiring yet another issue of fiat money: to keep the Just Price (business subsidies) and the National Dividend (consumer subsidies) in line with Real Credit (the total capacity – measured in money – of the economy to produce). Social Credit means State credit and inflation.

Fourth, I have shown that Major Douglas did not understand that the rate of interest is an inescapable aspect of human decision-making and not merely the product of a money economy, let alone fractional reserve banking. It is an aspect of time. (Remember my Roll-Royce example: we all want delivery today.) Because he did not understand that the interest rate is a discount which we always apply in to the present value of future goods compared to the present value of present goods, he did not understand the structure of production – not just under capitalism but under every possible economic system. He therefore misunderstood the function of saving and investment – thrift. He was opposed to thrift, the basis of economic growth.

Fifth, Major Douglas did not understand the source of profits under capitalism, namely, the correct forecasting and accurate implementation of a plan of production to deliver consumer goods in the future. He did not understand that profits come to one producer only at the expense of another producer, who did not see the economic opportunity: underpriced factors of production. He did not understand that each producer's profit motive is the consumers' hammer which they hold over the heads of producers: "Do what we want, at a price we are willing to pay, or else you lose!"

Sixth, I have shown that there is no break in the flow of funds under free market capitalism. In Appendix A, on Major

Douglas' A + B Theorem, I showed that this theorem had nothing to do with bank credit's effect on the flow of funds. I also showed that the theorem was incorrect with respect to the flow of funds.

Seventh, I have shown that profits under the free market are compatible with gradually falling prices as scarcity is steadily overcome. I therefore applaud falling prices that fall because of rising production and a relatively stable money supply. Falling prices under these conditions is the mark of man's progressive overcoming of God's curses in history. It is because I believe that it is beneficial for men to work toward the total abolition of the cursed aspects of scarcity, even though total abolition will occur only after the Final Judgment, that I applaud falling prices. Social Credit rejects falling prices.

Finally, I have shown that Major Douglas was an anti-Semite. While some of his followers are aware of this, and no doubt have committed themselves to the Social Credit movement because of it, I think most of the Christians who are associated with Social Credit would not agree with Douglas on this point.

I have done a great deal more than this, but this brief list should be sufficient. If I have in fact done what I have listed here, then Social Credit is revealed as fraudulent: wood, hay, and stubble. It deserves to be abandoned. I call upon you to abandon it publicly. You won't, of course. Therefore. . . .

What You Must Now Do

Those who have committed themselves to any cause for many years rarely abandon it. We see this in the case of Christians who predict the return of Jesus to bring the Rapture on a certain date. These predictions are always proven wrong on the predicted day of the so-called secret Rapture.[8] Does this per-

---

8. Dwight Wilson, *Armageddon Now! The Premillennial Response to Russia and Israel Since 1917* (Tyler, Texas: Institute for Christian Economics, [1977] 1991). Dr. Wilson is premillennial.

suade the former prophets to abandon their system of prophecy? Never! They just draw up new prophecy charts. Or their disciples do. I think it is the same with Social Credit. Thus, you have the following options in dealing with *Salvation Through Inflation*: the silent treatment, the "water torture" strategy, the "North has misinterpreted Douglas" strategy, and the strategy of incoherence.

The Silence Treatment

You can pretend that I did not write this book. Say nothing. "North? Who's North? Never heard of him." Most of my critics over the years have taken this approach. A variation of this strategy is this: "I will not dignify nonsense with a response."

But I don't think you will adopt the silence strategy. Leaders of religious cults are incapable psychologically of remaining silent when someone attacks The Founder in a full-length book devoted to challenging The Founder. Neither will you remain silent. In fact, I think several of you will respond quite rapidly in your newsletters, perhaps even coordinating your responses just to keep your answers consistent. I think some of you will make it your life's work to refute this book, month after month. If this book is correct, then anyone who has read it and does not agree with it must justify himself in public to his little band of disciples. So, you will have to respond. But are any of you intellectually capable of writing a whole book to refute my book? That is the question. More about this later.

The Newsletter Version of the Water Torture

This is the approach I think you will choose. Just keep replying to me in one article after another: drip, drip, drip, until your readers have had enough. "No more! No more! We won't believe North's arguments any more. Just stop it!"

The main problem with this approach is that I have written a book, not a newsletter article. If it becomes obvious to your followers that not one of you can answer me in an equally detailed book, keeping your arguments internally coherent, maintaining the cohesion of your entire reply, then your more sophisticated followers will catch on: you can't answer me.

Can one of you answer me? In a book? That is the question.

"Douglas Did Not Really Mean This"

I have filled my book with direct quotations from Major Douglas' books. I have let him speak for himself. It will be difficult for you to persuade your readers that I have quoted him out of context, since I have quoted from all of his books to prove my case. Therefore, you will have to show that Douglas really did not mean what he wrote. That will be a very difficult task on your part. Also, you may wind up the way theological liberals have: abandoning the message of the Revealed Word by completely revising its meaning.

"North Has Misinterpreted Douglas"

This is probably your safest approach. While it will not be easy, due to my continual word-for-word citations from Douglas, perhaps you will be able to confuse at least some of your readers. After all, so few of them own all of Major Douglas' books. They have not read them. Maybe you can show that two or three my interpretations of his words are incorrect, or are at least open to question, especially on some minor point or other. Then you can write something like this: "We see that North has completely misinterpreted Douglas and Social Credit." You have this much going for you: Douglas' language is so often confusing that your readers may not figure out that I have interpreted him correctly and you haven't.

I wonder, though, how you are going to deal with his continual attacks on the Jews. That will take some doing. He was so clear on this point – just about the only topic he was clear about.

Incoherence Will Distract the Troops

This tactic has been basic to Social Credit ever since 1917. Social Credit is incoherent: *inherently* incoherent. Its more recent public defenders have matched the original incoherence of The Founder. They, too, are remarkably, systematically incoherent. They spin vast webs of verbiage to entrap their hapless followers. They recite Major Douglas' slogans as if these were New Age mantras for meditation: "A plus B, A plus B, A plus B. . . ." Or: "Effective demand, effective demand, effective demand. . . ."

The problem with this tactic is that my book is clear. It is clear because economic reasoning is clear. Social Credit is unclear because it is not economics.

My Public Challenge to All of You

Here is my personal challenge: *Gentlemen, you do not have a system of economic analysis which enables you to answer my criticisms.* I will put it even more bluntly: Social Credit is not an economic system at all; it is a detailed psychological justification for retreating from the moral battles of this world.

Fact: whenever a Social Credit politician wins an election, he does nothing to implement Major Douglas' proposed reforms. There is a very good reason for this: the original Social Credit system cannot be implemented because it is not a system of economics. Social Credit has for decades been a vote-getting slogan – a name without political content – for a few Canadian politicians, and a responsibility-avoidance scheme for the vast majority of its professed disciples.

Thus, Social Credit is not a national reform program; it is a psychological justification for remaining on the fringes of culture: pointing the finger and calling others to leave the fight for systematic *moral* and social reform. Social Credit is an anti-reform movement disguised as a monetary and moral reform movement. It is a movement that plays at reform in order to escape the hard work of systematic organization and reform. It has no blueprint except the unworkable Scottish reform plan.

If I am incorrect about the economics of Social Credit, one of you should be able to write a book to answer *Salvation Through Inflation*, line by line, argument by argument. But I warn you: you had better make certain in advance that your representative really does speak for your movement. I will write a book in response. If I can refute him, I thereby have refuted the rest of you. So, it would not be fair for the rest of you to come back with this lame response after my response appears: "Answering that book doesn't count. Its author really doesn't represent Social Credit."

I want to see a Foreword to your designated representative's book: a signed statement from two leaders per nation – England, Canada, Australia, New Zealand, and South Africa – which affirms that his book constitutes your collective response to *Salvation Through Inflation*. If there is no signed Foreword testifying to your designation of the author's position as the intellectual representative of Social Credit, I shall pay no attention to the book. No one else should, either. If you cannot agree on what is wrong with *Salvation Through Inflation*, then Social Credit is not a developed economic system or movement.

Here is my challenge to all of you: choose your representative, identify publicly him as your representative in the book's Foreword, and the two of us will then do intellectual combat.

Please understand: my designated weapon is the book. I expect one of you to respond in a book, not just a series of highly selective newsletter articles written only to one's flock. Let your followers see if one of you can handle my arguments. I don't think any of you can. I now offer you an opportunity to prove me wrong. Will you accept my challenge?

This enterprise will cost you no money. The Institute for Christian Economics will finance it. Just have your designated representative write a response to *Salvation Through Inflation*, up to 150 double-spaced manuscript pages (Word Perfect 5.1

default format or its equivalent). I will then write a reply no longer than 150 double-spaced pages. Then each of us will write a 50-page response to the other's essay.

Is one of you is willing to accept this challenge? Can he get ten of you to agree that he is your representative? I don't care if all of you act as a committee to write the response, but put at least one person's name on the manuscript. Someone should be made responsible. (I hope Mr. Pinwill will accept my challenge, and ten of you will agree to have him represent you. His book initiated this confrontation. He should now complete it.)

If no one accepts my challenge, then all of you, not to mention your followers, should devote your lives to something other than Social Credit.

If I do not receive a positive reply agreeing to this public debate by September 30, 1993, and the completed 150-page manuscript by December 31, 1993, then in 1994, I shall begin advertising *Salvation Through Inflation* as follows:

> **The Devastating Attack on Social Credit Economics That No Social Credit Leader Has Been Willing or Able to Answer!**

Now, which of you will accept my challenge? Contact me at:

Institute for Christian Economics
Post Office Box 8000,
Tyler, Texas, 75711, USA.

One last reminder: should you fail to respond in detail, coherently, and in a book, then the best and the brightest of your followers will abandon Social Credit as a lost cause. They are awaiting your response. For that matter, so am I.

APPENDIX C

A BIBLIOGRAPHY OF FIAT MONEY REFORMS

The fiat money reform program developed by Major Douglas was one of many such proposed reforms during the 1920's and 1930's. This had been preceded in the United States by the populist free silver and fiat money reform proposals of the post-Civil War era.

In addition to such popular American works as W. H. "Coin" Harvey's *Coin's Financial School* and his other books, which sold in the millions during the presidential campaign of 1896.[1] The work of Alexander Del Mar deserves mention. Del Mar had been the Director of the U.S. Bureau of Statistics. He believed that the government should issue fiat money at a rate of 3.3% per annum,[2] a proposal which Milton Friedman has long echoed, beginning in the 1950's. He wrote numerous books on the history of money, including *Money and Civilization* (1886),[3] *The History of Money in America* (1899),[4] and *A History*

---

1. See also W. H. Harvey, *The Remedy* (Mundus Publishing Co., 1915), and *A Tale of Two Nations* (1894), reprinted in 1931 by the Mundus Publishing Co., Monte Ne, Arkansas.

2. Del Mar, *The Science of Money* (New York: Macmillan, 1896), p. 200.

3. Reprinted by Omni Publications, 1975.

4. Reprinted by Omni, 1966.

of Monetary Crimes (1899).[5] His bibliography reflects his wide reading.

Beginning in the years preceding World War I, Professor Irving Fisher of Yale University began recommending that governments regulate the supply of money so that domestic prices can remain stable. He published his major book on this reform in 1934, dedicating it to President Franklin Roosevelt.[6] Fisher is generally regarded as the founder of the index number, a way of measuring aggregate (average) prices nationally.

In the 1920's, there was Arthur Kitson, Douglas' contemporary, author of *Unemployment* (1921), which was published by Douglas' first book publisher, Cecil Palmer, the year after the firm published Douglas' *Economic Democracy* and *Credit-Power and Democracy*. Kitson also wrote *The Bankers' Conspiracy! Which Started the World Crisis* (1933). There was Frederick Soddy, who won the Nobel Prize in chemistry in 1921. His book, *Wealth, Virtual Wealth and Debt* (1926), was dedicated to Kitson. Soddy's work soon led to the creation of the Technocracy movement, an economic system described by Soddy in the second edition of his book as "the new American doctrine of social and industrial salvation. . . ."[7] In 1921, the English publisher Jonathan Cape released Charles Percival Isaac's book, *The Menace of Money Power*. He attacked free trade and "aggressive financialism." In the United States, Carl Strover, a Chicago lawyer, wrote and self-published *Monetary Reconstruction* (1922), which proposed fiat money to create a stable price level, a proposal which he believed superior to Irving Fisher's scheme. In 1937, a much larger book by Strover appeared, *Monetary Progress*. In between,

---

5. Reprinted by Omni, 1967.

6. Fisher, *Stable Money: A History of the Movement* (New York: Adelphi, 1934).

7. Soddy, *Wealth, Virtual Wealth and Debt* (2nd ed., 1933), p. 19. Reprinted by Omni Publications, 1961. See Frank Arkright, *The ABC of Technocracy* (New York: Harper & Bros., 1933).

in 1930, he had two articles published in the *Prairie Farmer*, calling for all prices to be fixed at the 1926 level.[8]

In the 1930's, there was A. N. Field.[9] There was R. McNair Wilson.[10] Gertrude Coogan's *Money Creators* appeared in 1935, the same year as G. G. McGeer's *The Conquest of Poverty: or Money, Humanity and Christianity*.[11] Elisha E. Garrison's *The Riddle of Economics* was published by Macmillan in 1932. It called for an elastic currency to promote economic exchange, with authority lodged in a governmental Currency Board. Charles Albert Hawkins published his own book in 1932, *Economic Slavery or Freedom: Business Depressions Their Cause and Cure*. Andrae B. Nordskog, the 1932 Vice Presidential nominee of the tiny Liberty Party, wrote a book in 1932: *Spiking the Gold: or Who Caused the Depression . . . and the Way Out*.[12] Also in 1932 came *The Siegfried Plan*, subtitled, *For An Honest Exchange of Values by The Issue of A Sound Money*, published by the Wigwam Press, Los Angeles. Amazingly, it had a Prefatory Note by Charles A. Beard, one of the most influential liberal political scientists and historians in the United States. In England, Frederick and Alfred Wigglesworth offered *The Gold Tangle and the Way Out: Meaning and Causes of the Great Industrial Collapse*, published in 1931, the year England went off the gold standard.[13]

In the United States, Francis Townsend's plan to create monthly money was reminiscent of Silveo Gesell's monetary theory. It became a popular movement from its inception in 1933 until World War II supplied all the fiat money necessary to overcome the Great Depression. Ten million people signed

---

8. See *Monetary Progress* (Chicago: American Money League, 1937), p. 5.

9. A. N. Field, *The Truth About the Slump* (1931) and *All These Things* (1936), both republished by Omni publications in Hawthorne, California, in the early 1960's.

10. Wilson, *God and the Goldsmiths* (1933), reprinted in 1961 by Omni Publications.

11. Both reprinted by Omni Publications in the 1960's.

12. Los Angeles, California: Gridiron Club.

13. London: John Lane the Bodley Head.

petitions favoring the program.[14] He was threatened with a 30-day jail sentence for his activities, but President Roosevelt signed his pardon.[15] Father Charles E. Coughlin attracted millions of listeners to his radio broadcasts. His publications included *The New Deal in Money* (1933); *A Series of Lectures on Social Justice* (1935);[16] and *Money! Questions and Answers* (1936).[17]

I hesitate to mention the writings of the bizarre Alfred Lawson, whose Lawsonomy movement gained followers throughout the 1930's. He had begun to write as early as 1904: *Born Again.* His 1931 booklet is representative of the decade's fiat money reformers: *Direct Credits for Everybody.* Lawson's books are still kept in print by his disciples.

An important political figure in this period was Republican Party Congressman Louis McFadden. He had been elected to Congress in 1914, served as Chairman of the House Banking Committee from 1920 to 1931, and was defeated by a Democrat in 1932.[18] Ironically, an even more vocal critic of the Federal Reserve was soon to become Chairman of the Banking Committee, this time a Texas Democrat: Wright Patman. He served in this position until his death in March, 1976. He was responsible for the detailed three-volume public hearings on the Federal Reserve System published by the Banking Committee in 1964, *The Federal Reserve System after Fifty Years*, and *The Federal Reserve System*, a study prepared for the Joint Economic Committee of Congress, published by the Joint Economic Committee just after his death. (I joined the staff of Congressman Ron Paul, a

---

14. Francis Townsend, *New Horizons (An Autobiography)* (Chicago: J. L. Stewart Publishing Co., 1943), p. 207.

15. *Ibid,* p. 211.

16. Both published by the Radio League of the Little Flower, Royal Oak, Michigan.

17. Royal Oak, Michigan: National Union for Social Justice.

18. *Collected Speeches of Congressman Louis T. McFadden* (Hawthorne, California: Omni Publications, 1970).

libertarian Republican Congressman, in July, 1976. Paul had won an unrelated special election in another Texas district shortly after Patman's death. Paul, as the most junior member of the Banking Committee, immediately became the main critic of the Federal Reserve System on the Committee. Patman had been an inflationist; Paul was a gold standard advocate.)

In the 1940's, another generation appeared. There was the liberal politician, Jerry Voorhis, who lost his seat in Congress in the 1946 election to an obscure California lawyer, Richard M. Nixon.[19] Gorham Munson dedicated his book, *Aladdin's Lamp* (1945), to Major Douglas' most tireless promoter, A. R. Orage.[20] Felix J. Frazer and Elsa Peters Morse offered *Tomorrow's Money* in 1948, published by the New Age Publication Co. The title of a 92-page booklet by anti-United Nations author George Cornelius Johnson made his position clear: *Gold Standard Money: Its Dupes and You* (1945).[21]

Whitney Slocomb's two-volume *Mass Production and Money* extended this tradition.[22] This was a follow-up to his 1955 book, *The Communist Constitution vs. the United States Constitution.*[23] Eustace Mullins, a disciple of the monetary theories of poet Ezra Pound, himself a disciple of Major Douglas, has continued to write books on the money question, beginning in 1954 with *The Federal Reserve Conspiracy*, published by The Christian Educational Association of Union, New Jersey. His *Secrets of the Federal Reserve: The London Connection* appeared in 1983, published by the Bankers Research Institute. In 1958,

---

19. Jerry Voorhis, *Out of Debt, Out of Danger: Proposals for War Finance and Tomorrow's Money* (New York: Devin-Adair, 1943. Note that this was one of America's two conservative publishers in this period, the other being Henry Regnery Company. See also Voorhis, *Beyond Victory* (New York: Farrar & Rinehart, 1944).

20. Gorham Munson, *Aladdin's Lamp: The Wealth of the American People* (New York: Creative Age Press, 1945).

21. Hollywood, California: Effective Thinking Foundation.

22. Meador Publishing Co., Boston.

23. Meador Publishing Co.

George Knupffer's book appeared, *The Struggle for World Power: Revolution and Counter-Revolution*.[24]

In the 1950's, the *American Mercury*, which had been a literate and highly influential magazine in the 1920's when it was edited by H. L. Mencken, was purchased by members of what can legitimately be called the fringe Right. Under the new editors, it began to move toward anti-semitism. The editors also began publishing a series of articles on the money question in 1957. These were compiled and sold as an inexpensive pamphlet, *Money Made Mysterious* (1959).

In the mid-1960's, by far the most sophisticated of the post-World War II efforts appeared: W. E. Turner's *Stable Money: The Conservative Answer to the Business Cycle*.[25] It appeared in 1966, the same year as H. E. Kenan's self-published book, *The Federal Reserve Bank: The Most Fantastic and Unbelievable Fraud in History*. Many books and pamphlets were written by Wycliffe B. Vennard, Sr. Omni Press published dozens of reprints of fiat money books in the 1960's.

In the 1970's, the books continued to appear. A dentist, Edward E. Popp, wrote *Money – Bona Fide or Non-Bona Fide* in 1970.[26] The next year, Charles S. Norburn and Russell L. Norburn used the vanity publisher (you pay, they publish) Vantage Press to bring out *Mankind's Greatest Step: A New Monetary System*. Charles Norburn followed in 1983 with *Honest Money: The United States Note* and in 1984 with *Honest Government: A Return to the U.S. Constitution*.[27] Also in 1971 came June Grem's *The Money Manipulators*, dedicated to Wycliffe B. Vennard.[28]

In 1980, Theodore R. Thoren and Richard F. Warner published *The Truth in Money Book* through Truth in Money, Inc.

24. Third edition; London: Plain-Speaker Publishing Co., 1971.
25. Ft. Worth, Texas: Marvin D. Evans Co., 1966.
26. Port Washington, Wisconsin: Wisconsin Education Fund.
27. Asheville, North Carolina: New Puritan Press.
28. Freeman, South Dakota: Pine Hill Press.

"Christian" Monetary Reform

There has long been an "underground" tradition paralleling the more secular fiat money reform proposals. This has been associated with Roman Catholic anti-usury authors and with equally anti-usury British Israel or Destiny authors. The most prominent Catholic author is Denis Fahay, whose book, *Money Manipulation and Social Order* (1944), was reprinted by Omni Publications in 1963 and again in 1986. Earlier, he had written *The Rulers of Russia* (1938), which was in its 16th printing in 1967. He listed these rulers; overwhelmingly, they were Jews.[29] This was an extension of his 1935 book, *The Mystical Body of Christ in the Modern World.*

In 1934 came Christopher Hollis' book, *The Breakdown of Money: An Historical Explanation.*[30] The author saw fit to cite favorably Ezra Pound's *Draft of XXX Cantos* praising the invention of paper by the Mongols (p. 48). He called for State control over finance and the revival of Christian faith (p. 210). A 1936 pamphlet, *Social Credit and Catholicism,* was written by Georges Henri-Levesque. He may be the only Ph.D. in economics (if he really had one) who ever defended Social Credit.

An early example of the Destiny viewpoint is J. Taylor Peddie, *The Economic Mechanism of Scripture: The Cure for the World Crisis* (1934).[31] A later example is C. F. Parker's little book, *Moses the Economist,* published in 1948 by the Covenant Publishing Co., London.

In 1962, Rev. George S. MacLeod wrote a foreword to *Money: A Christian View,* the First Report of the Christian Doctrine of Wealth Committee of the Congregational Church of Scotland.[32]

---

29. Fahay, *The Rulers of Russia* (3rd ed.; Dublin: Regina Publications, 1967), pp. 7-13.

30. London: Sheed & Ward.

31. London: Williams & Norgate.

32. Glasgow: William Maclellan.

Conclusion

I have compiled this brief bibliography from my personal library. For every title listed, I suspect there are three more, especially from the 1930's. But this list should be sufficient. The demand for monetary reform was high in the era of Major Douglas' prominence. The free market responded to this heavy demand, as it usually does. There were many rival suppliers, each with a theory supporting the necessity of the civil government's issuing of fiat money in order to keep the economy growing.

The undisputed winner and still-reigning world heavyweight champion in this competition was John Maynard Keynes. But he appeals only to liberals.

Members of America's far right – the racist, pro-Hitler far right – can still buy books by Gertrude Coogan, "Coin" Harvey, Father Charles Coughlin, Wycliffe B. Vennard, Jerry Voorhis, and even Major Douglas' *Monopoly of Credit* and *Economic Democracy*. See the 1992 Noontide Press catalogue, pp. 7-8. Address: 1822 1/2 Newport Blvd., Suite 183, Costa Mesa, CA 92627.

APPENDIX D

A BIBLIOGRAPHY OF FREE MARKET MONETARY THEORY

You may be saying to yourself, "Maybe this book is correct, but I need more evidence." I am including a brief list of books on free market monetary theory so that you can pursue a program of self-education. I recommend reading these books in the order in which I present them.

Until those leaders who publicly defend Social Credit have replied in detail to these materials, the Social Credit movement will remain little more than the curious passtime of people who are not serious about either economic theory or economic reform. At best, it will be a movemant composed of dedicated but totally self-deceived people whose candidates for political office are unlikely to be taken seriously. Even if a Social Credit government should be elected, its leaders will discover, as William Aberhart discovered in the 1930's and 1940's, that Social Credit has no blueprint for monetary reform.

Free Market Monetary Theory

Rothbard, Murray. *What Has Government Done to Our Money?* (1963). Auburn, Alabama: Ludwig von Mises Institute, 119 pages.

Sennholz, Hans. *Money and Freedom* (1986). Spring Mills, Pennsylvania: Libertarian Press, 88 pages.

North, Gary. *Honest Money: The Biblical Blueprint for Money and Banking* (1986). P. O. Box 7999, Tyler, Texas: Dominion Press, 160 pages.

White, Andrew Dickson. *Fiat Money Inflation in France* (1912). Irvington, New York: Foundation for Economic Education, 80 pages.

Prices and Price Controls (1992). Irvington, New York: Foundation for Economic Education, 169 pages.

Rothbard, Murray. *Man, Economy, and State: A Treatise on Economic Principles* (1962). New York: New York University Press, chapter 11, pages 661-764.

Groseclose, Elgin. *Money and Man: A Survey of Monetary Experience* (1976 edition). Norman, Oklahoma: University of Oklahoma Press, 306 pages.

Rothbard, Murray and Garet, Garrett. *The Great Depression and New Deal Monetary Policy* (1980). San Francisco, California: Cato Institute, 129 pages.

Hodge, Ian. *Baptized Inflation: A Critique of "Christian" Keynesianism* (1985). Tyler, Texas: Institute for Christian Economics, 274 pages.

Hayek, F. A. *Monetary Theory and the Trade Cycle* (1933). New York: Augustus Kelley, 239 pages.

Skousen, Mark. *The Economics of a Pure Gold Standard* (1988). Auburn, Alabama: Ludwig von Mises Institute, 158 pages.

Mises, Ludwig. *Human Action: A Treatise on Economics* (1966 edition). Washington, D.C.: Henry Regnery Company, chapters XVI-XX, pages 327-586.

Mises, Ludwig. *On the Manipulation of Money and Credit* (1978). Dobbs Ferry, New York: Free Market Books, 296 pages.

Mises, Ludwig. *The Theory of Money and Credit* (1953 edition). Irvington, New York: Foundation for Economic Education, 493 pages.

Capitalism as a Moral Order

The Morality of Capitalism (1992). Irvington, New York: Foundation for Economic Education, 150 pages.

Griffiths, Brian. *Morality and the Market Place* (1982). London: Hodder & Stoughton, 160 pages.

Griffiths, Brian. *The Creation of Wealth* (1984). London: Hodder & Stoughton, 160 pages.

SCRIPTURE INDEX

Genesis
- 1:26-28 43-44
- 2:16-17 44
- 3:17-19 41, 44, 144, 173
- 13:2 48

Exodus
- 20:9 144
- 20:15 183

Leviticus
- 19:36 50

Deuteronomy
- 8:17-18 41, 47
- 18:20ff 17
- 25:13 50
- 28:1-14 45
- 28:15-69 45

I Samuel
- 8:7 143

Psalms
- 12:6 48
- 19:9-10 48
- 66:10 48
- 106:15 143
- 119:72 48
- 119:127 49

Proverbs
- 8:18-21 49
- 10:20 49
- 16:11 50
- 16:16 49
- 18:17 xxxi
- 20:10 50
- 20:23 50
- 25:11 49
- 26:17 265

Isaiah
- 1:22 49, 227, 240
- 1:24-28 240
- 1:25-28 49-50
- 5:20 165

Daniel
- 5:27 20

Micah
6:11 50

Matthew
4:3-4 81
5:45 43
6:11 82
10:28 214
12:36-38 21
17:27 48
20:10-15 178
25:20 1 42
25:24-27 141

Mark
2:27 210
13:5 ix

Luke
12:47-48 78-79, 142

Romans
5:8 46
6:23 46

I Corinthians
3:12 xx

Ephesians
2:8-9 x
2:8-10 46
2:10 x
4:14 32

II Thessalonians
3:10 101, 145
3:10-14 212

I Timothy
6:10 47

James
2:20 x
2:24 x
4:1 143, 241
4:17 241

I John
1:9 47
4:1 17

Revelation
13:16-17 106

INDEX

Aberhart, William, 23, 57, 238
activism, xiv
Adam, 45, 87
Alberta, xii, 1-2, 28, 29, 56-58
armament, 146
auction, 45, 88-89, 113
authority, 102, 197-98, 206

Bank of England, 137, 166-67
bank run, 12, 230
bankers, 217, 221
banking
  abolition of, 69-70
  central, 11
  commercial, 148
  credit failure, 121
  depositors, 206
  Douglas vs., 90-91, 204
  exploitation?, 180-81
  fractional reserve, 137, 148
  fractional reserves, 160-61, 229-230
  Jackson vs., 11
  loans, 59
  millennium &, 217
  nationalized, 148
  panic, xvii
  real bills, xvi-xvii
  State, 42, 152
baptism, 22
Bell, Daniel, 94
Bell, Don, 8
Bible, 17-23, 43, 210
Biddle, Nicholas, 11
blueprint, 55-80, 185-86
boom-bust, xvi
buggy whip, 229
bulldozers, 169
bureaucracy, 72, 188-192, 196
Bush, George, 10
business, xvi

capacity, 97-98
capital
  allocating, 152
  financial, 168
  goods, 121-24
  growth &, 151
  human, 200
  monetization, 62
  national, 200
  real, 168
  return on, 171
  valuation, 61-64
capital goods, 121-24, 169
capitalism

- A & B Theorem, 260-61
- capacities, 97
- capacity, 94
- central flaw?, 100
- competition, 89
- consumer sovereignty, 94-95
- critics of, 42-43
- democratization, 255
- depreciation, 122
- distribution, 108
- Douglas vs., xxi, 165
- Douglas' history, 166-69
- flaw of, 243
- flow of funds, 243, 260-61
- hatred of, 2-3
- historic productivity, 136
- number-one evil, 165
- number-one flaw, 120
- output, 109-10
- pricing, 127
- secret of, 124-25
- self-destructs?, 120
- sovereignty, 87-88
- stock market, 87-88
- wages, 251

castle, xiii
causation, 242-44, 260
central banks, 102, 103, 148, 230
chemistry, 18-19
church, 168
coal, 147
coinage, 49-51
Cole, G. D. H., 37
commodity futures, 148n
Communism, 56, 121
community, 58-60, 203
competition, 89, 130
computers, 121, 122, 151
conservatism, 15
conspiracies, 4-10
conspiracy, 84-85, 142-43, 221
conspiracy thesis, 4-13
consumer credit, 244
consumers
- credit, xviii, 190
- demand, 197
- democracy, 219-20
- hammer, 76, 95, 103
- sanctions, 215
- sovereignty, 94-95, 102-3, 116-17, 145-46, 187-88, 206, 215, 218, 228-229
- tyrants, 103

consumption, 133
Coogan, Gertrude, 14
corporation, 166-69, 171, 239
corporations, 86-87
costs, 119
Coughlin, Father, 91-92
Coulbourne, Maurice, xxv-xxvi
Council on Foreign Relations, 7, 9
counterfeiting, xvii, 51, 230
creation, 20
credit
- A & B Theorem, 253
- consumer, xviii
- defined, 147
- individuals, 152
- money &, 152
- not mandatory, 253
- political, 153
- private, 150
- risk-avoidance, 189
- savings &, 152

credit masters
  above voters, 191
  bureaucrats, 77-78
  centralization, 186
  fear of, 216
  formula, 228
  free market, 190
  hammer, 186
  hierarchy, 218
  inventory, 186, 234-35, 258-59
  powers of, 60
  representation, 193
  sovereign, 203-4
  valuation, 200
crisis, xx
cults, 242
curse, 44, 45
cycle, xvi

Darwin, Charles, 78
Darwinism, 20, 211
decapitalization, 199-203
decentralization, 185, 186
deflation, 12-13
demand, 113, 195-97
democracy, 90, 153-54
demons, 143-44
depositors, 204, 206
depreciation, 122-23, 151
depression, 112
distribution, 106-18
dividend, 66-67, 169, 172
division of labor, 112-13, 145, 147
dole, 73-75, 78, 213-14 (see also National Dividend)
Douglas, C. H.
  A & B Theorem, 243-57
  Aberhart &, 57
  anti-banking, 204
  anti-biblical law, 83
  anti-Christianity, 101
  anti-democracy, 190-91, 193
  anti-Semitic, 220-23
  anti-taxes, 214-15
  anti-work, 144, 211-12
  bankers = owners, 90
  biography, 34-35
  blueprint, 185-86
  capital goods, 256
  capitalism is bad, 165
  capitalism's failure, 111
  capitalism's flaw, 242, 252
  capitalism's history, 166-69
  conspiracy theory, 221
  consumer credit, 234
  consumer sovereignty, 206
  consumers' democracy, 153
  contradictory, 251-52
  credit policy, 162
  cultist, 242
  Darwinist, 211
  decentralization, 185-86
  democracy, 90
  diagram, 256-57
  dividend defined, 177
  dividends & income, 172
  dividends & wages, 172
  dole, 213-14
  elitist, 190-91, 206, 228
  entrepreneurship, 119
  errors of, 268-71
  ethics, 210
  exploitation, 182-83
  exploitation theory, 180, 247

Fascism &, 198
final judgment, 220
flow of funds, 230-31, 239, 248-52
formula, 150, 243-44
fractional reserves, 149, 161
freedom & authority, 197-98
gold, 150
good intentions, 189, 192-93, 226
Hidden Hand, 84-85
hierarchy, 218
incoherent, 236-37
individualistic language, 161
interest, 179-80, 256
Jewish Question, 222-23
Keynes &, 120, 131-32, 139
machines, 170
magic pill, 149, 199
majority rule, 193
Marx &, 180, 183
millennium, 224
mistakes of, 244-46
money, 147
money-changers, 199
moralist, 82-84, 212-13
nationalization, 185, 198
philosophy of, 28-29
poverty theory, 216
pragmatist?, 82-84
productivity, 216
productivity estimate, 173
productivity estimates, 110
Protocols of Zion, 222
public interest, 192, 194
purchasing power, 130, 135, 241
ratio, 150
Real Credit, 243
Salvation Army, 213-14
sanctions, 209-25
secrecy, 34
smash-up, 218-19
"socialism," 197
systems, 210
thrift, 132-35
"tickets," 155, 166, 231-32
underconsumption, 165, 230, 252-53
underproduction, 181-82
wages, 172-73
work, 174-75
dross, 49-50

economic growth, 121
economics of scale, 129
effective demand, 195-97
Eisenhower, Dwight, 6
elastic currency, xvi
Eliot, T. S., 37
elite, 190-91
Emperor's New Clothes, xxix-xxx
England, 137
entrepreneur, 119, 120
entrepreneurs, 76, 128
entrepreneurship, 175-77
entropy, 125
Establishment, xiii-xiv, xxxii, 6
ethics, 212-13
exploitation theory, 247
expropriation, 217

factory, 115-16
fads, xv
faith, xi

Fascism, 194, 198, 237
fiat money, xi (see also money)
Final Judgment, 125, 210, 220
finance credit, 243
financial credit, 99-100
flow of funds, 124, 172, 230-31, 239-40, 243, 248-52, 254, 260-61
Ford, Henry, 126-27
formula, x, 81-82, 150, 203, 228, 243-44
fractional reserves, 229-30
free market
  auction, 113, 155
  capacity, 94
  competition, 89
  consumers' sovereignty, 90
  credit, 190
  economic order, 227-28
  (see also capitalism)
freedom, 187, 197-98
French Revolution, 62-63, 67, 199-200
fringe, xiv
fundamentalist, xiii
funerals, 128

Gantt, H. L., 109
geology, 19-20
German miracle, xx
Gesell, Silvio, 196
ghettos, xiii
Gilder, George, 127-28
gold, 47-48, 136-37, 150
gold standard, 11-12, 99, 102, 137-38
Goldwater, Barry, 5
good works, 46
grace, x, 46-47, 144-45
Green Shirts, 91-93
greenbacks, 12
greens, 3
Gresham's law, 51-52
growth, 125, 137-38
guild socialism, 145
Gurdjieff, G. I., 37-38

hammer, 76, 95, 103, 186
Hargrave, John, 92-93
Hayek, F. A., 257
hell, 214
Hidden Hand, 84-85
hierarchy, 84-85, 87-88, 153, 218
Hitler, Adolph, 29
Hobson, J. A., 130, 131
human capital, 200
humanism
  Establishment, xiv
  fads, xv
  fringe, xiv
  truth, 20

ideas, xix
ignorance, 111, 114
income, 73-75
Illuminati, 5, 11
inflation
  cause & effect, 52
  decapitalization, 199-203
  limit?, 201
  limits &, 203
  National Dividend, 67
  redistribution, 52
  tax, 67
  wealth redistribution, 202,

205
inflationism, 227-28
information, 111-13
innovation, 76
Insiders, 4
intentions, 189-90, 192-93, 194, 226
interest
  Bible &, xviii
  defined, 179
  diagram, 257
  theory of, 233-34
  zero, xviii, 4
interest rate, xvi-xvii, 69, 135
inventory, 186, 200, 234-35, 258-59
investors, 206
invisible hand, 85

Jackson, Andrew, 11
Jastram, Roy, 137
Jesus
  demons, 143-44
  "formalism," 213-14
  parable of employer, 178
  parable of talents, 141-42
  profits, 142
  representation, 87
  words of, 81-82
jet propulsion, xxv
Jews, 4, 13, 220-23
John Birch Society, 5
Johnson, Hewlett, 38-39, 180
Johnson, Lyndon, 5-6
Just Price, 199, 206, 235

Keynes, John Maynard
  deflation, 120
  disciples of, xxiv-xxv
  Douglas &, xii, xxii, 131-32, 139, 196
  effective demand, 196-97
  mixed economy, 196
  policy, 134-35
  strange bedfellow, 15
  success of, xix
  thrift, 132
  underconsumption, 132
Knight, Frank, 176, 202

law, 21-22, 46, 63
Law, John, 227
liability, 168-69, 171
loans, 100-1, 160-61, 173-74, 190
"lubrication," 231
Luther, Martin, xxix

machinery, 169-70
magic pill, 199, 242, 261
magic word, 81-82
Mairet, Philip, 37
majority rule, 193
managers, 88-89
Marx, Karl, 5-6, 42-43, 56, 84, 149, 180-81, 194, 196, 199, 217
metal, 233
millennium, 217-18, 224
mining, 233
miracles, 19
Mises, Ludwig von
  central planning, 192
  consumer sovereignty, 95
  profit & loss, 26
  underconsumption, 14

mixed economy, xxi
monetization, 62
money
  banks create, xvi
  claim on wealth?, 147
  conspiracy &, 142
  credit &, 152
  defined, 116-17, 147, 154
  doesn't disappear, 123
  elastic, xvi
  features, 48
  fiduciary, xvi
  follow, 108
  free market, 3
  held by someone, 253-54
  interest rate, 233-34
  land &, 63
  lubrication, 231
  metals, 233
  mining &, 233
  most marketable, 27, 47
  neutral?, 202
  not a legal claim, 154, 159
  omniscience &, 26
  paper, 60-61
  profits &, 123
  purchasing power, 135
  safeguard, 63
  safeguards, 61
  scarcity &, 232-33
  shortage, 123
  tax payments, 232
  wealth incarnate, 47
money changers, 199
monopoly, 187
Morse, Jededigh, 11
Mullins, Eustace, 32
Mumford, Lewis, 37
Mussolini, 32

national defense, 146
National Dividend, 65-68, 235
National Socialism, 205
nationalization, 185, 198
natural law, 22
natural resources, 76
nature, 44-45, 52
Nazis, xxi
needs of business, xvi
neutral mind, 21
neutral science, 20
neutrality, 83-84, 191
New Age, 35-36
New English Weekly, 38
Nietzsche, F., 36
Nisbet, Robert, 1
nuclear physics, xi
nupticism, 211

Old Man River, 124
omniscience, 26, 128, 196
Orage, A. R., 35-38, 188, 211
output, 109-10
ownership, 43-44, 64-65, 75, 86, 90, 107, 114

parable of employer, 178
parrots, 88-89, 113
Penty, A. J., 36
personalism, 4
philosophy, 28-29
Pinwill, Charles, 265, 265-67
planning, 227
politics, 219
popes, xxix
Populism, 12-13

Pound, Ezra, 32-33, 37, 207
pragmatism, 83
price competition, 130
price controls, xx, 52, 70-72
prices
  counterfeiting, 51
  expanding output, 121
  falling, 119-40
  Ford cars, 126-27
  information &, 111-13
  producers &, 115, 118
  ratification, 229
  ratification of, 115-16
  relative, 201-2
  supply & demand, 130-31, 195
  zero?, 122
producers (accredited), 153
production, 106-7
productivity, 173
  demand, 113
  falling prices, 121
  machines, 170-71
  poverty &, 216
profits
  consumers' hammer, 76
  Douglas' blueprint, 71, 216
  entrepreneurship, 76
  innovation &, 76
  Jesus' view, 142
  money supply &, 123
  perfect knowledge, 128
  quest for, 76
  residual, 71, 76, 176
  sanctions, 87
  source of, 175-77, 244-45
property, 44
property taxes, 73
prophets, 17
Protocols, 222
Proudhon, P. J., 14-15
public interest, 194
punishment (see sanctions)
purchasing power, 130, 135, 241
Puritanism, 213, 238-39

Quigley, Carroll, 6-7

real bills, xv-xviii
Real Credit, 96-99, 100, 150, 187, 203, 243
real estate, 64-65
recession, 101-2
Red Dean of Canterbury, 38-39, 180
reform, 189
reformers, 56
regeneration, 241
relative prices, 201-2
representation, 89-90, 102, 191, 193
Republican Party, 5-6
responsibility, 206
retirement, 65
revolution, 29
reward (see sanctions)
Rhodes, Cecil, 7
rich, 173, 254-55
risk, 189
Robison, John, 11
Rockefeller, Nelson, 6
Rolls-Royce, 179
Rothbard, Murray, 107, 257
Round Table, 7

Salvation Army, 213-14
sanctification, 56
sanctions
  bureaucratic, 192
  denial of, 25-26, 33, 77
  economic theory, 215
  final, 33, 125, 142
  historical, 55
  political or economic, 209-25
  reform, 189
  scarcity, 44
  taxation &, 215
  work &, 144
Satan, 81-82
savings, 152
scarcity
  Adam's curse, 44
  defined, 121, 197
  economics &, 88
  escape from, 45-46, 121
  "illusion," 25-26
  money &, 232-33
  sanction, 215
  zero price, 121, 197
science, 19-20
Scotland, 58, 61
seat, 154
seats, 116, 156-58
self-deception, xii-xiii
Shafarevich, Igor, xix, 81
shoes, 117
shovels, 169-70
silver, 48-50
sin, 46
Skousen, Clem, 7-8
Skousen, Mark, 132-33
Skull & Bones, 6
Smith, Adam, xv-xvi, 41, 85, 215
Smoot, Dan, 8
Social Credit
  Achilles heel, 98-99
  altar of, 23
  anti-depositor, 90
  appeal of, 14, 237-38
  arbitrary, 66
  authority, 86-87
  bad system, 226
  blueprint, 55-80, 185-86
  capitalism's flaw, 100
  centralization, 85, 197-98
  challenge to, 274-76
  collateral, 99
  community, 58-60
  conservatism vs., 15
  consumer credit, 244
  debate tickets, 157
  defenders of, 271-74
  deifies the State, xx
  dilemma of, 196-99
  distribution, 108
  dole, 213-14
  early converts, xxviii, 2, 31-33, 37
  economists ignore, 267-68
  elite, 190-91
  evils of, 77
  financial credit, 99-100
  flow of funds, 254
  followers, 24
  formula, 228
  free market language, 75-76
  gold, 150
  Green Shirts &, 91-93
  guaranteed income, 73-75
  incoherent, 236-37

innovation, 76
inventory, 200, 258-59
long-term goal, 212
magic pill, 145, 149
main problem of, 192
millennium, 217-18, 237-38
mistakes of, 244-46
mixed economy, xxi
money as tickets, 154-58
moral heart of, 205
National Dividend, 65-68, 172
National Socialism, 205
natural resources, 76
number-one criticism, 111
number-one reform, 98, 197
one man show, xxiv
one-State world, 151
philosophy, 33
political sovereignty, 153
post-reform A & B, 259-60
price controls, 70-72
private credit &, 150
profit theory, 176-77
profits, 123
profits guaranteed, 216
public interest, 194
purchasing power, 111
questions, 27-28
ratio, 150
real bills &, xv-xviii
Real Credit, 96-99, 100, 243
religious movement, xxviii
representation, 191
retirement funds, 65
sanctions, 77
scarcity, 25-26
small, xi
socialistic, 75-78, 205
State bank monopoly, 69-70
State power &, 153
strategy of, 271-74
supreme mystery of, 249
technicians, 93-94
underconsumption, 100, 165
unique?, 228
utopian, 24-27
valuation, 200
wages, 72-73, 172-73
welfare State, 78
why *Social*?, 186
work, 211-12
(see also Douglas, C. H.)
socialism
Douglas &, 197
guild, 145
heart of, 188
premises, 75-78
society, 186-87
sovereignty, 87-88, 144-46, 153
(see also consumer sovereignty)
Spadaro, Louis, xviii, xxvii, 14-15, 229
specialization, 113, 117
spoons, 170
State
balancing agent, 227
bureaucracy, 188-89
counterfeiting, 51
debt-free, 204
planning, 227
price control, 52
society =, 186-87
source of assets, 204-5
wealth redistribution, 205

statistics, 61, 151, 171
stock market, 87-88
style, xii

Taft, Robert, 6
talents, 141
tariffs, 112
tax (inflation), 67
taxes, 73, 112, 214-15, 232
Taylor, Frederick, 109
teaspoons, 170
technicians, 93-94
tenant for life, 74-75
theater, 116
theosophy, 39
thermodynamics, 125
"thieves," 90-91, 103
Thomas, Dylan, 38
thrift, 132-35, 152
tickets, 154-58, 166
"tickets," 231-32
time's arrow, 125
totalitarianism, 187
trade unions, 72-73
trespass, 44
truth, 20-21, 22

underconsumption, 13-14, 132, 243, 252-53, 165
unemployment, 169-70
unions, 72-73, 250
usury, 141
utopian, 24-27

valuation, 200
value, 159, 220
Veblen, Thorstein, 93-94
vision, 55

wages
  A + B Theorem, 247-48
  Douglas on, 72-73, 177, 180-81
  lowering, 172-73
  machinery &, 169-70
  Marx on, 181
  United States, 171
warehouse receipt, 64, 153, 155, 156, 232
water/wine, 19
wealth, 43, 115, 173, 147
wealth formula, x
wealth redistribution, 202, 205
Welch, Robert, 5
welfare State, 78
wine/water, 19
work, 101, 144, 174-75, 211-12
World War I, 102

ABOUT THE AUTHOR

Gary North received his Ph.D. in history from the University of California, Riverside, in 1972. He specialized in colonial U.S. history. He wrote his doctoral dissertation on Puritan New England's economic history and the history of economic thought. A simplified version of this dissertation has been published as *Puritan Economic Experiments* (Institute for Christian Economics, 1988).

In the late 1960's, he and R. J. Rushdoony founded what has become known as the Christian Reconstruction movement, also known as theonomy.

He is the author of approximately 35 books in the fields of economics, history, and theology. His first book, *Marx's Religion of Revolution*, appeared in 1968. His *Introduction to Christian Economics* appeared in 1973, the year he began writing a multi-volume economic commentary on the Bible, which now covers Genesis, Exodus (three volumes), and Leviticus. He was the general editor of the Biblical Blueprints Series (1986-87), a 10-volume set.

Beginning in 1965, his articles and reviews have appeared in over three dozen newspapers and periodicals, including the *Wall Street Journal*, *Modern Age*, *Journal of Political Economy*, *National Review*, and *The Freeman*.

He edited the first fifteen issues of *The Journal of Christian Reconstruction*, 1974-81. He edited a *festschrift* for Cornelius Van Til, *Foundations of Christian Scholarship* (1976). He edited two issues of *Christianity and Civilization* in 1983: *The Theology of Christian Resistance* and *Tactics of Christian Resistance*. He edited *Theonomy: An Informed Response* (1991).

He is the editor of the monthly financial newsletter, *Remnant Review*. He writes two bi-monthly Christian newsletters, *Biblical Economics Today* and *Christian Reconstruction*, published by the Institute for Christian Economics.

He lives in Tyler, Texas, with his wife and four children.